Motivating with Love

A Memoir

Mary D. Nelson

Brigham Young University

This book is lovingly dedicated to my late husband, Colonel Howard B. Nelson (USAF, retired), my loyal supporter, lover, and friend, who tried to make me believe I could do anything.

Library of Congress Cataloging-in-Publication Data

Nelson, Mary D. 1913–
    Motivating with love: a memoir / Mary D. Nelson
        p. 348
    ISBN 0–8425–2372–3
    1. Nelson, Mary D., 1913–. 2. High school teachers—
United States—Biography. 3. French language—Study
and teaching (Secondary)—United States—Case studies.
4. Teaching—Case studies.   I. Title.
LA2317.N45A3   1989
373.11'0092--dc19
[B]   89–10021
                                                     CIP

Brigham Young University, Provo, Utah 84602
© Mary D. Nelson 1989. All rights reserved
Printed in the United States of America

Contents

Acknowledgments

This book is the result of a solemn promise to my late husband and appeals for help from former students and colleagues.

Many others, all friends, have helped and encouraged: Janice McAllister and Cheri Anderson Loveless, who edited and critiqued the manuscript; Jane Goll, headmistress of Westminster Private School, Annandale, Virginia, who read and critiqued the manuscript for value of content; Linda Allen Schoelwer, former student, who critiqued from her remembrance of what she had lived in my classroom; Kathryn Yeates, who typed the manuscript and read parts of it to her teenage children; Howard T. Nelson, my son, who read the manuscript and encouraged its publication; Yvonne Houïs, former professeur at the Sorbonne, a great grammarian and friend; Peggy Teeters, author of *Getting Started in Writing,* my teacher and friend; Howard A. Christy, senior editor of Scholarly Publications, Brigham Young University, Provo, Utah, a friend who advised, edited, and guided me to publication; Gayle Maxwell Belcher, who created the dragons for the cover and chapter frontispieces; Andrew Robertson for creation of the interior cartoons; Bruce A. Patrick, Graphic Communications, for cover design; Louise E. Williams, assistant editor of Scholarly Publications, Brigham Young University, for interior design, copy editing, and typesetting; and Anne Slater, free-lance editor for Scholarly Publications.

To all of them and others, I shall be forever grateful.

Foreword

Madame Mary D. Nelson and I met for the first time in August of 1963 when Fort Hunt High School of Fairfax County, Virginia, opened its doors. At that time I was new to organized guidance. My first assignment, the ninth grade, was my field for work. Madame Nelson was one of two full-time French teachers assigned to the foreign language department, but the school grew. As the years passed, both of us developed an understanding, a rapport, and a respect which are useful and necessary in education. I came to appreciate in her a resolute standard of quality in teaching rarely developed by most teachers. I came to realize that many of those qualities are unique to an individual's character. Constantly Mary D. Nelson set the parameters which were acceptable. She insisted that each person with whom she came in contact search the inner self for values, strengths, and weaknesses. When I became the Director of Guidance for the school, it was a pleasure for me to observe her classes.

One year Madame Nelson decided to try her system of teaching with a captured group of superior athletes who were recalcitrant learners. For a large part of the first year, the threats to leave the program were frequent. She, however, had the charisma through which she could prod, cajole, and enlist the support of parents, counselors, and administrators in order to keep the group together. They learned.

At any time that Madame Nelson was approached in a parent-student conference, an administrator-teacher conference, or in a classroom observation, she was thoroughly prepared. Her sense of organization and thoroughness were impeccable, and it was actually thrilling to watch her skillful manipulation of a lesson plan. It was a rare student who didn't tremble a bit if his or her preparation was lacking. There were those who couldn't find the strength within themselves to overcome weakness in assiduity and who couldn't face the day-to-day pressures of the French lesson Nelson style. It was a very small percentage, though.

In my many conversations with Madame Nelson, I came to realize that teaching French was for her not an imparting of knowledge; it was an imparting of herself and all that she believed. She understands that Providence has given her a mission and imposed a responsibility. Madame Nelson is rock-sure of her position in life and is brilliant in her understanding not only of French, but of the psychology of the persons she has as students. She knows the weaknesses to which people often fall prey. Her strength is passed on to those who need it and accept it.

In her tenure at Fort Hunt High School, Madame Nelson became widely known and acclaimed. Her students regularly won prizes in the state, region, and nation. She received the diplôme supérieur from the Sorbonne, Paris, a B.A. in French language and literature from George Washington University, and an M.A. in foreign language methodology from Brigham Young University—her thesis exploring the motivational aspects of teaching French. She served two years on the National Committee for Test Development for the National French Contest. She established the first test center for the National French Contest and the National Spanish Contest for Northern Virginia and directed the test center for the National French Contest for several years. With a handful of her colleagues she founded the Northern Virginia Chapter of the American Association of Teachers of French and was its first president. She served her school for four years as a delegate to the Fairfax County Teachers' Assembly and became a consultant for French to the Advanced Placement Program at Princeton.

Her regular summer study every other year at the University of Paris enriched the lives of her students.

CARL SCLOEMER

Mount Vernon High School
Fairfax County, Virginia

*Language is the speaking
testament of dead and
living societies.*

Frédéric Mistral

Preface

Ce que nous savons,
Ce n'est qu'une goutte d'eau
Ce que nous ignorons c'est l'océan.

That which we know is only a drop of water,
That which we know not is an ocean.

The most important aspects of reality are off limits to scientific mastery. Reality remains, in a sense, a mystery that cannot be achieved or understood by critical analysis. Teaching, or the act of teaching, carries its pedagogical rules that can be learned and analyzed; the how of transference of knowledge from the mind and personality of the teacher to the students somehow remains a mystery. It, too, is a chemistry beyond analysis.

The goal for teachers is the solution of problems and the building of the self-esteem and the confidence of their students in their ability to learn. Writing an explanatory book will help, but the hidden chemical mystery of learning remains. It is individual and unique to each teacher and each student.

Education must be concerned with fundamentals and lasting values that are not affected by transitory circumstances. Recognizing these lasting values is part of the burden and the responsibility of all teachers, but especially for teachers of teenagers.

The teenage years are a terrible time of turbulence and frightening decisions. Caught between the world of protected childhood and the mocking and indifferent adult world of our urban societies, the adolescent is faced with the terrifying specter of rejection or isolation. "To be or not to be" is indeed his dilemma. However, teachers who have strong moral values will provide a sure sanctuary of acceptance and encouragement for their indecisive charges when acceptance by peers and by authority figures beyond the home becomes a pressing need. All the teachings, admonitions, and standards of parents and extended family are brought into question as these young people begin to establish themselves as individuals in a somewhat alien world.

This need for acceptance is not unique to adolescents but prevails in all creatures at all ages regardless of the species. But in human kind, and especially in teens, there arises a different need as well: the innate desire to be unique and different, but nevertheless accepted.

In a sense, the adolescent is at war with himself, filled with the conflict of emotions struggling for dominance in his life and in his decisions. It is my belief and my experience that dedicated, caring teachers can and should be the vital link between the world of fortress–childhood in the home and family and the adult world of decision making and acceptance of responsibility for one's behavior in the realm of school and work.

What kind of link shall we be? Shall we play the role of the welder, the unifier, the fortifier? Shall we play the role of the icon-breaker, the disrupter, the cynic, the intemperate disbeliever in the worth of the cultural roots of the society we call our own? Shall we build bridges over chasms, real or imagined, of the past and link present to future?

Teachers who mark the lives of their charges will choose a role. Those who choose none will mark no path, forge no link with the past and the tomorrows of their students. They will have the same effect as a five-minute shower, giving no depth of moisture, quenching no thirst of growing things. They will waste public funds and the precious time of their students. Teachers who choose to be a unifying link of the best—not the worst—of the past to the best of the present and the future, will heal any generation gap. They will make sense out of imagined and real family and societal restrictions, of standards of morality and decency, and the push and shove of peer and societal pressures to abandon the good in family teachings and in society. These teachers will have deeply rooted standards of their own and serve as models to their students of the best in traditions and ideas that have been the élan vital of civilization. They will teach their students to think, but they will, above all, recognize and teach the necessity of having *something to think about.*

Therefore, the curricula they prepare will deal with more than the mere teaching of skills; they will provide for their students the meat and drink of the ideas, art, beliefs, and mores of the past and link them with present and future. These teachers will recognize the role religion has played and continues to play in the workings of a society and the relations between nations and human beings. Bluntly and briefly, I believe that teachers must be well founded in the humanities and they must care deeply about their charges. They must be more than computer programmers, athletic coaches, business teachers, language teachers, mathematicians, artists, or historians in the simple, functionary sense. They must be mind stretchers, inspirers, archeologists searching the intellectual gold of the human potential of each student. They must be true believers in the infinity of the possibilities of their students, who, among other reasons, will achieve in order to fulfill the prophetic hopes of their teachers.

I am an unashamed "square" who practices and believes that the classroom should be the forum for the best in our culture or in the culture of the foreign language we teach. Anything or everything is *not* admissable. There is no time to waste on the sleazy, the aberrant, or the vulgar. These elements will and do manifest themselves outside the classroom. In life, as in art in all its forms, there will always be contrasts of good and evil, good taste and poor taste. The classroom should uplift and reinforce the best in human nature and cause its occupants to ponder. Just what do we think about when we don't have anything to think about? This should always be a question teachers should never cease posing to themselves and their students.

Socrates firmly believed that the peccadillos and capricious behavior of the gods should not be taught to the young. I concur. We are not without pagan gods, equally capricious, today. The classroom is for learning the intellectual discipline of organized, exacting scholarship. It is no place for lassitude and sloth. School can be pleasurable; but, unfortunately, Americans too often equate pleasure with cheerleading, sex, athletics, dating, and frivolous amusement. If American primary and secondary schools are to be rescued from the ignominious bottom of academic ratings among leading nations, much more serious attention must be given to scholarly pursuits in the classroom, and more time outside of class must be given to reinforcing what was begun in class. We cannot wait to make up deficiencies at the college level. Too many students never make it into the colleges and universities and, worse, many leave secondary school with no skills at all—not even the ability to communicate, read or write well, or analyze and solve problems of any complexity. Unnecessary and meaningless words are constantly sprinkled through the speech of teens who model their language on what they hear on television. Those who teach it should learn to skillfully use the language of the culture in which they live.

Caring, dedicated teachers, well prepared to teach their area of expertise, will be the decisive factor in the regeneration of America's primary and secondary schools and bridge the chasm between the world of protected childhood and the real (sometimes seemingly unreal) adult world of work. Teachers who understand and accept the responsibility of their role will be the mysterious leaven in the cake of academic success. Thus, fulfilling their moral contract with the future of their students, they will keep their rendezvous with history.

This memoir is my attempt to keep the promises I made to my students and colleagues through the years to "write it down," tell the why, the motivating elements in my life, recount the joys, and tell the stories. In no way, in any of my instructions, do I mean to imply that I have said it all or that my techniques are necessarily better than others. What I *do* claim is that the ideas and techniques I outline in this volume have evolved from a lifetime of application and adjustment—always through trial and often enough through error—and that they *work*.

When I began teaching, there was no book, no methods course that helped me or guided me through that first year or any subsequent year. I erroneously concluded that my textbook was my method. There is still no basic guide that will help calm the panic of a beginning teacher or hint at methods of how to teach and that have proved themselves by producing results—excellent results.

Teachers don't write memoirs. They are too exhausted at day's end—late evening—to do anything except go to bed. When they finish their careers, they still don't write. By then they will have passed the two-million-memo mark. Enough! they think.

I write because of solemn promises made to my husband, many students now teaching, and colleagues. I also promised, and threatened, my students that I would keep every memo and that they could count on being in print someday. They found that exhilarating. Imagine, having Madame write about them; being immortalized on paper! They outdid themselves in proving themselves memorable.

This book is necessarily brief. Teachers do not have the time nor do they have the inclination to read a tome of long explanations. They need a reference book that succinctly explains the methodology involved. I invite readers to try the methods and suggestions herein because they have worked for me. My students have regularly returned to tell me so, even to citing, point for point, what has worked best.

This book comes from the trenches of pedagogic slogging in "mud"—sometimes up to my armpits. The ivory towers didn't even glimmer in the distance—hence the memoir orientation instead of a scholarly, scientific approach. The results of past students will have to be my proof for the doubting. They helped prepare what happened to me throughout the thirty-odd years of my teaching. They also gave me the certainty that what I was doing was not only working well but was correct, especially in the areas where I seem to be most inflexible.

For example, the inflexible rule ("as certain as death and taxes") of a verb quiz each Monday evolved as a result of my attempting to give homework on new areas over Saturday and Sunday; this prompted a belief that continuous thinking about the new language would ultimately enhance the learning (and *using*) experience. Early in my career, too many students arrived unprepared or poorly prepared on Monday. I refused to consider the first day of the school week as merely start-up day, as many colleagues advised; the verb quizzes on Monday obliged students to constantly review, at least in their minds, what they thought they knew. They were forced to *think about that verb quiz even if all they did was worry*. At least worry is thought provoking. But more often than not, worry was soon replaced with increased confidence and anticipation as the course unfolded. Simply stated, it worked.

I have recently learned that there are scientific studies on the idea of "pre-experiencing," or review in the mind, of something we have done and practiced and will do again. Performance is enhanced and enormously improved as a result of this pre-experiencing. I know it worked. My students' comprehension and use of the verbal structure dramatically improved when Monday instead of Friday became the consequence day for the verb exam. Dealing with the verbal structure four days and then consequences of an exam on Friday sent too many students home miserable for the weekend.

Dialogues and speeches were done on Friday, never on Monday. All week the students could consult me or their peers and have speech or dialogue done on Friday. Everyone looked forward with great anticipation to dialogue or speech day. This was always the occasion for a good grade—great motivation in itself. Performing gave pleasure to the students and me. We laughed together. If they were prepared they went home happy. None failed. Victory!

The other three days of the week were varied in the activities of grammar (new and old), new vocabulary, review of old vocabulary, reading aloud, text commentary and questions, and dictations practiced and graded. These three days sandwiched between two standard, unchangeable days, gave my students a better chance at success in learning the language. Only those who refused to do the work failed. They were few. I found that these few failed for one of two reasons:

1. They wanted to prove something to parents. They could defy them and the parents were helpless.
2. They refused to discipline themselves to consistent study, always necessary for any kind of scholarship. Their habits remained erratic in many areas. Failure was never due to lack of ability.

Students who received an "F" learned some French, but they also learned a valuable lesson for life: Refusal to do something one is obliged to do brings unpleasant consequences.

I told my students that God expected me to do my own scholastic spade work; I appealed to Him for help in influencing their lives for good. I reminded them that I was there to teach them the immeasurable joy of work and experience joy by being able to speak the beautiful French language. I told them that I did not want to leave them the dull grey smudge of the memory of a year badly spent but rather to carry away that bright rainbow of victory and its pot of gold—fluency at year's end. To accomplish this we would all work and sweat together. (We never perspired in my classes.)

Swatches of that rainbow will appear early for students whose teachers are committed and determined to teach the academic discipline involved while at the same time caring deeply for their charges. Academic work can be as pleasurable as football and cheerleading practice are claimed to be. Why shouldn't the teachers be as demanding as the coaches? They are expected to win games. What school brags about a losing team?

In our primary and secondary schools we should put the emphasis on teaching young people to discipline themselves to cultivate the mind to work and to study, to problem solving and to believing in themselves. Games end with the blowing of a whistle. Life goes on long years after a student's departure from high school and memories last forever. The taste of excellence can be savored forever provided we do not content ourselves with mediocrity in ourselves or in our students.

This book treats several areas:

1. *My philosophy of teaching,* which is briefly stated in the preface and which is touched upon in various chapters dealing with specific topics.

2. *General techniques* of classroom management that could be adopted by any teacher and especially by a foreign language teacher.

3. *Specific areas of difficulty* in teaching French. Even these can be duplicated in any foreign language. Let us remember that English is a foreign language to some Americans, and I do not necessarily mean recent immigrants.

4. *Memoirs:* Memories of other times, students long gone, difficult times, miracles of change I saw in my adolescent flock year by year which have constantly risen to the surface of my mind and heart as I have written. I could not write them all, but the writing has called up the joy I found in teaching and in seeing miracles developing before me.

The chapters are each designed to be a separate entity so the entire text need not be consumed in order to glean teaching ideas.

It is my wish and my hope that these pages may help beginning teachers to get their sea legs in the constantly rocking boat of academe and encourage them to remain in the classroom with dedication and increased caring. May they inspire those about to abandon ship to take a new look at the joys and satisfaction that inevitably come to the caring believers in the divine spark in man and the necessity of fanning this spark to a flame in the classroom.

For administrators and guidance counselors who may read this book, my wish is that you might comprehend a little what fun *and joy* you are missing and have missed as a result of leaving the classroom.

The moral force of America is not yet spent in my view, but the engine that generates the power needs an overhaul.

May those who read this—teachers, administrators, counselors, or parents—be inspired enough to want to be part of the renaissance I see ahead for America's public schools.

MARY D. NELSON
Vienna, Virginia, 1989

1

Creating an Image

Have you ever wondered how others see you? Do you know the effect you have on others?

Teachers must take their image-making seriously. After my first several months teaching French, I was forced to recognize the images my students had of me. Their impressionistic masterpieces were displayed by the art department on one entire wall of our high school. The personality they painted became the talk of the school—an instant celebrity. Obviously many of my students were studying art. Their work dominated the exhibit.

There I was: A dive bomber of many hues, a bloodshot eye staring from a storm-swept sky, lightning with many pointed darts, a mass of swirling clouds and some blue space—truly an electric personality, even thunderous.

I was shocked. I saw myself as a rather mild individual whose heart was brimming with love and complete acceptance for every student. I had to take a closer look at myself. I knew that I was well prepared to teach the French language as a result of my three years in French schools in France, but these pictures revealed me as a person—not my professional preparation. Did these impressionistic gems represent repressed fear of Madame in the artists or just excitement about learning? Did the students enjoy this highly charged personality and atmosphere they had painted? I had to do some soul-searching and ask myself whether I wanted to be a light bulb or an electrical socket in their lives.

My students were waiting for my reaction after I had returned from this museum promenade. I told them it was one of the most exciting displays of artistic expression I had ever seen and that I was delighted to be their subject. I learned some important lessons that day. First, I learned how great it is for students to be able to tease a teacher and have the teacher join in the fun. They were delighted with my reaction. Second, my students were forming a visual and sound image of me. I came on like lightning and thunder. And third, I had to be prepared to project a personality or image of my own choosing and convey what was in my heart. Being perceived as an electric personality did not trouble me, but there were other things I wanted them to learn. They had to see my heart, understand that I loved them regardless of what grade they earned in French. But how? I would have to earn their respect before they could understand how much I cared about them and what we were doing.

Those first few weeks I resolved to make each precious minute count for something of value from first bell to final bell. They would gradually learn to enjoy hard work because I did. That disease is catching. We are what we do as well as how we appear. They would be workers too. There would be no shallows, no doldrums for our French boat. We would reach our snug harbor—fluency by springtime, I hoped. My list of interesting things to do in class would never exhaust itself. The atmosphere, as well as I, would be electric, exciting, I resolved, and I would tell them I loved them at least once a week and show them every day.

Some years later the parents of one of my students confided in me that their daughter had told them that she would never drop French, although she was always complaining about the work I expected her to do (she was with me four years). Her surprised parents asked why. "I can always count on something happening in Madame's class. I am never bored and that's more than I can say about my other classes."

It often takes time for teachers to learn that they have chosen the correct path in all they do. I rejoiced in my beginning resolve. Remember that adolescents rarely tell their teachers that they like to work.

That first year I had to make the important decisions for the techniques I would use to communicate to my students my care and concern for them. How could I *show* my love for them? They would spend one hour a day, five days a week with me, more time than many spent with their own parents. Children and parents can inhabit a house and not pass much time together after the children reach school age.

Examining my behavior and how I communicated love to my husband and our son, I convinced myself that my students had to be treated as members of my family. The techniques had to be the same. I would tell my charges that I loved them—not liked—but loved them. My love would be personal. My *likes* would be confined solely to their work and its quality—never to them as people.

Sometimes I did not like what my husband and son did, but I loved them unconditionally. I would have to tell my students often that I loved them. My behavior had to reflect this love. My husband and son needed the same kind of verbal and behavioral reinforcement in what I said and what I did. I remember our son at five years of age. He had done something that had displeased me. I explained to him that what he had done was wrong and that he must not repeat that behavior because he had been taught not to do it and why. I kissed him and told him that I loved him and forgave him. Now he should pray and ask God to forgive him, too. It was bedtime and my husband and I left our son's room. Not long after we heard weeping. We returned to ask our son what was wrong. "I've prayed and prayed and God hasn't said a word," he said. I comforted our troubled child by telling him that he would hear with his heart and understand the Lord's answer by how he felt.

My students would understand my love by what I said and did. I couldn't leave it up to God to speak to my students or to do my work of loving and forgiving, but I would, and still do, need divine help to continue my committed course. My behavior and my words had to be sincere, believable to my students. Being credible would take careful thought and constant attention to how my students behaved—not just how they worked. They would need to feel part of my family—a believable part.

The many faces we construct to mask ourselves and to hide our inner feelings disappear like mist in sunlight before the piercing eyes of adolescents. We may deceive children for a time, but never adolescents. The nascent, struggling adults within them easily discern our facades; they have already learned to form some for themselves, and they doubt, a normal state for this age. The thirsting of their soul for credible models of their culture will not be quenched by masks, puppets, and nonbelievers. The north star of the adolescent is not yet firmly fixed. Their search for models to guide them through shoals of doubt is relentless until they steady their course. They are constantly searching for a believable self and a worthy self-image. Therefore, our image must be believable, firmly anchored in the basic cultural values of the society in which we live and which we are morally obligated to personify and to represent.

That first year I made some commitments to myself that I endeavored to keep and remember:

1. I would always be willing to learn from my students or others. I would be a scholar.

2. I would never *blow my top*. When I wanted to play a memorable "scene," I would act it to the hilt—for a *cause*, not a *trifle*.

3. I would be willing to sacrifice my ego to save face for a student.

4. I would treat students with respect, hoping that they would respect me because I would demand something of them and myself every day.

5. I would laugh at myself when occasion demanded. That would always relieve tension. A good story about my own mistakes would help them to bear their own and help us grow fond of each other as the year advanced. This would help each class become a small community of souls, all striving for the same goal.

Mirth is the magic ingredient of progress. It destroys false gods and pompous fools, and clears cobwebs from the mind. My students had many occasions to laugh, but I wanted to be remembered because I had taught them something and loved them.

One year I was so intent on getting students to remember that the feminine adjective for *old* in French had an extra "i" in it that I conceived the notion of calling myself la vieille dragonne (the old dragon). A tradition was born—no, it became a legend. That was one thing I never had to repeat three times or ten times. Talk about image! That did it. My students smiled whenever they heard it. They fabricated stories about their legendary beast, played dialogues, wrote skits with someone gladly assuming the dragon role. What sense of power! Long years later, tales of La Vieille Dragonne were told again and again, not just by my students, but others as well who had only known me by reputation. The huge, spotted, red, green, and yellow dragon my students presented me one day hung from the ceiling of my room for years with a sign hanging from her neck—"Entrez, mes enfants. Je vous accueille à bras ouverts. Ne parlons que cette belle langue française." (Enter, my children. I welcome you with open arms. Let us speak only this beautiful French language.) My door was often decorated by paper dragons made by my students. Dragons

La Vieille Dragonne—the red, green, and yellow
dragon presented to Madame Nelson by her students

appeared on cakes, notes—all done by students who knew that I would comment and praise their artwork. I became memorable. My students gave me a logo.

One year as a result of an administrative memo about students smoking, I did a dragonish thing. As I was passing the door of the boys' restroom, two students said, "Madame, there are some fellows in there smoking." To do the unpredictable was expected of me. "Gentlemen, go in and warn those students that Madame Nelson is coming in," I told them. They did. I immediately followed them and asked three unbelievers to please follow me to the vice-principal's office. They came along like lambs, too stunned to protest. I walked into Monsieur K.'s office and announced, "I found these three gentlemen smoking in the boys' restroom." My equally surprised superior was momentarily speechless, then he bent over some papers on his desk to hide his smile and asked without looking up, "In the boys' restroom, Madame?" "Yes sir," was my reply as I went out the door.

The news of the Old Dragon's restroom visit moved with hurricane swiftness through a student population of two thousand and a teaching and support staff of well over a hundred. I went my way in the "eye" of the momentary storm. No one ever discussed the incident with me, but for days I was greeted with smiles and unspoken questions from colleagues. I never mentioned the episode to anyone but my husband, who listened with appreciation and made a request I always remembered: "Darling, please never change. Don't change being unpredictable." I never again visited the boys' restroom, but legend had it that such a visit had high priority on my unpredictable list.

Teachers sometimes play one role in the classroom and another when they are elsewhere. I found that being myself inside and outside the classroom was the only way I could live. I was Mother to our son, Grand-mère to grandchildren, and Gorgeous to my husband. Only intimate friends called me by my name, Mary

7

D. However, I was Madame Nelson everywhere else, even to my husband if he happened to be speaking of me to acquaintances or associates. We both had been reared to believe that we admitted people to our intimate circle only after much time. The unfortunate, and, in my opinion, almost impudent practice so prevalent in America of strangers calling people they have just met by their first name offends me. I found that maintaining a dignified but always cooperative and concerned presence in everything I did and said on all occasions with parents, administrators, colleagues, and students was the best path for me. I was comfortable and happy and worked best in a businesslike atmosphere. Other teachers may choose other methods.

I was a French ambassador in and out of my classroom. I was Madame. In everything I said and did I created a French aura about me. In all my note writing to students, parents, administration, and colleagues, my signature was Madame. A certain aura is a must for any teacher.

Some personal examples:

An urgent message came to me from our principal. He wanted me in his office right away. We were showing French films that day and I was reluctant to leave. My messenger assured me I had to come at once. I arranged for a teacher to replace me and went to the principal's office. As I hurried along, I wondered what had happened that had so upset Monsieur T. This was so unlike the man. My wonder ceased when I walked in and Monsieur T. presented the minister-counselor of a major South American embassy to me. He had obviously intimidated my good principal. This man's rigid, military stance and stern stare gave away his dictatorial attitude. I met his gaze with a stare more frigid and haughty than his, then I extended my hand in the typical gesture of a French upper-class woman. This was more eloquent than words.

He clicked his heels, took my hand, and bowed over it. I

began in French; he responded in French. Not one word of English passed my lips. My attitude was polite but distant. His complaint was that we were showing a film of unfair propaganda against his country. I asked him if he had signed the consent form allowing us to show films of our choosing to his son (his son was not my student). He had. The film, however, was biased, he protested. I said that I knew that. I reminded him also that in a free society we entertained many ideas and points of view in order to be able to teach our students to discern truth from propaganda or fiction. Then I asked if he had seen the film. He had not.

"How interesting," I replied. "You see, sir, it is anti-American, anti-U.S. propaganda. How odd that your informant interpreted the fictitious South American dictatorship to be your country. We shall remove your son from the showing of the film and provide instead a class in grammar review for him. However, you shall explain to your son why we are obliged to do this. We do not accept this kind of censorship."

I arose to take my leave and again extended my hand. He took my hand and bowed and murmured, "That won't be necessary, Madame."

As I raised my eyes to look at my smiling principal, who had not understood a word of French, I was reminded of the satisfied whisker-licking and tail-switching cat who had just caught his mouse. Monsieur T. had understood the changed tone of voice and body language of his previously protesting assailant.

On another occasion our school was going through its evaluation year in order to be certified. The foreign language department had evaluated itself. We were critical of our weaknesses and noted what we did well. We rated ourselves at good, plus a few points.

The evaluating foreign language team arrived to give us a thorough inspection of several days. The leader of the team was the chairman of the foreign language faculty of one of the prestigious universities of our state, a Dr. B., a German name I thought. I was correct. I heard his German accent as the introductions began. Cultural remembrance rose within me, filling me with rebellion and thoughts of the invasion of France by German troops three times within seventy years.

I extended my hand, palm down, and spoke to him in French. M. S., the guidance director, protested, "But Madame, perhaps Dr. B. does not speak French."

I replied in French, "My dear M. S., every cultivated European speaks French."

Dr. B. bowed and never spoke a word of English to me during the evaluation. He loved it. He was flattered. I tried to forget the visions of invading German troops and decided a temporary truce would be in order. After all, de Gaulle spoke English but refused to speak anything but French with official visitors. Why shouldn't I?

Image making? Indeed it is. Furthermore, the impression is lasting.

One day a disgruntled parent came to the guidance counselor of her child to lodge a complaint against me. The parent did not want to face me.

"Why this 'Madame bit' with Nelson?" she began as she sat down.

The counselor contemplated her visitor for a minute and replied, "Because that is who she is—Madame Nelson."

I never heard the complaint of the parent, but my guidance counselor friend delightedly told me the story and assured me that the parent went away satisfied with the counselor's explanation of my grading system. She perhaps felt no fear in facing a "Mrs.," but didn't want to face a "Madame." This can be a useful technique for self-protection.

Whatever beast—elephant, stampeding buffalo, dragon, or

donkey—you may choose to personify for your students, be memorable, lovingly memorable, inside and outside of the classroom. You may decide that you do not wish to assume the image of an animal, but bear in mind that people and especially children and teens find animal images interesting and lovable. Whatever image you may choose to make for yourself, please remember to love your charges unconditionally. Be able to grade yourself with "F" in the three graduate courses of pedagogy: F=Firm, F=Fair, and F=Friendly. Perhaps you should add two more that you construct for yourself: F=Funtastic and F=Fabled.

Foreign language teachers must be able to interpret the values of another culture through the barriers of another tongue. Whatever political or religious styles of living and thinking that are unique to teachers cannot and should not be preached as the only ones acceptable to their captive students. Those are issues, not values. Issues can only be intelligently chosen and conclusions reached if built upon values—the basics of honesty, decency, and the moral values upon which a culture is founded. These all imply standards—high standards—not bumbling mediocrity. They must be taught in the classroom as well as at home. Teachers are not fence sitters here, unless they want to disappear as no more than a blip on the mind screen of their students. Even the curriculum content of a teacher who has no values will be "gone with the wind" in five years or less.

Teachers who have no basic values usually see nothing to value. That will be the image they project. Students will soon recognize what value they assume in a valueless system. They cannot be deceived, nor will they be nourished at a time when their hunger is greatest. Adolescents want to make sense out of life, even though rebellion bubbles constantly in their veins. They want to see and experience compassion at times when all they feel is defeat. They want to see someone who is courageous enough to take a stand when they lack courage about honesty, decency, morality. They want to experience triumph based on what they accomplish by their own efforts. They want someone to expect something of them. They want to anchor their north star regardless of their pendulum swings from pole to pole. They want teachers they can trust, teachers who are honest, fair, scholarly, demanding, yet understanding and friendly—but never buddies.

Teachers who take lightly or shrug off this unwritten moral contract of passing to their charges the values, traditions, and moral baggage of a culture cheat their students and deny themselves joy in their work. They care not at all for their own image. The metabolism of history will not write the names of such teachers, even on the sand. They never were because they never did, or never stood. Teachers who think that curriculum content alone will engrave their image on the mind and heart of their students delude themselves. The shadow, larger than life, they could cast on the future thought and behavior of their students will be transparent—not even vaporous.

People who choose the teaching profession are, in my opinion, basically idealists. Teachers' salaries could attract no others. However, I am persuaded that beginners tend to look at the "fruits" of pedagogy without examining the roots, the nurture of the vine, the back-breaking endurance necessary, as well as vagaries of climate and season. The preparation for planting is even less considered.

Take your image-making seriously if you would teach. This requires careful thought and preparation and constant attention to signs of deterioration.

Bursts of feeling when we see our own emotions filtering, changing, enlarging, or concentrating will undo us, cast aside our masks, unless we have already decided and chosen the direction and goal of our teaching and accepted the responsibility of our moral contract with the future.

In word, in dress, in behavior, in thought—be the warm, re-

12

sponsible, caring human being you want your students to be. I respectfully submit that this is the only realistic, workable formula for any teacher of any discipline at any level of learning. Try it. It works! Your image will be lasting. Memory links us to the past and the future. Samuel Johnson said, "It is indeed the faculty of remembrance which may be said to place us in the class of moral agents."

Your students will remember you, remember almost all you taught them, and will return to tell you how you influenced their lives. This formula will produce ripple effects in other areas of your students' lives. In your retired years, your memories will be sweet.

2

Order in the Classroom

Teachers have several workdays to prepare to receive their students on the first day. Those workdays should be used for thorough preparation—not idle chatter.

Get acquainted with your students. Have on hand enough three-by-five-inch index cards for all students in all classes. On these cards the students write their name, class period, date, and schedule of classes. On the back, the parents' names, address, and telephone number, and the number of years, if any, the student has studied French. The students then write hobbies, interests, and the name of their guidance counselor. Is there a parent who speaks French?

This information gives the perceptive teacher a quick glimpse into the personality of the students and sometimes conditions at home. The parents' names are vital; there may be a divorce.

Caution: Wait one week or ten days before studying these cards. Form your own opinion of your young charges; then go to the record on the three-by-five-inch cards. In the event of a student's hasty decision to drop your class, call home to encourage the parents and the student. It will do wonders in building your image as a caring teacher and often save a student with great potential.

Have a list of necessary class supplies required of all students and explain why they are necessary for the student. The list should include:

1. A loose-leaf notebook large enough to hold all papers, all exams, all verb quizzes, and all instruction sheets you will give every student. Have a model of what you expect.
2. Pencils and pen in a plastic holder anchored in the notebook. Again, have a model of what you require. They should also have a red pen. This will be used to correct papers in class.

The notebook is to be brought to class every day without exception. Inspect it occasionally to see that there is proper order of all papers. Announce inspection several days in advance (usually). All papers will be dated the day you give them to students (verb sheets, explanations, class rules, etc.). Tell them that you keep your own log notebook of all daily paper shuffling in addition to your lesson plan book. Tell them also that in your grade book, all quizzes are numbered and dated and will correspond to their notebook (see "Grading and Communication," chapter 3).

Explain the need of records. Good records save time—and they teach. They provide a road map that will help build trust. Guidelines and trust work together to promote self-confidence in the students' ability to learn French. They protect the student and you as well. You must always know where you are going and where you have been. A lesson plan book is not enough. There are interruptions, emergencies, and sometimes changes. All should be noted and reflected in your daily log notebook as well as in your grade book. The students' notebook will be the basis for review all year.

Take roll orally every day. Insist that your substitute do the same in your absence, marking absences or tardies.

Make eye contact as you take roll and expect that students reply "présent" or "présente." The importance of this cannot be underestimated. You, the teacher, are legally and morally bound to know whether the students assigned to your charge are indeed

16

present or absent. This roll taking soon conveys a hidden message: *"I am important to Madame Nelson. She cares whether or not I am there."* You will learn their names quickly, a very important consideration. I have heard too many students complain about uncaring teachers: "Why, Madame, he doesn't know who is there. He never takes roll."

Do not substitute body count for oral roll taking. Oral roll-taking and eye contact provide the teacher another psychological tool for communicating caring concern: "Où étiez-vous hier? Vous m'avez manqué" (Where were you yesterday? I missed you). It gives the student the occasion to say: "J'étais malade toute la journée" (I was ill all day long) or something else.

The absence of a student can be marked by a small red zero in the upper right corner of the grade box, the tardy student by an "x" in the same corner. For very late arrivals I filled in the small red zero. Have *some* system of marking tardies and absences. You won't remember at the end of the class or end of the day, so it must be done when taking roll. In the event of a hasty exit from school, you will be expected to know whether all students are present, so a marked book is a must. It is carried out of the building in your hands for fire drills or the real thing.

Insist that students be on time. My door was locked immediately following the bell. A tardy student was obliged to knock in order to be admitted by the student who sat by the door. Thus a student could not slip into the classroom unnoticed. The door was closed at the ringing of the bell and anyone who knocked was tardy. Three tardy arrivals meant detention. Write this down in the rules of your classroom on a sheet given out the first day.

There should be homework. Friday morning before class, *write* the following week's schedule of events for every level of French you teach *somewhere in a place visible to all students*. List by day of week. You do not have blackboard space for this. I had a large tablet (27-by-36-inch) anchored to the wall on which

I could write with a magic marker in script large enough to be seen anywhere in the room. Telling them about homework will not work.

For the first three days, I reminded students that assignments were their responsibility, and then I ceased oral reference to future work, exams, and the like, unless I wanted to indicate something unusual about what was written. Due dates for reports for advanced classes were posted well in advance on the large tablet. What was listed comprised only the homework expected, exams, speeches, and reports. It did not list all the activities scheduled in my log and plan books for the entire class period.

Avoid preoccupation with time. The large clock face in my classroom was covered by a sign that read: "Etes-vous pressés? Alors, revenons aux moutons." (Are you in a hurry? Let us get back to the sheep [business at hand].) In the event of my absence, students always took the sign and hid it behind cabinets or just left it on a desk. I always pretended great surprise and blamed such behavior on some strange student who had come in. Sometimes the students named the culprit—the substitute teacher. My invariable reply was, "Ma foi, pas possible!" while pretending surprised sorrow. The sign was never stolen. There were always several in reserve. The students were aware of this. I never showed irritation, but my remark, "Les enfants seront toujours les enfants, hélas" (Children will be children, alas) left its mark on my students. They loved this little game—and paid attention during class!

Do not waste time beginning. This is important. Be prepared to go to work at once when the bell rings. You can prevent waste of time after taking roll by saying, "Numéro un" for a verb quiz. Require that dialogues, reports, and speeches be placed on your desk as the students enter the classroom. Sheets to be passed out for inclusion in notebooks should have been placed on a table (card table will do) in the middle of the room. Students

18

pick them up themselves. Corrected exams should be placed in a desk file marked with each period. Don't waste time passing out corrected exams or papers. Let the students find their own papers. Learning responsibility is a long and daily lesson.

Teach your curriculum content. Teachers of any academic discipline should concentrate on teaching the curriculum of what they are charged with teaching and abstain from criticizing or commenting on other teachers' domains. You have quite enough in your own. Your class time is too limited and too precious to waste on other areas if you are criticizing and not complimenting and approving. *Scrupulously avoid commenting on other teachers' methodologies* or criticizing your superiors or any student absent or present. You can listen to students without replying to any such comments from your students.

An orderly, professional classroom requires extreme self-discipline by the teacher in what is said and done. Students imitate what they see and hear. *Remember that you control your classroom in order that learning may be the rule.* Teachers must learn to control themselves in behavior and speech if they expect and teach order and control in their students.

Assign student assistants. Most high schools once had study halls where students were supposed to study, but often didn't, in the free hour that was built into each student's schedule. Teachers were assigned to monitor these areas like gendarmes, requiring silence and not much moving about on the part of the students. Many discipline problems arose from this practice. In addition, the space required for several hundred students at one time was costly since these areas were not available for more productive activity.

Why do I say *more productive?* Isn't study productive? Indeed it is if self-initiated. We cannot *make* students study; five or six teacher-gendarmes stalking about can hardly be effective. Students must be persuaded to study by their teachers.

19

Studying French aloud not only aids analytical thought, but employs the sense of hearing, which greatly increases the value of the sense of sight. But my students could not study aloud in study hall.

How gratified I was when our system abandoned this futile study hall practice. Some students were allowed to leave school one hour earlier because of no sixth period. Others could not. Student assistants became the rule in our system. In our school, assistants eventually received one hour of credit.

My student assistants literally gave me the gift of a twenty-eight hour day for I usually had at least four assigned to me. However, they had to meet several requirements:

1. They had to know how to type.
2. They had to have some previous exposure to French—at least one year.
3. They had to report to me on their assigned hour as faithfully as they did to class. Dismissal from my charge would be the result of the first truancy.
4. They had to arrive on time.

The teachers were charged with the legal and, in my view the unwritten rule, moral responsibility of knowing where these students were during the hour that they were assigned to us. The additional requirement by the school was that the students be accepted by the teacher as assistants before they could be assigned.

When this program began, I was astonished at the number of students requesting to be my assistants. They readily accepted my requirements and I embraced them gladly, always grateful for their work. Some were my own students the year of their assistantship, some had been my students, but some had never been my students. They typed exams, work sheets and letters, corrected the recopied verb quizzes (if able), ran errands, picked up my mail, and tutored others if they were able.

Were they trustworthy? A thousand times yes. Was the security of my exams ever breached? Never. The only exam my assistants did not always type was the end-of-the-year final, and sometimes they did that if they were not in one of my classes. I usually did the copying of exams, but that would depend upon who happened to be my assistants. Breaching the security of any exam with me would have been exceedingly difficult, since my students knew only the principles involved on an announced exam. They also knew that my methods of examining were extremely varied and usually oral and then written. They were also aware that I would be armed with stacks of different exams that would examine the same principles of grammar and comprehension. Students could only safely predict that I had many ways of examining what they knew they had to know. My student assistants were as intent as I in keeping things moving and orderly in my classroom. On some occasions I was called away briefly just as class was beginning. I knew that upon my return roll would have been taken and any other detail of class management accomplished that assistants might do.

I posted work assignments for my assistants at least two weeks in advance. I planned so far ahead that they were able to chart their time for both my work and their own studies. When they needed the entire hour to study, they knew they could have it if they asked. They knew that, owing to advance planning, my work plans would not be neglected.

These student assistants did the enormous work of letter writing that the launching of a new chapter of the American Association of Teachers of French entailed. They handled the paper load during the years I was president of the chapter and the many years I acted as chairman for the Center for the National French Contest in our region. In only one instance were my assistants not employed while I served on the National Committee for Test Development for the National French Contest; they could not type my confidential report and recommendations to the committee. Even then my assistants might have participated for I was obliged to submit more than one example of the area that fell to my charge since the choice for the National Exam was always unknown to me. Teachers who have not helped in professional activities beyond their classroom domain are unable to estimate the innumerable hours that these areas require.

Doing this greatly enriched my life. My worthy and hard-working student assistants allowed me this extra dimension during my career. On holidays and at year's end I gave them a money gift and a note of thanks—small pay for the great service they provided me, their peers, and my colleagues. They paid me the tribute of feeling free to sit among my students occasionally if there was no work to be done, even though they may never have studied with me. Their faces remain in my memory still, but some of their names have danced from my brain.

In a school where black students were no more than a hundred in a student population of about two thousand, I was blessed with two black assistants of unusual devotion. Why do I recall this here? These two young ladies kept me informed of what was going on in the small black community whose students came to our high school. They did not serve as my assistants the same year, but many years apart. The first worked with me at a time of great unrest among the black students. A few of these students (not mine) had decided that being uncooperative with the learning process to the point of disruptive and insolent behavior in the classroom and perpetual truancy was their route and their obligation. One day my assistant said to me, "Madame, if the principal and vice-principals don't stop being scared of the black kids and start shaping them up, this school is going to be in big trouble."

"Afraid? For Heaven's sake, why?" I asked.

"I don't know, but they are," she said. Her tone of voice dripped disgust.

Gail had been my student the previous year in French III and as a result of my encouragement had gone to French IV. I was not teaching that level that year. I made a mental note of what she had said and concluded that she was sending me another message. She had been the witness some time earlier to a little exchange between me and a vice-principal with whom I disagreed when he had the temerity to charge into my room and ask me in front of Gail why I was not doing something to which I had objected because of a violated principle. This man expected to intimidate me with his outrageous demand. Gail had noted my calm, determined reply and refusal and the lack of knee-trembling on my part. She realized that tiger behavior in anyone moved me not at all, except to a disgust equal to what I detected in her voice. I decided that I would pass on the warning to the administration. I quoted my black assistant to another vice principal who appeared to listen. Whether that bug-in-the-ear did some burrowing into the thought process of our authority figures, I do not know. It may have taken a few more bugs to help things simmer down with the few disruptive students, but simmer down they did. Order gradually became the rule.

The following year I was invited to come and have lunch in the home economics department by three of my black colleagues, one of whom taught in that department. I was surprised to find that I was the only one they had invited. We talked and laughed about many things during the short time we were together. During the conversation, one of them remarked, "Madame, you wouldn't believe it, but some of our biggest white male colleagues are terrified of our black boys. Thank God you're not."

They noted my surprised look as I replied, "How ridiculous. I can't imagine why anyone should be afraid of black boys or white boys, they are all boys to me—not yet men. They will behave as gentlemen if we expect that of them. If they don't, then they remain boys and should be treated as such."

We all smiled our appreciation of each other. My colleagues

23

had given me an unspoken message and I had returned the favor. My remarks acknowledged that I knew that black males resented being called "Boy" at any age and that I intended to treat students equally. Boys were boys, whatever the color of their skin—be it black, white, brown, yellow, or black and blue—until they became men. The interior color of what was between the ears of all my students was certainly green, and I tried always to remember that was true for me, too. My three friends had already concluded that I knew the significance of the word *boy* to black students, but they needed assurance. They became my staunch supporters.

The other black assistant who helped me many years later had never been my student, but she was one of the most efficient I ever had. She didn't need pictures or any explanation from me about my methods and my insistence on order and discipline. She had already informed herself elsewhere. She was with me the year of "Athletic French" (see chapter 8) and gave my four black athletes in that class much stern advice about "shaping up." She, accompanied by her first child, came back to see me some years later. She was memorable, intensely and fondly memorable.

America is in sad shape if we allow fear to enter the thinking of those who are charged with our schools—in our classrooms or in our administrative areas. If a white teacher cannot teach a classroom of all blacks, if a black teacher cannot teach a classroom of all whites, if a teacher cannot see that all the students are together green between the ears, cannot teach without fear, and cannot teach without prejudice or discrimination, then our brains in this country need some interior decorating and a little rearrangement of the furniture. We should bear in mind that all babies are born without pigmentation of the skin. The pigmentation takes place hours after birth. We all arrive on earth pink. It is my belief that this can and must be believed by all if excellence becomes more than a dream. Alexis de Tocqueville (*Democracy in America,* 1835) is sometimes quoted as writing, "America is great because she is good." However, he noted that America could remain great or become great if she escaped the tyranny of the majority that our system of government might engender.

I submit that we must escape the tyranny of minorities and the tyranny of a thin majority as well. Our schools must be the forum of teaching more than the first-person singular pronoun, *I, I, me, me.* We must help our students learn to understand that *I, I, me, me* cannot be the only rule, but allow the plural, *we, we, us, us,* regardless of color, race, or appearance to dominate our thinking to the extent that we admit that excellence requires work—striving on an individual level *for everyone.* If we are all equally mediocre, then excellence can never be considered as a required product for the vast sums spent on education. We shall remain the joke of the world—low man on the totem pole of academic excellence in primary and secondary schools.

3

Grading and Communicating

Teachers too often use their grade book as a club or a threat. This is wrongheaded and self-defeating—to the teacher and to the student. It leads to rebellion in teenagers and trouble for any teacher who may harbor desires for vengeance for any cause whatever. However, friends of mine have sometimes expressed their fear of going to see a teacher to express their concern about their unhappy child. Indeed, they feared their child might suffer as a result of their complaints about anything. This is foolish for parents. My advice to them was always, "Go see the teacher but leave your sword at home. There are always three points of view: the teacher's, the student's, and the parents'. *Consider the teachers your allies and return the favor by saying you are theirs.*"

It is my belief that early in the year teachers and parents should establish their support of each other to promote the well-being of the young people in the classroom. Everyone involved should understand that *grades do count for something;* they measure and evaluate work done and its quality—nothing else. Grades are an imperfect tool to record everything that has been absorbed or not absorbed by students. But until we develop a brain scan for every cell, grades will have to serve.

Grades are the students' responsibility. Students should understand from the first day that the scores in the teacher's grade

27

book are their responsibility—not the teacher's. These mathematical symbols will measure work and its quality, not the beautiful faces and the delightful personalities of the students. Teachers should tell their students just that, and the telling should be done with a smile, not threats. Winning friends and influencing students require the same techniques in the classroom as in the business world.

I assure anyone who reads this that transferring the idea of responsibility for grades from the teacher to the students can and does work. It worked in my classes, and I began the transfer of responsibility the first day. I reminded my students of this regularly: the fifth week of every quarter, during any student conference, and at the year's end. Any colleague I knew who mumbled threats about grades reaped a bitter harvest.

Teachers must also bear in mind that some parents may be extremely protective and suffer ego problems if their children bring home a grade they feel is unworthy of the intellect of their offspring. These are normal reactions. Parents, as well as students, may need reminding that *grades have very little to do with intellect.* Two of the most intellectually endowed of my students regularly received, and richly earned, poor grades in French because of sloppy, indifferent work. They refused to do consistent, organized homework. In some other classes they were able to slide by with a "B" or even an occasional "A," but not in French. Their parents had some difficulty with this, but my students did not and told me and their parents that they received what they had earned.

I wanted the respect of my students. I always told them that I was willing to wait for them to love me, but I valued their respect—the only reliable basis for love. Therefore, their grades would be earned, not given.

Consumed with the desire that their son or daughter should shine at any cost, some parents have even pressured principals to change grades on school records. I know that this happened in some cases. It never happened to me for very good reasons: (1) I would have screamed from the housetops; (2) my students would have complained; (3) my students regularly engaged in evaluating themselves at the end of each quarter and at year's end; and (4) my records were meticulously kept—grade book, interim reports on each student, any memos on absence, truancy, or behavior problems, plan book, and log notebook. The parents, students, and all administrative personnel were aware of my record keeping. There was no secret nor any unpredictability about Madame's records.

The Grade Book

A teacher should never allow students to consult the grade book alone or in groups. A student could look at the book with me after I had covered all names of other students. The grades of each student were individual concerns and thus the business of the student and the teacher alone. It was confidential information. Occasionally I have had parents ask for the grades of other students in the class of their child. I always expressed surprise at such a question and invited the parents to consult their child for such privileged knowledge. My concern at that conference was finding some means for better performance of their son or daughter. This question arose three times only during all my years in the classroom, but it can and does happen. Be prepared to deal with it firmly and diplomatically.

The grade book should never be in a secret code. It should be understandable to anyone. Grades should not be just checks or an "X," but *should* have a mathematical meaning.

Any code for absence, tardy, or cut should be explained. Such codes should be explained at the bottom of each page, not just the beginning of the book; thus they will be understandable to any administrator or guidance counselor. I used a small red zero in the upper right corner of the box for any day absent. If the student arrived late in the hour, I filled the zero with red. A tardy was recorded with a small x. If the student cut the class, the red zero filled the entire box.

Each grade in the book has a reason for being there. The type of exam, oral or written, is noted at the top of the column of the boxes for the grades for that day. A verb quiz, both oral and written, would have "verb" and the number of the exam that corresponded to that quiz in my log book. An exam on grammar would have "pronouns, rel." or "pronoun ob.," etc., plus the number of the exam. Idioms would be "Id" with the number of the exam in my log book. Dialogues, speeches, and reports were written as well as oral, and marked as such. These alone did not bear numbers but did have the name of the dialogue or report. The grades for all of the above were always recorded in black ink. At the end of every quarter, I added two grades, sometimes three, for the quality of oral class work, that is, response to questions and participation in class discussion. These grades were recorded in green ink. The final grade for the quarter was recorded in red ink. Teachers quickly learn the value of using different colored ink for quick identification of that which is on a page and its reason for being there. Keeping a careful log book that corresponds with a student's notebook and further explains your grade book saves time, charts the course of your work, and will provide a ready source of accurate information for you, the students, guidance counselors, and parents. This is separate from your plan book.

Your grade book must be guarded carefully. Never, never leave it at school. Some teachers have lost their grade book as a result of this careless practice. Do not lend your grade book to anyone, even to a substitute (this person may sometimes be a parent). It never leaves your possession until the end of the year after all final grades are calculated and it is turned over to the vice-principal charged with the security of this privileged information. Anyone who examines it during the year will do so looking over your shoulder.

Any counselor or administrator may request all the grades for a particular student at any time, but that request will arrive on a memo. You are obliged to reply promptly with your own memo with proper explanations. Be prepared to do this. You owe it to your students, to the parents, and to your superiors.

Your grade book will be at home with you if you become unexpectedly ill; therefore, *some record of all your students must remain at school in your desk at all times.* I kept a second grade book at school. No grades were ever recorded in it, but it was the same type of book with all students' names and their student number beside each name in the same class order as my grade book. The code for absences, tardies, or cuts was indicated and explained. I also indicated several students in each class who would be able to help the substitute teacher. I told my students that I *expected* their cooperation with my replacement whenever I might be absent and also that of the students who were responsible for helping. My students thrived on my confidence in them. They knew that I would expect and receive a written report on every class and would praise their exemplary conduct, or lack of same, and suffer any consequences that would automatically result if trouble arose.

Exams

Students should receive their exams back after grading as quickly as possible. This requires work at home by the teacher, but whoever said that teaching is not work? Disabuse yourself of the wild idea that work ends for a teacher with the final bell for the day. Guidance counselors and administrative personnel may sometimes leave the classroom because of the after-school workload, but they give up other time. They must work most of the summer instead. Do not be deceived. Let this be a salutary warning to those who think that teaching is an easy way of earning one's living. There may be "baby-sitters" pretending to be teachers in the classroom, but I am convinced they either have a bad conscience or no conscience. They reap no rewards except oblivion.

Dedicated, caring teachers work harder, longer hours than students. I learned to cut down on my at-home work by giving shorter quizzes oftener, and by correcting these short exams in class by exchanging papers immediately after a quiz. My students learned more and retained more of what they learned. I always checked these papers.

Students wrote their student number *(note that they did not write their name)* on their papers with date, level of study (I, II, III, IV, V), and hour of the day. All this information was written in the upper right corner of the page. On a quiz, students were expected to write with a pencil in order that they could erase and correct their answers, thus there would be no difficulty for anyone to read what was written. Writing with a pen, I found, produced a scratched and often illegible mess that no one could read. What could not be read was automatically incorrect. I picked up the papers after the quiz and redistributed them myself. Students did not correct neighbors' papers. The students doing the correcting then wrote their name in *red* ink at the bottom of the page on the right and corrected the paper with the red pen or red pencil each student was required to carry to class every day.

Why am I so precise about the position of students' numbers and correcting students' names? This consistent method saved me time when I went over the papers myself to record grades and check errors. Student numbers protected the identity of students. The student doing the correcting was immediately identified to me and to the owner of the paper. When I reviewed the paper before entering the grade in my book, I saw the work only, not the face of the owner. I knew the student corrector and also whether that student was a dreamer. Students quickly learned not to be careless about what they did on other students' papers. They suffered consequences from two sources: (1) with their peers, who would complain if their papers were incorrectly done, and (2) with Madame, who lowered a grade if blatant carelessness was evident.

Exchanging papers with this method not only taught students to listen and to look carefully, but helped them to discipline themselves to be responsible for what they did to others. It also taught them to care about their own grades. Who wants to be classed as an incompetent know-nothing by one's peers? Mediocrity might be the norm of peer pressure in some schools, but I never saw it. My students learned to make themselves a class community quickly. Before leaving class on a quiz day, they went through the stack of papers to find their own and to note who had done the correcting. *Caution:* The teacher must immediately secure these papers in his/her briefcase and be sure all papers are accounted for. Occasionally a jubilant student carried off a paper with a good grade. The poor paper never developed legs. That kind of behavior produced a blank, a zero, in my grade book. Warn students of this. Rarely did this occur in my classes, but I was diligent about protecting students' papers. They went home with me and my grade book.

Teach students how to take your tests. Teachers construct many kinds of exams and quizzes. Therefore, it is my belief that teachers should teach their students how to take exams and should give practice exams of every type expected. In tests of multiple choice, I taught my students to learn to eliminate what they knew to be incorrect and then to proceed to the possible correct answer unless they knew it at first glance. Students beginning the ninth grade are not always prepared for every type of test. It is our responsibility to be as diverse and varied in our testing as we can possibly be. However, teach students your diversity before they are burdened with trying to guess what your testing procedures will be.

Reuse your exams. The order of questions might be rearranged or not, as you see fit, but I always numbered them. For example: If a list of questions was rearranged, the test bore the original number with the addition of a letter: Test 1 rearranged would be marked 1A.

Teach, then test. Teach and retest. Move forward but look back and examine the kind of progress *all* your students are making—and the progress *you* are making as their teacher.

Computing Grades

Don't grade on the curve. Students always wanted to know how I graded. The usual question was: "Do you grade on the curve?" My invariable response was: "Yes, I do indeed." The next question was: "What are the percentages?" I replied: "My dear students, you all make your own individual curve. If you all make 'A,' then we shall have one hundred percent 'A's.' If you all make 'F's,' then we shall have one hundred percent 'F's.'"

"But, Madame, you can't fail a whole class," was always their surprised chorus.

"I have never failed a student in my life." I always replied. "Students fail on their own. They get no help from me. But wait a minute, are you telling me that we can't have all 'F's'? Then we cannot have all 'A's.' Fair is fair. How about all 'A's'? It's your choice." That ended the matter. However, I learned from my students that some daredevil teachers had announced to their students the percentage of "A's," "B's," "C's," "D's," and "F's" that would occur in that class. I always warned students never to announce to me such a teacher's name. I wanted to consider my colleagues intelligent enough to know about self-fulfilling prophecy. Students do want to prove a teacher or parent correct—even an outright idiot.

Give grades only for accomplished work. Students never received grades for just coming to class ("warming the bench"). All grades were the result of having done something. However, a special grade, a zero, was reserved for any and every cut. This zero was never erased. It carried as much weight as an exam with 100 on it (see below for an example). I communicated this bit of information the first day orally, then later on by mathematical example on the board. Truancy was never a problem in my classes. Hell was preferable to a zero for a cut. They could eventually escape the Inferno, but that zero burned forever. I explained that I wanted to give them strength to fortify themselves against any temptation from their peers, but a better reason was that I wanted to remind them that I missed them when they were absent. I told them that I wanted them to feel loved.

Score by number with 100 the perfect score. I found that numbers from 1 to 100 served my purpose best. This system allowed my students to compute for themselves how near they were to earning an "A" or "B." A system of 0 to 4 does not permit this. They knew their own strengths or weaknesses and often could estimate to the microsecond how much more time they needed to study in order to put themselves in the next grade bracket. They always knew exactly where they were.

The first week I always gave them an example of the weight I gave to each exam or quiz, usually equal weight. For example, in the case of five equally weighted quizzes, one of which was failed or inexcusably missed:

	Score	
Quiz 1	100	
Quiz 2	0	
Quiz 3	100	The accumulative score would
Quiz 4	100	be 400 + 5 = 80 = C
Quiz 5	100	

In the case of four equally weighted quizzes:

	Score	
Quiz 1	100	
Quiz 2	100	The accumulative score
Quiz 3	0	would be 300 + 4 = 75 = D
Quiz 4	100	

They quickly saw the necessity of many grades for each quarter and the hope of recovery from one or two poor grades. They also saw the advantage of a repeated test if they reviewed and reviewed, as well as the value of avoiding a zero for cutting class. They could measure their own progress and cheer themselves along the way. Teachers should recognize that every one of us needs to feel victorious now and then.

I valued progress and the desire to improve, and for an incentive I would stretch the fraction of an average score to the next higher whole number if the student was putting forth effort to learn. For example, a score of 86.1 would be stretched to 87. A consequence of daydreaming could mean the loss of that tenth with the result that the 86 would be final. At Fort Hunt High School the difference between 86 and 87 was the difference of a whole letter grade.

On dialogues, reports, and speeches, I accorded a numerical grade. Therefore, A = 95–100, B = 87–94, C = 80–86, D = 70–79, F = anything below. This was the standard scale in the system used at Fort Hunt High School for many years. Teachers had the liberty of altering this slightly (at their own risk). Students sometimes complained that 95 was just a low "A." My response was an explanation of how I was treated in the French schools with a system of 0–20. One memorable professor announced with finality what would prevail in his class as a result of some students' complaints. I quote and translate: (Only French is spoken in schools in France, much to the wonder of some of my monolingual friends.) "Twenty is for God, nineteen is for me. Be content with fifteen." Then he glared. He didn't smile. "How dare his students question him" was the unexpressed thought behind that glare. A glare was respected and even expected in French schools. I delivered this little explanation with a smile. That behavior was more acceptable to my students. "One hundred is for God, ninety-nine for me. Be content with ninety-five."

The military recognizes the psychological advantages of decorations. Covering chests with medals for service beyond the call of duty in time of danger produced warriors of determination and great valor. Making it through the mine fields and exploding bombs of a foreign language classroom presided over by a demanding Old Dragon merited awards, decorations, and good grades. My students felt victorious with a "C." I always told them that the work of civilization was done by people who earned "C's." That was always victory in my book. They had endured and improved. They would be valuable to the world. They were to me.

One year a brave student who had survived the year with a skin-of-his teeth "B" at fourth level, laboriously burned into a wooden plaque Dante's words that decorated the portals of Hell: "Abandon all hope all you who enter here." John presented this plaque to me with a pleased smile at year's end. I never commented on John's grammatical error (in French) then or ever, but quickly decorated and saluted him in the French manner—a kiss on each cheek and the typical French handshake. John was proud of himself for having survived a hard year, and grateful to me, and I was proud of him and told him so as I "decorated" him. Cardboard medals can be struck with a little effort and were always valued by my students. I found occasion often to decorate my valiant strivers. An embrace and handshake French style were frequent and fun—usually expected. John's plaque hung above my classroom door for years, the object of amusement and comment for all students as well as for me.

Drop the first few grades and the one lowest grade during the term. The first two weeks of grades of the *first quarter only* were noted in my grade book *but erased* when computing the grade for the quarter. This gave students at lower levels a short time to accustom themselves to my testing techniques and to be consistent in their study habits. *The lowest grade of subsequent quarters was erased—one grade only.* This encouraged review.

The final grade for the year was usually computed by counting each quarter as one fifth and the final exam at year's end as a fifth. My final exam was usually broken up into three parts given over three days and divided by three to equal a final fifth. *I do not believe in all-morning or all-afternoon endurance trials.* I examined frequently enough every quarter to measure what had been learned throughout the year. This system worked well for me and my students. They were better motivated to regular study, which is the essence of scholarship. I wanted to teach them the pleasure of study and work as well as the French language.

Communicating Grades to Students and Parents

At Fort Hunt High School, at the end of the first five weeks of every quarter, students received an interim report which was usually sent only to students doing poor work and who might be in danger of failing. These interim reports were often called failure notices and were handed to the students in front of their peers so everyone in a class usually knew who received a warning notice. Every school system obliges teachers to send an interim report on a failing student. But I did not like this method of warning. In my opinion it discouraged, never encouraged.

Send a billet doux. All my students, I decided, would receive a notice; and I changed the name of this report from interim, or failure notice, to *billet doux,* which means love letter in French.

Did this involve much work? No, on the contrary. Instead of my computing averages that carried a letter grade, I shifted the burden of doing these math problems to my students. On my note paper that carried my name and some counsel, I wrote the student's name, the date, and all the grades earned to that date. Quickly going down my grade book page I listed each student's grades in a whole class in less time than it took to compute the average on two students. Guiding my eye with a white sheet of paper (to be sure I noted the grade boxes correctly for each student), I could finish five classes in about thirty minutes. I noted work missed as a result of absence (which was recorded as a zero until made up) and told students to calculate that zero equally with the other grades, then to figure their average without the zero. Students quickly made up their work in order to transform that zero into something of greater value. The students transferred the grades received on my note paper to a formal billet doux that I devised to encourage them regardless of their grades (see Figure 1).

They evaluated their own work, pretended they were Madame Nelson who was evaluating them, and checked areas where they could praise themselves or set new directions. They filled out two copies of this love letter and returned both to me. That evening I inserted a carbon between the two copies for each student and made my evaluation with checks and added a note of "Bravo" for work well done, or noted counsel when improvement was needed. This method "saved face" for the students doing poor work and gave me the occasion to give each student some attention, a pat on the back, some encouragement, suggestions for improvement when appropriate, and an expression of my hope and my joy.

One copy of this billet doux was carried home by the student for a parental signature and was then returned to me. The other copy remained in my files in the event of a lost report or parental

Figure 1

Billet Doux
(Interim Report)

Evaluation Form

Conseiller_____ Date_____

Le Français_____ de Madame Nelson   Nom d'élève_____

Student's Evaluation—circle appropriate item   *Grades to Date*

a. I always—rarely—usually do my work.

b. I always—rarely—indifferently learn speeches.

c. I come for help during the break—after school when needed.

d. I make up work—allow work to accumulate when absent.

e. I review regularly—never.

f. I pay attention—dream in class.

g. I do my best—I do not try.

h. I have cut class _____ times.

Madame Nelson's Evaluation

a. Always prepared—usually prepared—rarely prepared.

b. Gives speeches well.

c. Always polite—not always polite.

d. Pronunciation excellent.

e. Needs to better pronunciation.

f. Needs help—but does not come for it.

g. Indifferent attitude.

h. Progress shown (please encourage).

i. I love your son/daughter.

j. He/she tries.

k. Should repeat next year.

Citizenship

a. His/her cooperative attitude and fine citizenship contribute much to the good order and the progress of the class.

b. He/she respects authority.

c. He/she frequently lacks courtesy and self-control.

40

Commendation

a. He/she shows initiative, skill, and thoroughness, and applies knowledge gained to new situations.
b. He/she begins and completes work on time.
c. He/she takes part in discussions and is helpful to the group.
d. He/she follows directions carefully.
e. He/she shows an improvement in effort.

Probable reason for low mark

a. He/she failed to have the necessary equipment and materials.
b. He/she fails to hand in assignments on time.
c. He/she frequently came to class poorly prepared.
d. He/she failed to complete the required work.

Madame Nelson's telephone number _____

Some of this was written in French for my students. I also wrote the counselor's name and student's name in French. Student and parents could add their own comments.

---

inquiry. This system worked well for me, my students, and the parents. It literally saved many students from a poor grade for a quarter, permitted parents an early and a regular report on progress, and established good relations between teacher, student, and parents. *I never questioned a parental signature.*

Students quickly learned the meaning and the value of being responsible for what they were doing. This billet doux was never called a failure notice in my classes. In the event of a poor grade, this report provided me with the occasion for a short after-school conference when I could pick up, dust off, bandage wounds, and smile words of encouragement and love. I was able to direct floundering students to setting goals for themselves and to advise on study methods. I was always able to prophesy success. I re-

Figure 2

My note paper, 5x7 or one-fourth of an 8½x11 sheet of paper, on which I wrote all grades for every student at the end of the first five weeks of every quarter. These grades were transferred to the billet doux by the student, who computed his own average.

MADAME NELSON
Fort Hunt High School

Trente minutes   *Tout ce qui n'est pas*
chaque soir.   *clair n'est pas français.*

fused to admit failure if students would work. Lack of work was always the reason for failure with me.

The billet doux also proved a time-saver for me. Parents could write messages to me on the returned report or they could call me. Conferences with parents, always time-consuming and often inconvenient for teachers and parents, were rare as a result of this method of communicating grades and progress to students and parents. The love letter literally resolved many budding problems. Students and parents looked forward to receiving these reports. Parents were told about them on back-to-school night and they were noted in the letter to parents that was provided that same night (see chapter 4). I recommend this means of communicating grades to parents and students.

Students should never leave your class with a feeling of having been unfairly treated. If a wide difference exists in your evaluation of a student's work, this problem should be resolved between the two of you on a one-to-one basis. Talk it over. Have students *write* the "why" of their conviction of unfairness, then read this together. Writing diffuses anger and puts everything into perspective. A student does not want to be perceived as unfair either.

Challenges to my grading system were never made to me by my students. I did, however, have a rare parent who challenged the grades his son/daughter had received. However, this challenge was never made to me, oddly enough, but to the chief of guidance. My records were never changed. There was overwhelming evidence in my records of the amount and the quality of the work done—by all the students of every class. Thus the work of the son or daughter of the complaining parent could be shown in detail—and compared with the performance of all the others, if necessary.

Again, keep meticulous and explanatory records. They are time-savers and student savers. They teach the necessity of being responsible for one's own behavior. Be fair! Happy grading!

4

Problems
Prevention: An Ounce

Communicate with your allies—the parents—early. Students, parents, all of us are always more comfortable in a game if we are certain of the rules. Knowing what to expect gives us self-confidence in our ability to move ahead or just to survive a situation or an endurance test.

Learning a foreign language is just that—an endurance test—for the student, for the parent, and for the teacher. Writing general rules and giving these to students and to parents always has a calming effect.

I always had a "letter to parents" prepared to hand to the parents on "back-to-school night" (an example is given at the end of this chapter). This letter should be filled with polite warnings of what it takes for success in a foreign language. I began this letter with a positive note of welcome and a promise of success if students, parents, and teacher all worked together and the students did what was necessary. I added a guarantee of success if these requirements were met:

1. Daily oral practice at home (sometimes nothing but review)
2. Repetitive work, that is, memorizing
3. Constant review in class
4. Consistent oral work in doing homework
5. Thirty minutes of study every day, seven days a week (there is

no rest if one learns to think, to dream, to speak this language)
6. No daydreaming in class

(See below for a further discussion of these points.)

The letter ended with an offer of extra help from me to parents and to students. My telephone number was listed as well as the hour I arrived at and departed from school.

The P.S. was a lifeline to me. It was a promise of an interim report during the fifth week of each quarter listing all the grades of the student for that quarter. Parents depended upon this report and often told me how much it was appreciated. The parents were not cast adrift but received a map that would chart the course of their son or daughter with whom they entrusted me in this sea of foreign sound and symbol.

Parents are naturally fearful for the well-being of their child who is casting off in unknown waters. Teachers should recognize this fear and learn to communicate confidence and calm. Teachers must recognize that parents inevitably will be allies or foes. There is no middle ground. It is the rare parent who is indifferent to the success of his child. There is too much ego involvement to permit total indifference. I have never seen it.

Inform parents that at least 40 percent of English vocabulary is derived from French. Students arrive with an immense baggage of words that are merely pronounced differently in French. Give examples by writing them on the board and invite them to join you in saying them aloud. Point out to them the numerous instances of the use of French in our political vocabulary, in the advertising of products in newspapers, magazines, and on television. Run through a few place names on the map of America: Des Moines (some monks); Terre Haute (high ground—the explorers must have experienced a flood); Coeur d'Alène (heart of Alene); Boise (wooded); Nez–Perce (pierced noses); Grand Tetons (large nipples—as on a mother's breast); Detroit (narrow strait or passage); St. Louis; New (Nouvelle) Orleans; Fort Vincennes. The country abounds in French names.

Many of the Founding Fathers were certainly familiar with French. Some obviously had read Montesquieu's *L'esprit des lois* (Spirit of the laws), published in 1748, which described the separation of powers in an ideal civil government. Books in French were in Washington's, Jefferson's, and Franklin's libraries.

Point out to parents that even French idiots speak French. On the whole, high school students are extremely able, certainly not idiots. So everything is possible provided consistent work is done.

By Christmas the students will be talking to their pets in French and reciting their dialogues and speeches in front of their mirrors with all the appropriate gestures of the French environment. Their homes will resound with French. (I always counsel that all work be done aloud—even a written assignment.)

Homework for the weekend should be verb review and that can be done while taking a shower, emptying the trash, walking the dog, or playing ball. I recommend it to be done orally because that is how a verb quiz should be done on Monday.

Ask parents always to give you a telephone call if they have questions or doubts. Name the time of evening when it would be best to call. This always saves time and calms parents' fears. (Requests for parent conferences occurred rarely during my career.)

A teacher who does not consider parents as worthy allies sows seeds of discontent that often produce a harvest of thorns for the teacher. Keeping parents informed is the most important ounce of prevention of trouble between parent and teacher, teacher and administration, and teacher and student. Once trouble and misunderstanding have begun, it takes much more time and emotional expenditure of energy to resolve the problem or to explain away and smooth out misunderstandings.

Communicate, communicate, communicate! Do it early and never stop.

Communicate the same message to parents and students.
What is good for parents is an absolute *must* for students. The
letter to parents must go into the student's notebook to be kept for
future reference. On "back-to-school night," be sure to take roll
of the parents who come to each class. For absent parents, give
their son or daughter a copy of the letter to take home as well as a
copy for the student's notebook. Tell the students what you told
the parents and then repeat it in detail the first few weeks of
school. The list should include the following:

1. *Class cuts are recorded as a zero grade and not erased.* The
   student suffers the consequence of that zero the *first time.*
   This will eliminate future temptation. It usually eliminated all
   temptation for my students. They knew the consequences.
2. *Speeches and/or dialogues are made up (if missed) in class.*
   They are *never made up after school.* This eliminates the
   temptation of suddenly developing a stomach ache the morning of the day this oral work is due. The consequence of giving two speeches the following week will be too difficult to
   face and will cause intense seizure of fear. Parents understand
   this well (see chapter 3).
3. *Notebooks must be kept in order daily.* One never would
   know when Madame might make a sudden inspection and give
   a grade for order and discipline. A notebook's order always
   announced very early whether the students paid attention and
   reviewed work.
4. *Daydreaming is not allowed.* Repeated failure of the same
   grammatical principles would indicate dreaming in class and
   no progress.

Parents must see the interim report. Tell the parents that a
billet doux will be given to every student in the fifth week of each
quarter, which must be taken home for a parent's signature. Failure to carry the report to parents should produce the uncomfortable consequence of a call home asking about the report.

The above always reassured the parents in my experience. It is wise to remember that a student, and especially an adolescent, is happier and more comfortable dealing with the teacher alone than with parents, teacher, and administration on the same problem. Invariably, the teacher and student can resolve a problem better alone—*if the teacher is viewed by the student as fair. See that you are!*

Truth and *consequences* **must apply to students and teachers.** You are part of the process of helping your students to live in the real world. You teach more than subject matter; you teach responsibility for one's behavior. You keep school, the ongoing learning process in life or school, moving every day of the year. School is over the last day of the year and so is work in your class, but learning goes on forever. Tell parents and students that learning responsibility is as important as French.

Students *earn* everything they receive as a grade—no gifts. To treat them otherwise is to insult their intelligence and teach them a lesson they should not learn: *"You are not capable of earning what you get."* This lesson destroys self-confidence and ambition. My students came back to tell me of the pride that they felt in a truly honest grade. They scorned the teachers who had given them grades that they had not earned. I learned this lesson my first year.

Students are honest until they prove themselves dishonest. I always told that to my students. They would never cheat until they are found cheating. No test, no lie is worth the consequence—my loss of confidence in them. They might need me as a character witness or as a reference for a job or entrance to college. Teachers must be honest, too. I always told them that I was ready to give them extra help or to find a peer tutor. Parents and students must know how you intend to operate—early.

The above are not just nine ounces, but a ton of prevention. It is important that you, the teacher, remember what you have prom-

ised, the warnings you have issued, and the consequences involved. A student of any age does not value, nor does he trust, a teacher who does not follow through keeping promises and instituting consequences. He will quickly learn how honest and consistent you are.

Note the following:

"I, Danny F., skipped class on Tuesday, October 10, 1975, for the first and last time."

This was signed and written by Danny. My invariable questions for an unexcused absence or why work due was not submitted: (1) Where were you? (2) What are your excuses? And the request: "Please date your paper, write what you must, and sign it," or if absent, "I missed you yesterday."

These gems were kept in my files by quarter and by class until the following year. They prevented problems and answered parental protests. They were there in order and easily retrieved. The students knew about my record keeping. Administrators, counselors, and parents soon learned this as well. I was usually left alone to teach and to help my students, which are the only reasons why teachers remain in the classroom year after year, and for which they were originally employed by the school system.

The above rules may seem harsh to some who erroneously believe a teacher should be a friendly companion who can be pressured and maligned if need be. These rules "kept the peace" in my classroom and prevented the trouble and the crises many of my colleagues endured too frequently, in my opinion.

Dedicated, caring teachers should communicate their love and concern for the students *at the beginning,* before the "First Judgment" (the first quarter interim report) arrives, before "back-to-school night" with parents. That first report will fall like a lightning bolt on the insouciant and careless during that fifth week when all grades earned that quarter will be listed and given to the

51

students so they can calculate with joy or despair their average to date. As previously stated, school systems require that an interim report on students with failing grades be sent to parents by mid-quarter. I sent them on every student. These reports encouraged instead of discouraged.

Remember that the grades of the first two weeks of the first quarter (see chapter 3) should be forgiven. I told my students this the first exam. This happens the first quarter only, but the students will keep these papers in their notebooks.

Keep your cool! Regardless of the "pit" a student may be in, smile and ask the student to come to see you after school the *next day*—not the day the blow is delivered. Digestion takes a little time, at least twelve to twenty-four hours, and thinking is improved after some reflection.

Always communicate caring and unfailing belief in success. See each student alone; never with a friend. Let the student begin and listen with the ear of the heart. Do not show disapproval or despair if grades are lower than expected. Students are usually in shock and must be resuscitated with tender, loving care if failure seems imminent. They will need to be picked up, dusted off, and assured that they are not dead yet and that the prognosis is good. Always predict success.

For conferences you should have all the test results of aptitude, pretesting (if any), and your positive observation of the student's *great intelligence.* I am not joking about this. If any student is *not* intelligent enough to do what you expect by the fifth week, you, the teacher, will have been able to discern that, usually without tests or going through the guidance archives. If you are not that observant, I suggest that you need to sharpen your wits and take a course in behavioral psychology.

What to do? Assure! Never admit the possibility of failure to enter your thoughts. Encourage! Then ask a few questions:

1. *How much time do you spend on homework?* You usually get

52

a straight and honest answer. When the chips are down, honesty is the best way out and students know that.

2. *Do you have television or radio in your room?* Parents are very indulgent these days. They think their children are absorbed in books when in reality the books might be upside down while a pair of earphones are clapped on the head. I always suggested that students either study in a public part of the home or with study or bedroom door left open.

3. *What do you intend to do about this?* Listen carefully and suggest a few things—the how of studying.

End the conference by asking the student to put his plans on paper and sign and date it. Then send the students away with a smile on their face, and yours, telling them you love them and know they can accomplish what they have planned and promised. File this paper for the future.

Early conferences with students who begin dismally can be the crucial difference that brings success. These conferences have "saved" and prevented or resolved problems early for me and my students. This is an excellent opportunity for a teacher to show love and caring and to build a student's confidence. Students who are faced with the reality and the consequences of their academic behavior early learn important lessons of responsibility. They think through and then write their plans for change and improvement.

Oral promises do not accomplish the same things. Gaps in memory, in the tape recording in our brain, are frequent and convenient if the agreement promises are oral for the student and for the teacher. We must never forget the power and "legality" of a written contract. It is vital in education and good interpersonal relations in any profession.

These written promises became a tradition in my classes. They worked for my students and some took on legendary proportions. Chapter 10, "Truth and Consequences," records a few of the typical gems that were written over the years.

To conclude, millions of Americans have been "exposed" to a foreign language in our public schools with little success. Why? In my experience, the dominant reason for this waste of time and public funds is the failure of teachers and students to recognize the need of *practicing*, reviewing the language on a *daily* basis in order to acquire fluency. (I talk to myself every day in three languages—aloud. I never mumble but often shout. I need to hear myself.)

The second reason for failure to achieve success is the curious and shortsighted practice of only two years of study, not the recommended sequence of seven. Alas and Alas!

It is the role of parents, teachers, and administrators to have the vision to see the need and the necessity of being fluent in at least one language other than one's mother tongue. Sometimes we sadly lack fluency in the language we call our own. Students will catch our vision if we are truly committed.

*Sample of a letter to parents
at the time of "back-to-school night."*

Dear _____ (Parents):

We are happy to welcome _____ (son/daughter) to French. I trust this will be an interesting and fruitful experience. It will be if we all work together.

I believe that all normally intelligent people are capable of learning a second language provided certain requirements are met:

1. The ability to listen and pay close attention must be a well-established *habit*. (Daydreaming is fatal in a foreign language.)
2. The desire to learn the language must be the student's own, not just the need of parents or the wish to fulfill college requirements. (Let us remember these requirements are necessary to graduate from college.)
3. Willingness to practice, repeat, and review areas one may feel are already learned. This is called "over learning"—if such a thing exists.
4. Consistent oral work—thirty minutes every night, seven days a week.

Students can practice verbal structure orally on pets, parents, and friends on weekends. Dogs and cats are wonderful listeners.

5. Attention to details, oral and written.

6. *Not easily discouraged!* Learning and polishing a language takes *years* of patient effort, determination, and *constant correction.* We study our native tongue for years and years.

This may sound simple. It is. I guarantee success if all requirements are met. Success does not necessarily mean an "A" or "B." A "C" is good success.

May I remind you that repeated absences are extremely damaging to foreign language learning.

I arrive at school at 7:00 A.M. every morning and remain until 3:15 P.M. every night in order to help struggling students and for makeup exams.

I rejoice in the success of my students and feel only sadness and loss when they do not succeed. My telephone is 000–0000.

Sincerely,

P.S. All my students receive an interim report at the end of the first five weeks of every nine-week period. Please ask for it and sign it so that it may be returned to me.

5

Beginnings

Teach the Language of Languages

Teachers who do not teach students how to answer their own questions do not teach. They leave their students literally helpless at year's end. It is something like feeding a baby with a bottle when the poor child has reached the age of being able to eat from a dish with a spoon. Babies soon experience frustration in their desire to be able to help themselves and so do students.

Foreign language teachers are the greatest culprits in this kind of teaching. The students are taught to memorize dialogues, and to memorize sentences without learning (1) the mysteries of how the sentence is put together, and (2) the dominant role of the verb in all expression, oral or written. Telling students that they will understand *later on* is not good enough. Sometimes "later on" never comes; it remains later on. Students cannot see around the verbal roadblock in their path and are often disheartened by the constant continuing mysteries of dialogue and sentence structure. Students are left unable to construct a sentence of their own making as a result. They are left with brute memory—a poor substitute for thought. In their native tongue they flounder all their lives.

One professor, who teaches a graduate course in advanced

grammar and composition at one of the best foreign language universities, told me some years ago that he found that most of his students, all majors in French and many already teaching it, had a poor knowledge of the verbal system of the language. I thought that he might have exaggerated a bit. Not so. The year I served as an advanced placement consultant for the southeastern United States for French, I learned how correct he was. The teachers who came to my seminars were often at sea in the verbal structure. They did not do well on the verb quizzes I gave them, the same quizzes I regularly gave to my own students. I used the same techniques for them as for my students. None of the teachers at these seminars had ever studied in France—almost a must if a teacher wants to be truly fluent—and to master verb structure and use. Still, study in France does not always guarantee a complete mastery of French verbs and French grammar if the period of study lasts only a summer or two after graduation. But constant and continued daily study will. Teachers of foreign languages shirk their duty if they are not scholars, continuing learners of the language they teach.

In addition to the verbal structure, all elements that comprise a sentence, oral or written, must be understood and taught by the teacher. It is unfair for teachers to expect students to arrive at comprehension by the analogy route, which is long and arduous. Students—young high school students and adults, sometimes with advanced degrees—in my experience have no tools to read the language map.

The thought and analyzing process of language begins early in children as they begin to speak. They have listened for a period of time, then they imitate but also analyze as they imitate. This analysis is not always evident except to careful observers of patterns of beginning oral expression. I remember the beginning speech patterns of our first grandchild. I was doing research at the time on the how and why of speech acquisition at the beginning stages of foreign language. My granddaughter, Elna, was experiencing triumph in her ability to communicate verbally. One day she was practicing her marvelous tool of speech and said to me, "He do it this way." I corrected her saying, "He does it this way." She considered me a minute, then said with an inquiring look, "We does it, grand-mère?" I then conjugated the verb *to do* in a sentence for her with all its persons, asking her to repeat after me. I did not explain the English verbal structure to her that day, but she learned how to deal with that verb for *I, you, he, she, we, you,* and *they.* The writers of foreign texts in the United States have overlooked this thought process and neglected the *all persons* approach to dealing with a verb.

Teachers of foreign languages forget or overlook something else. They assume that all students, young or old, arrive in a foreign language class knowing the "language" *of* language. Texts will not explain *how* to teach this mysterious lingua franca of the foreign language realm. The first day, beginning teachers of any foreign language will walk out of the classroom dazed and baffled by the blank stares of American students, young or adult and sometimes with a Ph.D. tacked on their names, at the mere mention of a past participle. I was. I have never known a foreign language teacher who did not complain that beginning students arrived with no comprehension of the language of language. What is an infinitive? What is a past participle? What is a present participle, an adjective, an adverb, a preposition, a conjunction, a relative pronoun? I had students who arrived at second-level French who asked me, "What is a pronoun?" "What is a past participle?" What were these unknown animals? There may be a few students who arrive equipped with this lexicon, but my advice is not to waste time trying to find them. They are too scarce. Feelings of despair and fury at former teachers of these students are equally a waste of time and certainly a waste of emotional energy. To expect a beginning foreign language student to

Madame, painfully listening to French being fractured by a student

understand the function of a past participle when they don't even know what a participle is, is simply unrealistic. *Assume they don't know.* Any who know will sit and gloat over their superiority and those who don't will be relieved that you did not ask for a show of hands.

Start from zero. Don't cast any stones at former teachers of these students. Don't forget that you will someday turn your students over to other teachers who may feel like throwing a few rocks themselves. Don't waste a single minute, but begin with a cheerful, positive attitude to teach the language of language. Your students will be attentive and absorbed and will learn quickly the necessary tools if you begin the first day with basic explanations and, above all, examples. They will also be relieved that all your first sounds and words are in English, but quickly give them the vocabulary in the foreign language as well.

Your students will leave class the first day feeling as triumphant as Molière's Bourgeois Gentilhomme in his play of a rich ignoramus after his first lesson. This gentleman wanted to educate himself in order to impress a new mistress with his erudition. His sly but observant teacher recognized that he had to assume that his student knew nothing (his assumption was correct), so he began by teaching this man with full pockets a few basics. Simple: what wasn't a vowel was a consonant, what wasn't poetry was prose. Wonder of wonders, this beginner had been speaking prose all his life. What victory this hilarious personage displayed.

Begin by telling your students that you are going to visit a wild jungle kingdom. Name all the beasts and describe how they look and act so that the animals may be tamed and made to perform as we wish them to do. They are going to learn how they sound for sometimes they change their songs or grunts or snarls. So we must comprehend that the meaning of all these sounds will vary with the time and the place and what they are doing. Games are usually fun if the teacher thinks and acts in full context with the game employed.

I always began with the following sentences, writing them on the board without comment: *(The words in parentheses were not written on the board.)*

1. She *gone* to town. (has)
2. I *written* her a letter. (have)
3. I *done* it yesterday. (have)
4. He *do* it often. (used to)
5. You *flown* a kite. (have)
6. She *do* it tomorrow. (will)
7. She *do* it often when she is young. (used to)
8. I *am going* _____ *write* it. (to)

The students were asked to correct the sentences without changing any of the verbs (the italicized words). They were asked to observe the correct time or tense of the action and to fill the blank. They could add any word, but they could not change the verb.

In sentence 1 students wanted to add *has* and sometimes *had*. I noted to them that *had gone* announced a different time than *has gone*. *Had gone* was farther back in time than *has gone*.

In sentence 2 and 5 they all quickly added *have* or *had*. They hesitated over sentence 3 but added *have* or *had*. They remarked that the sentence sounded "funny." I then asked them to consider this: "Have you done it?" "Yes." "Yesterday?" "Yes." I asked them to change the verb. "I *did* it yesterday" was their reply. Then I asked them to consider this: "Have you done it?" "Yes." "I have done it—yesterday." Adding "yesterday" *immediately* sounded funny but hesitating a second before replying "yesterday" (by inserting a dash) made *sound* sense.

I pointed out that meaning and *sound sense* of correctness could be affected by tone of voice and hesitation before or after a word. Changing the verb to I *did* it yesterday required a change of tense in English as well as French from the *past indefinite* (passé composé) to the *past definite* (passé simple). This was correct in speech in English, but the past definite or passé simple was not used in French in conversation. It was necessary for this sentence to be understood in French in order to read a newspaper or a book but not to speak. They would need to understand it orally in order to comprehend classic theater or a lecture at the Sorbonne.

In sentence 5, *have* was quickly added, and *will* to sentence 6. Sentence 4 and 7 caused some pondering, but students soon added *used to do* and *was* young. I told them both verbs were in the same tense. In French only one word would represent *used to do* and *was*.

I told them that *gone, written, done,* and *flown* were past participles; all verbs had them. Then I asked what *write* was in sentence 8 and why did they need the preposition *to* in the blank. Some bright stars knew that we were dealing with the infinitive form of the verb, but this knowledge was not widespread even in adult classes. They were quickly able to see that past participles required a helping or auxiliary verb to make sense in English. This is not true of all English past participles, but always true in French. I chose what could be comprehended at a glance. The students noted also that the form of the auxiliary verb was controlled by the subject and that all infinitives required the preposition *to* in English. They do *not* in French or any other language in order to be classed as infinitives.

This exercise may seem ridiculous to some who read this, but I could actually see light bulbs snapping on in the brains of my charges by the gleam in their eyes.

Students also noted that verbs announced different time values, not always the present—the only reality for teenagers—but other tenses: completed action, past continuing action, future, conditional (a maybe tense), past historical action. With more examples, they could see requested or commanded action of the imperative and later uncertainty or wished-for action in the subjunctive. They will have soon acquired the vocabulary of the verbal jungle of unknown animals after you have written and commented on these few simple examples and comparisons. Examples of all tenses can be used to help clear up confusion.

Tell the students that all the verbs they will study will be first written in the infinitive with no *to* for French and that at the same time they will learn the past participle as well. I never taught or introduced an infinitive without its necessary past participle that would require an auxiliary or helping verb unless the past participle changed its spots and became an adjective: the *finished* letter, the *handwritten* letter, the *typed* letter.

The Insect Jungle of Auxiliary Helpers in English

The peculiar plenitude of helpers or auxiliaries of the English language confounds any foreign student beginning the study of English. While this idiosyncrasy of the language is usually absorbed with great difficulty by immigrants or foreign students, native speakers of English take this difficulty for granted. They take this "for granted" idea with them when they begin the study of a foreign language and apply the idea when they translate verbatim (which can rarely be done with the verbal structure). It is wise, therefore, to dispose of this confusion the first week. List on the board all the possible auxiliaries of English.

"Do" as an auxiliary. I *do* speak well.

Other examples:

must	used to
should	ought to
would	may
will	might
shall	to have
	to be

Only the verbs *to have* and *to be* are auxiliaries in French. None of the others exists as auxiliaries in French. The idea is in one word.

Do must have the preposition added *(to do)* in order for it to become an infinitive. Point this out to your students. Verb endings in French indicate the infinitive and the time or tense of the action of the verb. Knowing this helps a student cross language barriers more easily.

French is basically a very simple language, much easier than English. Again, even French idiots speak French.

Explanations such as the above calmed fears and prepared a smoother road for my students. Many of my students doing poor work in English returned to tell me that their English grades had improved after starting French. Interesting concept, but it is my belief that all classes taught in a student's own tongue should fortify and improve a student's knowledge of the most important tool he possesses—his ability to communicate and understand others. But a foreign language class fortifying a student's ability in English? It does indeed, in my experience, but this idea is not widely accepted by those who decide curriculum content in the United States in our public schools. The prevailing attitude resembles Marie Antoinette's reply when she learned that the peasants had no bread: "Let them eat cake." (Let them speak English.) Students should indeed speak English in our society but another language as well. Our nation is no longer an island with impenetrable borders. How are our people going to communicate with unknown aliens in space? They should carry a whole trunk full of other languages in their baggage as well as English.

Going from Zero to Something

Getting a beginning language class to the stage of comprehending teachers in the foreign language they teach takes a bit of doing, but it can be done—and quickly.

The first day I quickly wrote on the board a list of "core" verbs necessary for me to conduct my classes in French. American textbooks ignore this. My students quickly copied them with their English meanings boxed in. This list remained on the board for the first six weeks; thereafter, it was erased because its contents had been learned.

Here are the core verbs. *Do not leave any out of the list regardless of your text.* They are basic to conducting your classes in French.

avoir = to have
être = to be
faire = to do, to make
vouloir = to want
pouvoir = to be able to
savoir = to know (as a result of learning)

connaître = to know by seeing
mettre = to put
voir = to see
ouvrir = to open
écrire = to write

aller = to go
venir = to come
sortir = to go out

partir = to leave
entrer = to enter

parler = to speak
écouter = to listen to
regarder = to look at
conjuguer = to conjugate

compléter = to complete
prononcer = to pronounce
fermer = to close
chanter = to sing

répondre = to reply

entendre = to hear, to understand

comprendre = to comprehend, to understand
apprendre = to learn

finir = to finish
s'asseoir = to sit down
se lever = to stand up

Regularly add any needed verb.

These verbs and their comprehension will prepare students to understand in French. English will gradually disappear. It will no longer be necessary to translate for the students to comprehend you. Conducting a class in English all year, translating all year, will produce students who will always expect a teacher to translate for them. They will not try to comprehend the spoken language for they know full well that their teacher will translate. It is wise to remember that textbook translations written beside the foreign language are not always exact, and that they vary from text to text. Therefore, the thought process of thinking in the foreign language must begin early in the first year. Teach your students to go to a large, not small, dictionary for translations. Have several on your desk. They will soon learn that words often carry a whole baggage of meanings, some the teacher should know or learn as well. Teachers should learn every day as well as their students.

I began the teaching of the above core verbs by conjugating *avoir = to have* and *être = to be*—the vital auxiliaries—in the present and past indefinite (passé composé). I listed the past participles by every infinitive as I explained and spoke, going from French to English in everything I said after teaching the language of language. Every verb was first listed in the infinitive, then with its past participle written beside it, whenever I added new verbs to the vocabulary.

Contrasting and writing the present and the past indefinite (passé composé) began with this core list. Students quickly learned that there were different time values of these verbs as a result of this contrast the first day. Waiting for the presentation of past tenses in the textbook is crazy, in my opinion. *Contrasts and comparing of tenses is a tool to end confusion early.*

The first two weeks I quickly added the *futur proche* (near future), a simple tense—and required for conversation. This cannot wait until midyear. Le futur proche requires *aller* in the présent (or imparfait—not yet introduced) plus the infinitive (never a compound tense of *aller*):

I am going to depart in a little while.

Je vais partir tout à l'heure.	Nous allons partir tout à l'heure.
Tu vas partir tout à l'heure.	Vous allez partir tout à l'heure.
Il (Elle, On) va partir tout à l'heure.	Ils (Elles) vont partir tout à l'heure.

67

Le passé récent (recent past) is equally of high usage and is easily grasped. Emphasize the necessity of the preposition *de* in order to guard correct meaning. It is *venir* in the present plus *de* plus the infinitive.

I have *just* finished.

Je viens *de* finir.	Nous venons *de* finir.
Tu viens *de* finir.	Vous venez *de* finir.
Il (Elle, On) vient *de* finir.	Ils (Elles) viennent *de* finir.

By the end of three weeks, the students will have a grasp of time as a result of the contrast of present and passé composé, le futur prôche and le passé récent. American texts do not introduce, nor do they contrast, the time value of verbs early enough. They present a new tense as a neat little package, a time bundle separate and apart. Error! Speech and language are not acquired that way. It comes pell-mell. It is the teacher's role to present and use core verbs in contrasted time values from the first few weeks. The teaching of tense as presented by the text will fall into place automatically. The students will encounter them as old friends they met the first three or four weeks. It is review to them. *Remember: Learning is achieved by constant review.*

I stopped all English translation after the first six weeks at first level. Students quickly saw that French was filled with cognates (the same word in English). At other levels I did not translate.

By the end of four weeks, write on the board the three verbs *parler, finir,* and *entendre* in the following tenses: Présent, passé composé (past indefinite), futur (future), conditionnel (conditional), imparfait (imperfect), plus-que-parfait (pluperfect), and impératif (imperative). Underline endings, show the source of the radical (root) for all tenses, and have students copy and translate meaning by each tense.

This is simply a partial preview of the verbal structure. Do not expect all students to absorb everything, but this preview will smooth the path ahead. You will have given them guideposts along the way that they will recognize as they come upon them in text or speech. Your struggle to teach students the time value of verbs will cease to be a struggle. You will move forward in your text with confidence and so will your students. The text will become a *tool* and not the guide; not the method. I assure you that you will cover all the required lessons in your text and do it well. Moreover, your students will have learned.

Beware: A text is never a method. You, the teacher, provide, define, and embody method. Supervisors, principals, and texts cannot. Don't argue, protest, or explain. If you are well trained and competent, you must be trusted, even the first year. Be confident. Keep your mouth shut and offer to test your students against any others at the end of the year. Your students will vindicate you. Believe, and do the above. It works. I encountered opposition, scorn, and jealousy at first. The success of my students silenced critics and enlisted student and parental support that lasted throughout my career.

One last word:

1. *Never, never* say that anything is difficult.
2. Encourage your students from day one.
3. Pound away on the core verbs the first four weeks in writing—and choral work.
4. Give practice verb quizzes after the first week (see verb quiz in chapter 11) or even the first week.

6

Techniques and Methods

How do techniques evolve? Or do they? Are teachers using the same methods they employed the first year or two? If they are, they have only one or two years of real experience even if they have taught ten or twenty years.

Since education courses deal largely in generalities, beginning teachers of foreign language, and perhaps other disciplines, enter the classroom with vague ideas of classroom management, how to get through unit one to unit fifteen, what to do with disruptive students, how to deal with the paper load from administration and supervisors, and how to measure their own progress.

My first year I felt lost. Most new teachers do. Memos spewed from administrative authorities and from the guidance department. In those days I had to calculate the days of attendance for all my homeroom students who were not my students at all and submit correct accounts of days present to a vice-principal who knew the correct answers. If I made a mathematical error, I had to do everything again. These results had to be submitted to the federal government in order for our school to receive "impact" aid for children of government and military people who move about a great deal. This change of station of these people could not always be correctly calculated by school systems, thus the aid for the sudden overcrowding of schools. The sudden disappearance of a military or a government installation caused much difficulty. Enrollment was hard to predict.

I rejoice that teachers are no longer charged with this horrible and exacting task. Whoever changed all that deserves a front seat in heaven and has my eternal gratitude. This work was not method—just frustrating to every teacher I knew who lived through that era. I never devised a method to do that work that made me happy. However, my role and my methods in the classroom continued to occupy me and to change throughout my career.

The first year I had to make the vital decision of what kind of an image I wanted to create, but being a caring and observant teacher did not teach my students French. However, *the manner with which I viewed my students and their learning needs did influence my methods.* These young people became sons and daughters of my adopted family, but I also considered them brothers and sisters in a divine family of a Heavenly Father. *Therefore I held myself accountable for what my students learned.* They must all be given a chance for success and certainly would succeed if they worked and if I knew how to teach. I assumed that they all wanted to learn French or they would not have been registered for a French class. Desire, I knew, would help them surmount any obstacle. How naive I was! I concluded that their enthusiasm would match mine in our approach to the language and that within six months they would have the same command of the language as I had had, for example, when I was launched into the teaching of a religious class to French women in France after that length of time. While I still had a lot to learn, and knew it, I nevertheless understood and taught in French in that far-off time.

Another error of assumption was the belief that, beginning on page one of the text that I was obliged to use, by faithfully plowing through to the end I would automatically be successful. The text was filled with English and the authors apparently expected the students to translate back and forth from one language to the other, which I had never done in my studies. My classmates in France had come from every major nation in the world and our teachers did not translate. They couldn't speak Japanese, Chinese, Arabic, Spanish, Italian, Hindi, and English. They spoke French from day one. I would too, I decided.

The first three or four days my students suffered a panic that I can only dimly imagine. I chattered like a magpie—a French magpie—and I mistook their stunned surprise for rapt attention and desire to learn. A guidance counselor soon came to see me. "Madame, if you will just speak English, everything will be fine," he told me. The poor man was trying to keep everyone from jumping ship. I considered his request, then said, "All right, I shall translate for the first six weeks or two months, but they will hear French every day. How else will they learn the language?"

Back and forth I went from English to French until they began to understand and to acquire a basic vocabulary. After the first three or four days of nothing but French, the poor lambs could catch glimpses of green pastures and calmed down. I realized that I had to do a good job of brainwashing to make them believe that they could eventually understand and speak French if I spoke the language. I assured them (again, my favorite expression) that even French idiots speak French—so they would have no problems since they were the smartest students I had ever seen. Teachers who discount praise and assurance and practice this daily, drip by drip, perhaps do not believe in the great potential young Americans have. They neglect the most certain method of learning—persuading students that they can do something.

Remembering my beginnings in the language, I brought pictures to the classroom—large ones—filled with all kinds of detail: large advertisements for home furnishings, children playing, families, anything that had something to do with their daily life. These immediately aroused interest. I asked questions about the pictures and answered them. Their new vocabulary was written on the board and they had to copy it just as I had to do in my classes (pictures or designs now appear in texts).

I soon learned that copying was an excellent learning tool; it reinforced oral and written learning. I continued this copying technique throughout my career.

That first year in one of my French II classes, I had a transfer student from another state. The doctrine being preached in the school system from which she came was: no books, no writing for the first two years. The poor student knew a dialogue or two, but when questioned orally, she was mute; she did not understand and could not speak, except a few memorized sentences. How grateful I was for the experience with this student when the same idiotic idea seeped into the thinking of supervisors and personnel in our system a few years later. I knew that *seeing* reinforced *hearing* and that *writing reinforced both*. Many years down the road, someone announced a "new" principle: Learning comes through the senses, all of them. Things like that made teacher conferences in this country difficult for me.

One year we were even told not to issue books until midyear. I ignored this directive and protested. My students were learning well and everyone knew it. My colleagues in the language department asked me what I was doing. Ignoring the directive, I told them.

The French tried this experiment in their school in St. Cloud. All students were foreigners, six hundred of them, and all they did was repeat and talk for six months. Another group of six hundred learned to hear, to speak, to read, and to write at the same time. At the end of six months the first group received a text and reading and writing began. At the end of the first year the group without books the first six months was still far behind the group that began by using all the senses for the learning process. I learned of this experiment the summer the results were announced to professors from all over the world who were enrolled in the summer course of study. In the United States the no-book theory still held some ground.

What is not perceived is not learned. Step one must be understood if step two depends upon step one. We often forget this in foreign languages and rely on analogy alone for students to comprehend orally. *Analogy alone does not work.* Poor results on tests of what we think we have taught should warn us that something is wrong in the learning process, not just lack of application on the part of the students. Methods need a closer look when poor results are the outcome of what we thought we taught. Thus, experimenting with methods of presentation using all the senses and *analysis,* not analogy, and measuring results should be our constant concern.

We can teach our students to see and to hear better and more perceptively by our methods if we *use all the senses at the same time.* Thus, the regular verb quiz, copying and then memorizing, dictating and writing what is heard, then correcting immediately will sharpen perception of ears and eyes and voice muscles as well as teach spelling, which aids and speeds pronunciation. *Rote learning* must be part of early language acquisition, but it must be made meaningful for students to analyze and to remember what they are memorizing.

Our methods will inevitably distill from our personality and how we were taught, whatever we are charged with teaching. We must be willing to learn from others and *constantly vary* how we present material, and *how we examine and measure the results* of our teaching.

Teachers who do not give frequent tests do not teach and never know whether their students have learned. They delude themselves by saying, "I covered the first fifteen chapters." When I hear this, I always ask myself, "Did you run, skip, or fly, and did the students learn?" *Good foreign language methodology automatically implies good measurement, good tests that both*

75

teach and measure, and which use all the senses.

Image

This word "image" means picture in French. When we see a picture or an image, a mental process begins—imagining or remembering. We put our own meaning on what we see. Pictures prick the memory, pull us into the past, project us into a near or distant future, or make the present come alive.

The first year I began using pictures to teach vocabulary, but I soon realized that a picture brought to class *by students* would allow them to acquire vocabulary that especially interested them. They taught this to their classmates and launched themselves into what I call "free" speech or saying anything they wanted to say about their pictures. This soon became a favorite technique for speech days, especially for levels I and II. We learned about their families, how their parents behaved if they asked to drive the car without a permit, what some suffered as punishment when they broke the rules at home. Unless the image was treasured by the family, students left their pictures in a box on one of the card tables in the center of my room. Occasionally, after a quiz I asked students to select a picture and speak about it without any preparation. They made up stories about what the picture meant and inspired me to start a story of my own and allow the students to continue it, saying anything that came into their mind.

Very early I learned to use myself as a figure or a player in a ridiculous situation. For example: Madame Nelson est sortie ce matin pieds nus. (Madame Nelson went out this morning in bare feet.) The students obligingly added all kinds of reasons, most of them amusing, why I had started or had come to school without stockings and shoes. Sometimes I was driving at excessive speed and was stopped by the police. Even the indifferent learners took part in this kind of an exercise of free speech. Listening to their

spontaneous flow of sentence structure allowed me many occasions to note (without a grade) what they were learning and remembering and how they constructed their sentences. Often I realized that I needed to do a better job of teaching, or to review, a
particular concept.

Contracting and Advanced Placement

At advanced levels and for an Advanced Placement class, my
students and I devised a contract. They were encouraged to contract for a grade. We very early examined the entire program for
the year in an AP class. The grammar structures we knew would
be examined were noted and written so that students could refer
to these on their own. There was always a list of literary works
that had to be read. One major work for each quarter was expected for everyone. In addition, they could choose a work they
wanted to read for each quarter. Any literary work that was read
required a three-page written summary and critique which also
had to be delivered orally, without notes, to me and, most of the
time, before peers.

Contracting can give teachers and students unusual opportunities for preparing for university work where supervision is not
very close. I found that students gained self-confidence and goal
setting became more habitual.

In AP classes my students and I read in class two classic plays
of the seventeenth century, *Le Cid* by Corneille and *Phèdre* by
Racine. Reading and discussing these two works of the golden
age of French literature greatly enriched the vocabulary of my
students and gave them a sense of the poetic beauty of the language that no other literary works offered, in my opinion. The
two plays also provided an understanding of the two threads of
philosophic thought: (1) We are masters of our destiny, and (2)
we are victims of the gods and can do little to change our des-

tiny. (These two thoughts still exist in good writing today.) My students were able to enroll in courses in literature and composition their first college year whether they were language majors or not as a result of their AP class—or just a fourth-year class. These two plays gave us much to talk about and to analyze regarding the problems of the human condition.

Peer Teaching: A Program for Individualized Tutorial French

One year I asked that French students at levels I and V be grouped in the same class. The French V students were all seniors and preferred a less accelerated pace than the regular French V class (see chapter 8). The French V students spent at least two days a week on tapes or in conversational grouping. Three days a week the French V students passed the hour with the French I students on a one-to-one basis, correcting written exercises, leading oral drill, or teaching and writing dialogues.

I also had four classes of French IV and III grouped with similar conditions. One year there were three classes of IV and V students combined. Another year there were two classes of French V and VI, and one of French II and III. This program continued for me over the last five years of my career.

Peer teaching produced four significant results. First, students received help from peers as soon as there were problems. Second, the students in the level above the one with which they were grouped took some responsibility for the success of the students they helped. *There often was a strong student helping a less motivated student of the same level.* Third, student tutors gave the time they would spend on break (fifteen minutes at the end of second period) helping one or several students who needed help. And fourth, the upper-level students took turns giving fifteen to twenty-five minutes to a student after school.

The French Honor Society can also be a useful resource to encourage peer teaching and learning. Being an honor student implies willingness to help others. The constitution of this society is "help for both teachers and students." At Fort Hunt High School, where I taught, I sponsored the French Honor Society and added by amendment to the school constitution the requirement that peers help and teach each other. The principal and foreign language department approved the constitution, and the honor societies of the other languages added the same section to their constitutions. We had that option from the national society plus setting our own grade standard at upper levels.

I had always despaired at the end of a year when final grades were calculated. All students would be going to the next level of the language but with varying degrees of mental baggage. They had all received the same exposure, but depending upon their work and willingness to learn the language, what they carried in their heads was not always the same. Since I had always insisted that dialogue grouping be mixed with strong and weak students, peer teaching was an accepted rule in any class. And the combined classes worked well for me. Only one such class posed difficulty—the I and V grouping. I tried it only once.

Disruptive Behavior: Learn to Deal with It

Rarely did I ever have to send a student to the disciplinary principal; but when any student from Madame Nelson arrived with a note, my administrative superiors always knew why—*insolence*. I began the year by telling my students that I would treat them as ladies and gentlemen and that insolence was the sin that I found hardest to forgive. It would always mean temporary expulsion. I also told them that I taught the cream of the school and would depend upon seeing exemplary behavior. However, I knew that my conduct had to be exemplary, controlled, and polite if I expected that of my students. They would emulate me, I knew, if I treated them with respect.

A teacher's behavior must be impeccable in and out of the classroom. *Never engage in an exchange of insults.* Never make an oral reply to insolence regardless of what the student said. An angry retort from a teacher only complicates everything. Unfortunate, unkind words cannot be wholly taken back by apologies. We, the teachers, must forgive and forget. The anger of the student can only be diffused by a teacher's self-discipline. The student will be helped and strengthened by a calm teacher, but he will be harmed by an angry, insulting one.

Courses in behavioral psychology and behavior modification, adolescent psychology, abnormal psychology, or reality therapy can prepare a teacher better than any methods course to formulate a sound plan of classroom management and teaching methods. They did for me. Methodology is affected by the personality of the teacher, and we should in turn consider and measure the personalities we teach. Let us learn to judge and measure well the personalities of our charges. It is never too late for teachers to acquire this kind of knowledge. Be Polite, Positive, and Prepared.

Only once during all my years in the classroom did I feel it necessary to accompany a student of mine to the disciplinary principal. Marie was a senior and editor of the yearbook. She was extremely able and her grades were "A's" and "B's." She was receiving a "B" in French III class, which was scheduled for the last hour of the school day. We were well into the last quarter when Marie started to present excuses asking to be allowed to leave French class about ten minutes early. Her excuses were signed by the teacher/sponsor of the yearbook, so I permitted her to leave on three occasions. She claimed that it was necessary to go to the Library of Congress, which I considered a valid reason. I usually refused any request from any teacher asking that a student be excused from my class. I did not ask other teachers to allow a

French student to be dismissed from their subject discipline and expected the same kind of courtesy from them. However, I knew that Marie was extremely busy and the deadline for the yearbook was drawing near. I honored three excuses, always on a Friday. When she presented the fourth excuse, I told her, "No, you cannot be excused early." I had suddenly been prompted not to honor this excuse. It looked like the others, but a peculiar sense of warning came over me as I looked at it, although it looked valid. I did not suspect it to be forged. I just said, "No."

I turned to walk back across the room, then heard the door slam. Marie had gone. I immediately stepped into the hall and called to her to come back at once. She came. The bell rang shortly and I turned to Marie and told her to come with me. She attempted to run, and I grasped her arm.

"Unhand me, Madame," Marie commanded. I stifled an impulse to burst out laughing and replied, "Marie, you and I shall walk arm in arm to Monsieur K.'s office."

My students filed past and I linked my arm into Marie's as we walked to the vice-principal's office. I told him that Marie had tried to leave class unexcused. I had refused to honor her excuse. I left. I was angry and my voice trembled, but I had in no way lost control of my voice or behavior.

On Monday, one of my colleagues, surrounded by several others, approached me in the front office. He began in a high voice intending for all to hear. "Madame, I hear that you *beat up* on our friend Marie. The whole school is applauding."

I was momentarily speechless, then I recovered enough to ask, "Where did you get this information?"

"Why, Marie of course. She has told everyone all about it."

"Well, Bert, you are misinformed," I said. "I understand better now why you historians get things slightly muddled."

I immediately went to see Monsieur K. and told him what Marie was telling all over the school.

"Well, Madame, you were pretty angry," he said.

"Indeed I was, but not half as angry as I am now to realize that you have believed her too," I snapped. "Monsieur K.," I began, "you will call every one of Marie's classmates down here and question every one of them. Then Marie shall sit in your office for three days' detention for which she shall receive three zeros. When she returns to my class, she shall not be allowed to be part of a dialogue group the rest of this year. She has not been doing her part. Instead, she shall make a speech on Friday on subjects that I will assign her. Monsieur K., this lie will be cleared up in this school and community or my attorney shall see Marie and her parents in court for character assassination—he will see in court anyone else in this school who willingly propagates this lie. My reputation is all I have of any worth and I shall defend it with a battery of attorneys if necessary and all my students as witnesses. I am a public servant but not a public doormat."

I closed Monsieur K.'s door vigorously as I left. I had delivered my ultimatum with sparks in my eyes and acid on my tongue. He had no time to reply. He had no defense and we both knew it.

Everything was done as I had expected it to be done. After three days Marie returned to class and did as I asked her to do. My colleagues stopped their tittering and greeted me with a different demeanor and renewed respect. The story finally unfolded. Marie had forged all her excuses, this according to her yearbook sponsor who had come quickly to inform me. I learned that she was sometimes difficult in her other classes and that the community of students and parents considered her a spoiled child and that she terrorized her spineless parents with her threats and tantrums. End of the story? No. The following year a parent of one of my French II students came to school and requested a conference with me and her daughter's guidance counselor. Mrs. T. wanted me to write a recommendation for her daughter to spend the summer in Holland with a prestigious overseas student program. She assured me that her daughter would be accepted because they (she and her husband) had friends who ran the program, but they needed a sponsoring foreign language teacher's signature. They wanted mine because I was "well known," she said. The things teachers learn by accident never ceased to amaze me.

I did a bit of mental review of their daughter's work in French—poor—and realized that this parent wanted me to be a party to a fraudulent recommendation. I finally began, "Mrs. T., your daughter is studying French, not Dutch or German. She is capable of unusually fine work but she is not doing it—by choice, not by lack of understanding. In this program the young people are expected to be worthy ambassadors of the United States, thus its prestige. If your daughter continues in French III next year with better application, I shall be happy to truthfully recommend her then for the French program. I cannot do this for a Dutch program." I hesitated a moment and added, "I know that you would not want me to lie for your daughter."

Mrs. T. dropped her gaze then finally looked up and said, "No, Madame, I would not want you to lie. We all know what you did for Marie last year."

The guidance counselor and I exchanged a surprised look. I excused myself and left. Monsieur V. later told me that he had learned that I was the only person who had ever succeeded in disciplining Marie and "gotten away with it." Two years later I learned that Marie was having problems at university level and had been hospitalized for psychiatric therapy. No discipline at home was sadly taking its toll. *Meaning in a life and integrity of reputation implies continuity of behavior just as does meaning in curriculum content.*

Only one other time did I have to decide what to do about a lie, this time a lie spread by two students and a teacher. They were confronted and the lie was retracted in a written apology.

One of my former students, now teaching, had to face a similar situation—accompanied by a physical attack. Her mother, a former colleague, called me and asked me what to do. My reply was, "Hire an attorney immediately and announce to the principal that your daughter will have her attorney with her for every conference with this student's parents, the student, or the principal." My former student had been requesting that this disruptive student be removed from her class and had been refused. With her attorney on the scene, calm settled miraculously and the offending student, who was addicted to attacking teachers, we learned, was removed from the class.

If teachers have a good reputation, they should be prepared to defend it against anyone. My courage gave colleagues courage. My first year a very fine teacher counseled me, "Madame, every day that you spend in the classroom with teenagers, be prepared to be driven to the wall. The day you allow them to drive you into the wall, get out of the classroom. You will no longer teach anything."

Helping Struggling Students

I wrote the following memorandum to our foreign language department one year:

> Double exposure and repeated effort usually lead to success. I propose that language teachers be scheduled to teach four classes each year with one open class. Into this extra hour, students who need extra help in foreign language can be scheduled and thus have two hours of a foreign language each day instead of one. Teachers would still be teaching the required five class hours and students having difficulty would have a better chance of success.

This proposal was never accepted. Public funds are more precious than assuring success in all students. This idea of an extra hour of exposure in French would not leave me. I proposed it to my students who were having difficulty and to their parents. Those who could rearrange their schedules readily accepted this arrangement. The guidance department scheduled these students into a lower level than the class in which the student was earning credit. I always taught at least three levels of French so the rescheduling usually posed few difficulties.

These students were obliged to do the work of both classes, but the lower level provided them with review of areas they had already covered, or should have covered, and gave them a better chance of success in the class at the higher level where they received their grade. Their work at the lower level was graded and evaluated, but no grade for this class could be recorded since they had already received a recorded grade and the credit for that level. These students were able to shine in the lower level class and make creditable and good progress in the higher level.

Students who came to me from another school system or from another school in our system sometimes found themselves in a precarious situation if they had been badly taught. It grieves me to write that many times this was the case. We taught the foreign language in the language—not English—in all our foreign languages at our school, and transfer students without this kind of background were always at a great disadvantage. They were discouraged, but our desire to help them, coupled with the above-described system of double exposure, proved successful for students willing to accept that arrangement. Sometimes, however, transfer students did not have this option in rearranging their schedules and were obliged to go back to a lower level. In that case we averaged the two grades for the same level for the recorded credit.

Only giving help after school did not always rescue students who were poorly equipped to do the same work as their classmates, but the above two-class arrangement worked well at our school. We wanted all students to succeed and we were all committed to foreign language study for every year of high school. A foreign language department without this kind of dedication to helping struggling students will soon lose students to that discipline and shrink in size rapidly. Our society is mobile. Students often attend more than one high school in four years; therefore, *schools should arrange some means of helping students maintain their credit from schools previously attended and encourage these students to go forward.* This help is especially vital in foreign language. Some schools teach foreign language very well; some do not. Unfortunately, standards vary even in the same school system.

One year my principal received a request from the parents of a student who was studying French in another high school of our system. They wanted their daughter transferred to my French V class. She would continue the rest of her classes in the other high school. The complaint of the student was that her French V class was conducted in English. According to my principal, this student was extremely able—she would be one of the valedictorians. He granted the request before he consulted me. I was appalled. I asked him if he had examined this student in French so he knew just where she was in comparison to my French V students. He had not, of course. He didn't speak a word of French (although he had a Ph.D.). I told him that I would have to examine her with her parents and a guidance counselor present in oral and written tests. It was agreed.

I gave her a dictation of average difficulty and interrogated her orally. The results were not brilliant; however, her eagerness to learn French was so evident and the desire of her parents for this transfer so intense that I gave my consent with one condition: her grade would be pass/fail. Thus, her grade point average would in no way be threatened. (Students in our system were allowed to choose pass/fail for one class only. Their grade was merely pass, which could be a "D," but not computed with overall average.)

I was frank with all those present: student, counselor at our school, and parents.

"You will be obliged to work very hard. You are behind my French V students, but I believe that your intelligence and your great desire to learn French will see you through. You will be obliged to read literary works, write a three-page report, and deliver this report orally without notes once every quarter," I told her.

After the first week, it was obvious to her and to me that her oral comprehension was minimal and that her understanding of the verbal structure and tenses was chaotic. She failed simple verb and grammar quizzes. I encouraged her every day. My students soon learned from our new student why she was there and sympathized. *But sympathy is a rotten teacher; in fact, it cripples the receiver.*

We continued to midway of the second week. She was becoming more and more depressed. Finally she approached me one day after school. She could hardly muster the courage to begin to tell me how defeated she felt. I tried to imagine the loss of self-esteem she might suffer if she had to return to her French class at her high school. I told her that I could see that she was ready to give up, but I still believed that she could do it if we changed something.

I told her to go home and talk things over with her parents and go through her schedule of classes carefully. If they could find some class that she did not need to graduate and could drop, then we could schedule her into a level III class of mine and fill in the areas where she was weak. There would be no credit, of course, for this class, but she could save herself in French V. She acted as though the weight of the world had suddenly lifted. The schedule change was made. I do not know what class had to be dropped, but her enthusiasm for French in the level III class was so catching that she inspired even the students addicted to sloth in that class. Her French V classmates went out of their way to help her write the reports, which she dreaded but did. She passed.

What happened to Bertie? She was accepted at the Naval Academy and continued her French. Her junior year she was among the few cadets chosen to spend the summer at a French school in France. With her kind of courage, I expect to hear that she is an admiral commanding a warship in the Persian Gulf!

Dialogues

Allowing or expecting students to write and perform original dialogues can be risky if begun too early in the study of French and if the students are allowed to write anything that catches their fancy.

Level I students do not know structure well nor do they acquire enough vocabulary early enough to be launched into original dialogue production without special guidelines and special subjects with attendant vocabulary. However, a teacher who ignores the innate desire of all human creatures to "invent" their individual expressions will stifle ambition "to fly," hinder progress, and dampen enthusiasm. Therefore, it is vital to regularly add, on verb quizzes or in answer to questions, special ways of saying things. Students should be encouraged to come after school to ask you how to say something they would like to say. Even acceptable slang expressions can be added. The student will leave you repeating over and over these sentences. What a sense of victory and triumph I have seen in students, almost as though we shared a special secret that they would reveal to classmates on the next dialogue day.

Copying and memorizing are essential exercises that prepare students to write their own dialogues. Beginning with the third week at level one, I had the students copy simple, short paragraphs about geography, artists, explorers, writers, and historical figures—all in French. They were not allowed to translate from English to French. This is an effective way to teach or reinforce history, geography, and art.

The students had workbooks with a short paragraph on the assigned subject. These paragraphs were copied three times without copy errors and memorized once a week at level I. I included the dates as listed. We used Amsco workbooks, which we found very good as resource material for all aspects of the French experience. They are self-help books. Our students bought them if they wished. There were some in the library. With the copy machines found in all libraries today, a student can quickly copy a page and be prepared with material for a week or two.

The first-level Amsco is unsatisfactory for cultural material since it is all in English. The second, third, and advanced or superior levels are excellent sources. All the cultural material is in French.

I cannot stress enough the necessity of *copying and memorizing,* beginning at level one and continuing through advanced levels IV, V, and VI. Free conversation gradually grows out of this. At advanced levels, the discussion of history, literary themes, philosophy, and art will be no problem. After memorization, students walk with confidence into the class conducted in French.

There are other benefits that result from copying historical material. The irregular verbs of the passé simple (past definite) are always used in these passages; for example: être, faire, naître, mourir, voir, venir. The students quickly learn the regular verbs, but copying the few irregular verbs in this tense opens the written page of newspapers, magazines, and literature to them. Newspaper and magazine articles are then comprehensible to even first-year students.

Free dialogue writing can begin toward the end of the first year. Whether this will be successful will depend on whether the students will accept guidelines for content.

I gave no credit for the quality of acting in a dialogue. Al-

though acting and body movement are marvelous ways to reinforce feeling and memory, nevertheless, dialogue is words and
proper use of the language. The entire dialogue was written correctly by every student and memorized by all those participating
in the group work. All copies were turned over to me at the beginning of class, thus they avoided the temptation to study while
other groups were speaking. I insisted that students listen atten-
tively to their peers. Since they had all received the same subject
for their dialogues, they learned from each other. For example:
"Accident en route" as the dialogue subject produced all kinds of
situations from hospital experience, police arrival on the scene,
death, broken heads and bones, and near escapes from disaster.
Students loved this. Dialogues captured their attention quickly.
They heard, saw, remembered, and memorized what they all had
written.

Sometimes I was the victim of an accident after I had given an
especially difficult test. On one occasion I was dispatched to the
moon with no hope of returning to the earth. I laughed as heartily
as the students, who appreciated my willingness to be amused and
even be delighted with their portrayals of a demanding teacher.
Welcoming such teasing, in controlled situations, enhances a
friendly atmosphere, communication, and trust. Adolescents do
not tease teachers who cannot laugh at themselves.

It is my opinion that texts printed in America present the language by the "spare parts" method, a verb here, a verb there, and
by the end of the first year the students are fortunate if they have
any idea of the conjugation of all six persons of the verb *aller* in
the présent, passé composé, and futur. The texts do not introduce
the complete conjugation of a verb early, even though one person
may appear in a dialogue or an exercise.

In order to control dialogue writing at levels I and II, I set verb
and vocabulary guidelines. Students first conjugated on the board
in all persons (I, you, he, she, one, we, you, they) any irregular

verb to be used in the dialogue to be written in présent, passé composé, imparfait, and futur. Regular *er, ir,* and *re* verbs almost teach themselves. I also drew up a vocabulary list for a situation that allows action. (Students love to play scenes with action.) They suggested any additions they wished.

I told the students they would receive a grade for the words they spoke, their accent, and how well they knew the dialogue. All members of the group had to know the entire dialogue and be able to change roles if asked to do so. Again, their ability as actors and actresses was not judged, which, in addition to not disadvantaging those with less showmanship, eliminated too much pantomime. We all applauded the great acting we saw, but walls had to talk, birds had to speak, even trees in a forest could not be mute if these were the roles being played.

All members of the dialogue group wrote the entire dialogue and surrendered their individual copy to me upon entering the classroom on dialogue day. The exercise of copying something from the blackboard or an exercise prepared outside of class was a learning experience in spelling and comprehension of the written word. Don't overlook this teaching occasion. It bears fruit little by little and will help speed your students to oral expression.

On dialogue day, speech day, or report day at any level (dialogues were gradually replaced with individual speeches or reports in advanced-level classes), I asked students to give close attention to peers during the entire class. Their desks were cleared of everything except a blank sheet of paper on which they were expected to accord a grade for each student they heard. They left these with me before leaving class. Giving each other grades always produced interesting results. Students listened more intently for correct pronunciation, grammatical construction, and content. Students using verbs and nouns they knew were unknown to their classmates wrote these on the board and defined the meaning in French.

I sat quietly at a student desk *behind* the student giving a report or speech. This is impossible in dialogue, but I tried to be as inconspicuous as possible. A teacher's stare may render a poor student mute and trembling. I remember an advanced student who arrived in my class at fourth level obliged for the first time, unfortunately, to make speeches and oral reports. He had the advantage (or disadvantage) of having had two older brothers who had been my students. His pronunciation needed correction. True to form, I corrected him. At the end of his speech, he turned to me and said, "Madame, this is going to be a long, hard year." I returned his gaze with a smile and replied, "Monsieur W., I shall endeavor to make it a great year for you. Courage! You will be able to do well everything I ask of you."

He did. He was an honor student. However, he was retiring and modest before his peers and in his classes, not given to showing off. He was a confirmed book scholar—a good one!

Examples of dialogue situations:

1. Un accident en route. This entailed vocabulary of all parts of the body, internal organs, parts of an automobile, roads and conditions, rescue attempts, and the like. The subject allows plenty of freedom for research on the part of students and great opportunities for peer teaching.
2. Visit to the dentist
3. Decorating a house
4. A voyage in a canoe
5. A voyage by train or airplane
6. A marriage reception
7. Breakfast in bed at home, hospital, or in a hotel
8. Visit to the hairdresser
9. Dinner with the family at home
10. A poor report card (or a good one)

The possibilities are endless. I found, however, that students readily researched and wrote dialogues that involved their daily life and activities.

Some cautions. The first attempts at dialogue writing should not begin until near the end of the first year of French, or perhaps after Christmas. The first attempts for my students were in class under my supervision. Gradually they did things outside of class. Another caution involves dictionaries. It is always necessary to teach students how to use a French–English dictionary, thus avoiding having such things as a disordered dining room described as a naufrage (nautical for shipwreck). I discouraged the use of tiny pocket dictionaries. They are misleading to beginning students.

I required known vocabulary and verb structure for dialogues when they first began. If any unknown vocabulary was used, it was written on the board at the beginning of the performance. I allowed the class members to form their own dialogue groups, but I remained alert. Some students were sometimes left out. I insisted that all students be included in some group—no more than four to a group. Occasionally I asked for a new group formation. As the year moved along, I called my most able students in to ask them to each form his or her own group in order to help students who were struggling. My students never failed to meet this challenge when I asked them to help others.

Original dialogue day became an exciting and anticipated day for students and for me. Students came early with props and costumes. Often I found myself asked to play a role with the script already written for me. Dialogue day was always on Friday, a pleasurable end to the week.

Helping students to write original dialogue is a fulfilling experience. It is a marvelous method to teach useful idioms. The students love to memorize these and usually remember. Bonne chance! Patience!

Free Speech and Spontaneous Dialogue

"Madame, how do you take them from zero to something?" was the question of a former student facing her first year as a teacher of French I. A greater dilemma is: How does one bring oral comprehension and speech to a class of French IV students who have been taught French in English? Sadly, this happens too often. When I encountered such a class, the students were mute; they looked at me with glassy eyes when I spoke French in class the first day.

Comprehension and speaking ability needed to increase quickly. I copied all the dialogues in our French I, II, and III books. There are usually twelve to fifteen basic dialogues in all texts regardless of the publisher. (There is a maximum of forty-five dialogues in the several commonly used text series published in the United States.) I compiled thirty-six dialogues that supposedly had been "covered" in the first three texts these French IV students had used.

The homework for performance in class was two dialogues a week, which the students recopied and handed to me, and then they stood in the center of the room and gave these dialogues orally without notes or help. Everyone memorized all roles in every dialogue. Before the first class period had ended on the first dialogue day, the students were all prompting each other and talking and understanding each other in that dialogue.

Three days of the week we used the Level IV text, reading the stories aloud. After a few lines or a paragraph were read, I posed questions on word definitions and sentence structure to which the students gradually learned to respond in French. Translation was not necessary. There is often too much English translation in texts published in the United States. I always used more questions than those following the passage.

Short dictées were also given from something we had read the day before or last week. Before thirty-six dialogues had been memorized, the students were moving ahead more rapidly than two dialogues a week.

Some techniques are applicable to comprehension at any level.

Below are some of the techniques that I found particularly useful.

I gave surprise dictées on dialogues students had memorized but changed the dialogue to a story. These were immediately corrected after papers had been exchanged. I picked them up and gave them a grade. One day of the week was devoted to quiz and verb drill. I had a blackboard on wheels that I rolled behind the student at the blackboard doing the writing as I dictated. Thus the dictée was there for all to see *after* we had exchanged papers. This is a regular technique in classrooms in France. There, the blackboard swings on hinges.

At the end of two months, Fridays were devoted to more serious and longer speech-making, and memorization was faster.

I drew up a list of historical figures the students were to study and asked them to *copy* pertinent facts about this person's life. In this speech, they were to have four important dates: birth, death, and two dates of prime importance in the person's life. (The students immediately wanted to know if I expected them to know these dates for exams. I always told them I would expect a few and warned them that dates which were turning points of history would always be expected. We would discuss dates in class at the conclusion of historical periods.)

Why dates? One might wonder. They all thought they knew their numbers; they had recited them off and on for two weeks the first year. It was my observation that much effort had been wasted on numbers after students learned to count to one hundred. They still could not *think* in French numbers. Within four weeks of reciting four memorized dates a week, the students forgot their fear of numbers and stopped much of their translating. I used this technique for teaching numbers at all levels and spent no time drilling numbers. The students had to memorize them for speeches—even first-year students.

As a practice drill for numbers, I picked up the verb quiz papers and recited the grades in French, asking for a quick translation into English. This oral recitation of numbers took place regularly for two or three minutes two or three times a week in all beginning classes. I then reversed the question: I recited grades in English and demanded a French answer.

When the students were sent to copy passages on historical figures, they found these in texts on history, literature, art, music, and the like in our school library in French. *I never permitted translation from English texts.* There should be encyclopedias in French, history texts, and so on, in any school library where the language is taught. If your library funds are too scant for the luxury of books published in France, then organize cookie sales, car washes, and film programs that will stock your library. We did it with a French film project. The students paid a small fee of $2.00 for a program of five rented films a year. The profits went to buy books for the library. Our library was well stocked with reference books published in France. Each year we added books from our film profits.

Film Project

We had written permission from parents for the showing and the rental of films from France. The film showing was considered a field trip and the entire department participated for four or five films a year. The films were shown every period so schedules were not disrupted. Each film was critiqued in English by a teacher for all assembled classes. Themes and cultural aspects were pointed out. In class, teachers then critiqued in French. Advanced levels were asked to note themes they thought they saw in the films and to critique them in French. These critiques provided occasions for vocabulary enrichment and the learning of idioms and the use of figurative language.

The films inspired classroom conversation at all levels. New phrases were picked up by students as a result of this exposure and were noted and written by teachers to add to their vocabulary. The soundtrack was French with English subtitles, *never an English soundtrack.*

The Verbs of Coming and Going
Les Verbes de Va-et-Vient

The verbs in this grouping have peculiar characteristics that should be taught at the same time. They are not listed together in American texts but as usual appear here and there with some left out of the first-year text.

Some of these verbs are to be found in the core group I have listed in chapter 5. Before two months had gone by in first-year French, I listed them on the board (to be copied) and explained the rules governing their use. As always, I contrasted the present with the past indefinite (passé composé) for every one of them:

aller = to go

partir = to leave

arriver = to arrive

sortir = to go out

rester = to remain ([rester] boxed because one is going nowhere)

entrer = to enter

monter = to go up

rentrer = to return (home)

descendre = to descend

retourner = to return

venir = to come

revenir = to come back

mourir = to die

naître = to spring forth, to be born

devenir = to become

passer = if it means to go from one place to another; a synonym of aller

The past participle of these verbs agrees in number and gender with the subject, and have être for the auxiliary in compound tenses, thus:

Elle est morte   =   She has died or she is dead. (The sentence is the same in French.)

Il est mort   =   He has died or he is dead.

If we go far enough back in English usage, we will find many of these verbs behaving in English as they do in French. Anyone who reads the Bible in the King James version will see and read similar structure. It is beautifully poetic.

When I taught these verbs as a group very early in the first year, my students were more able to grasp their meaning and to remember their behavior. It gave me the occasion also to teach the meaning of *again* in many verbs. I would add *re* to mourir, remourir, to die again—each time they faced a verb quiz; renaître = to be born again, resortir, repartir, redevenir, remonter, redescendre, repasser.

Some workbooks list almost all these verbs at the same time, but I have never seen a book that lists all the possibilities with the addition of *re* as a prefix except for those verbs of the first list. This was an early and useful technique for me.

Proficiency and Aptitude Testing

A foreign language department whose teachers take the measurement of progress in learning seriously should test all students at the beginning of the year with the *Pimsleur Aptitude Battery Test*. This test is not to discourage students but to indicate particular areas of weakness or strength. Students with difficulties can then receive remedial help in order to experience success in the foreign language. (The test is available from Psychological Corporation, 555 Academic Court, San Antonio, Texas 78204–0952, telephone (512) 299–1061.)

The aptitude test does not test a specific language. We tested our entire foreign language department. I shared my findings with the English teachers and enlisted the English department in my crusade to improve vocabulary, to understand sentence structure, and to recognize syllables in English. Any improvement will automatically carry over to the learning of foreign language.

If there were students who were having unusual learning difficulties, I asked that they be tested by the remedial teacher. As a general rule, students always responded and cooperated with this interest in their welfare. Remedial work thus began early and extra help brought some measure of success to students who had a learning disability. My sharing also alerted the English department to some students who had not yet been tested by them (see chapter 7).

Students met with me privately to discuss their individual score on the Pimsleur aptitude test. I was able to suggest changes of how to improve vocabulary in English. The study of French or any other language improved students' sound discrimination, their ability to hear sound-symbol and syllable association, and their understanding of the structure of a sentence. This carried over to English classes.

The section of the Pimsleur aptitude test which is designed to measure the interest of the students in learning a foreign language is *not* accurate, I found, as a result of two experimental classes. The desire to learn French rose and fell as a tide, depending on whether the students had experienced success or failure in recent previous endeavors. (I tested them several times during the year in those two classes with the interest part of the test alone.)

The aptitude test must never be used as an instrument to advise students to drop the study of a foreign language. It is unreliable in measuring desire and determination to work. Aptitude increases as students continue in their study of a foreign language. This was noted as a result of testing my students with the Pimsleur Aptitude Battery over a period of four years as they moved to a higher level or repeated a level. In my experience, the aptitude test score invariably correlated with the difficulty students experienced in the early stages of learning. But as the students learned the art of listening intently and improved their comprehension of structure, difficulty diminished. Desire to learn and hard work always brought a measure of success. A teacher should consider success as any passing grade, even a "D" if it is *earned.* As stated previously, the work of the world is accomplished by students who have received "C" or even "D" in many areas but have used these skills, however average they may be (in our measurement) to achieve great things. Teachers value too much the students of "A" and "B" work. They forget that the struggles of students receiving a "C" or "D" can bring the sweet taste of success to those who persevered in their battle. I rejoiced with these students. I praised their striving and always held out hope of greater achievement. These students were encouraged to continue the study of French to upper levels even with a "C" or "D." Skill in a foreign language will open doors to them regardless of the profession they follow.

Proficiency Testing: Pretesting and Posttesting

Pretesting with the proficiency tests of the Modern Language Association Educational Testing Service, Cooperative Test Division, Princeton, New Jersey, or Berkeley, California, can give teachers and their students a base by which posttesting can be meaningful at the end of the year. There are two levels of these tests. These tests are standardized; therefore, (1) the tests must be kept in the guidance department, (2) test answers can never be given to the students after the testing if the exams are to be used again, (3) teachers must not examine tests before or after testing, and (4) if possible, the tests should be administered by guidance personnel.

My students' pretest and posttest scores were given to the students at the end of the year. They were thus able to see progress, sometimes dramatic progress, between the pretest scores and the end-of-the-year scores. These scores were kept on five-by-eight-inch cards and kept in the foreign language department until graduation. They were then stored with the records in the guidance department.

These tests examine listening, reading, and writing comprehension in separate parts. I never gave these tests a grade that carried weight in the work average for the year. They were useful to me, the student, and the administration in evaluating progress. I used them to encourage students to continue to the next level of learning. They can be useful to administrators in evaluating the effectiveness of foreign language teachers. Some teachers may feel threatened by such an idea, but we must be as responsible and accountable as the students we teach.

Caution

A wise teacher never wholly equates a grade with a student's ability and/or aptitude. Many factors will have helped determine a student's *desire to learn:*
1. Work habits formed long ago
2. Ability to listen
3. Ability to *hear* and make sense

The last two are not the same. One can listen but not hear; that is, understand. I learned to play detective when grades did not equal potential or when they suddenly or gradually declined. There were always reasons for a poor grade in aptitude testing, proficiency testing, or regular testing during the year. Here is what I found that influenced scores:
1. Habitual use or abuse of drugs
2. Conflict in the home between parents of different views or too permissive or too harsh rules
3. Divorce (Adolescents do not handle this well. I have seen this problem send the student into the drug culture.)
4. No academic expectation from the parents
5. Low self-esteem in the student who has been reared in a negative atmosphere
6. Unrealistically high standards and expectations of the parents even for learning-disability students

7. Illness
8. Excessive time demands from athletic coaches
9. Inability to read and write English well

There are others. This should be enough to help a beginning teacher become aware that students are the product of their environment, their home especially, the pressures of their peer group, and habits of acting and thinking often deeply ingrained.

A caring and concerned teacher can:

1. Build students' self-esteem
2. Counsel students on use of harmful substances
3. Encourage parents to encourage students at home
4. Be a friendly counselor when the student feels that no one cares
5. Secure remedial help
6. Be alert for a learning disability

We all live on hope for better tomorrows. We all need to be valued and loved by another human soul. A caring teacher can provide a firm anchor to an emotionally bewildered student. Sincere caring by teachers will influence the most reluctant student to try to please the teachers and not to disappoint them. Our role is to see that with all our measuring and testing, the potential of our charges does not forever remain merely potential.

Paradis Terrestre
L'Antre de la Vieille
Dragonne

Aux grands maux
les grands remèdes.

7

Problems

Prevention and Resolution

I have selected from my files documentation of some examples of serious problems that quite likely will come up during the career of every teacher. The problems—at least the problems indicated on the surface—are repeated absence, poor performance, confusion about life, and negative outside influences. Correspondence and dialogue is quoted liberally in each example—or case. Each case is titled with the first name of the student who experienced the problem.

Ted

To: Carl S.   Date: le 29 Sept. 1976
         Director of Guidance

From: Mary D. Nelson

Subject: Ted D.

Ted has been absent since September 21. He has been marked absent for only Monday the 27th on school rolls. I have talked with Mrs. S. (counselor) who told me Ted was in guidance (not with her) to talk. I called home but did not reach him until Monday. I talked with him. He said, I have a family problem. I can't talk much now. He promised to come to see me and explain. He has not appeared. I want to know *what* is going on.

Was Ted my problem? The school year had just begun; there was a mountain of work before me and there were the usual problems in foreign language classes that the teachers must face: calming students to listen in a language not their own; getting students accustomed to a routine of work instead of the fun and games of the summer vacation; recovering from the shock of overcrowded classes, the endemic plague of all language departments in secondary schools; and persuading *myself* that with luck and much divine help I probably would survive the year, albeit with my annual accumulation of the usual baggage—more grey hairs and an extra portion of wrinkles.

Was it my problem (as well as Ted's)? And, was Ted worth the effort? Yes to both! All students are worth the effort, including those with problems.

Ted had spent the previous year with me and had done well. Something must be wrong at home.

To: Mr. S. C. [vice-principal]   Date: le 6 October, 1976

From: Madame Nelson

Subject: Ted D.

Since Monday 29 Sept., I have talked with C. S., Mrs. S., and Roving Leader R. about Ted. I reached Mrs. D., Ted's mother, on Monday evening by telephone (4 Oct.) and told her Ted had not been in French class since 21 Sept. She seemed very upset about Ted's behavior. Her husband left home last spring. They are getting a divorce. She has been obliged to go to work. She was grateful for my call. She insisted Ted speak to me on the telephone. I told him I was shocked that he would not come to see me. He promised he would.

The dates on these memos should be noted. There is nothing in my files to indicate Ted was missed by anyone except a curious French teacher.

One must understand, however, the problems of a large suburban high school in an area where families are very often transient. Administrative personnel are inundated the first few weeks of school with new students arriving in an already overcrowded school. This, in turn, creates new teacher problems—not enough were hired. The "bare-bones" budgets that schools are required to live with do not allow for any extra teachers. The counting is always the other way.

Thus, the moral and legal obligation that falls upon a teacher for every student in every class should be carefully observed. Every means possible should be used to communicate with a troubled student and to tell him, "You are important. I miss you."

Ted spent a miserable year with both parents telling him horror stories about the torments of their lives. His academic year was miserable as well. He was constantly trying to flee from anything that required thought.

He did come in to talk. I listened and hoped that listening would help lighten the burden he bore—loving both parents and not wanting to take a stand against either one. I found this behavior typical and expected in divorce situations. The students involved often felt guilty and unloved.

Caution: As these cases unfold, note how important it is to keep good records.

Wesley

To: Madame Nelson   Date: April 21, 1978

From: Mr. V. [guidance counselor]

Subject: Wesley C.

His mother called Dr. M. [principal] to ask for an explanation of why Wesley received an F in French and why he still had an Incomplete for the 2nd quarter. Mr. C. asked me to look into it. Please come by so we can form an answer that I can relay to the parent. Thank you. (P.S. She is under the impression that Wesley meets with you every day during break and also has a tutor to help him with French.) I spoke with Wesley. He has great respect for you. He is also frustrated that he is not achieving better in the class.

* * *

To Mr. V.   22 April 1978

Memo from Madame Nelson:

Wesley *had* a tutor, Ron, but Ron just stopped. I didn't know until about three weeks ago. He had three students to teach. I have found another tutor for him, but Wesley made no effort to find help although I have a list of tutors posted in my room. I had to go and find another for him. They have just begun.

Please go through these records *carefully*. I am fond of Wesley. I have outlined what he must do and told him time and time again to come with his questions. He is a gentleman, but does not communicate with his parents.

* * *

(Promise written by Wesley G.)

Wesley G., le 18 Oct. I will come three days a week for help in verbs. During the break and one day after school. Review verbs out loud at home.

* * *

Note date, this came about after I *begged* him to come. I think he can be saved *if* Wesley will do as I ask. The Incomplete was the result of my allowing Wesley to make up things much later than he should.

* * *

Je parle français un petit en classe. Je parle anglais souvent avec mes amis en classe. Je fais mes devoirs souvent mais quelque fois Je ne comprends! [*sic*]

My note: Wesley had help to write this.

Below are Wesley's grades and average which he wrote himself: for the nineteen graded exercises—28, 76, 18, 95, 43, 39, 86, 55, 47, 48, 48, 50, 52, 52, 34, 25, 79, 70, 39; total 984. Thus, 984 ÷ 19 = 49.9, or 50%. (The correct average is 51.8 percent.)

Students always figured average on interim. I never did because this average was never recorded on the permanent record. Students often made small errors, as Wesley did above.

Wesley's promise:

> I will have to study verbs at home. My speeches will have to become longer and my pronunciation will have to get better. I will have to practice my speech aloud at home. I will have all of my homework done and on time. I will come three days a week during the break. I will make my work up on time. The main things [*sic*] is to know all of the verb tenses!

* * *

> Wesley G., Jan. 29, 1978. I had a chance to go back to Level II, but I didn't want to go back to Level II. I have been told to come in during the brake [*sic*] and after school. I have to study more after school and tape my speeches. I don't think you should change the way you have been teaching. It is up to the person to bear down and get to work. I don't know what I deserve—whatever decision you make goes.

* * *

To: Mr. V., Counselor   Date: Jan. 29, 1978

From: Madame Nelson

Subject: W. G.

You have a copy of this and so does M. B. I told M. B. that Mrs. G., the mother, would not come in. She would ignore my request for a meeting. I have talked with Wesley many times and begged him to come before or after school as well as during the break. He has been referred to the remedial English teacher by me.

* * *

Wesley G., April 13, 1978. I received my grades because I did not study enough for verb quizzes. Also I didn't study enough for Pronouns Objects. I thought I did pretty good speeches.

In November I sent the following Student Evaluation home. French was mixed with English on the evaluation. The students loved to translate at home. (My comments for items 5 and 6 were always at the right margin.)

<u>Student Evaluation Form:</u>   WESLEY C.
<u>November</u>

__1. I always, rarely, usually learn speeches.
__2. I come for help during the break; after school. *sometimes – W.C.*
__3. I always, rarely, usually do my work.
✓4. I make up work, allow work to accumulate when absent.
__5. I review regularly, never, sometimes.
__6. I pay attention; I dream in class. *?? (Madame Nelson's remarks)*
__7. I have cut class ∅ times.
✓8. I do my best.

<u>Madame Nelson's Evaluation</u>

__1. Always prepared. __ Quelle joie! Préparé d'habitude, Rarement préparé(e)
__2. Gives speeches well *On parle bien.*
__3. Always polite, Toujours poli(e), not always polite.
__4. Pronunciation excellente.
✓5. On a besoin d'améliorer la pronunciation.
✓6. Needs help but does not come for it. *Wes does not always*
__7. Attitude indifférente. ?? *come for help. He can*
✓8. On fait des progres, but please encourage. *do better if he*
✓9. J'aime votre fils/fille. *reviews. I must beg*
__10. On essaie. *him to do this. He must*
__11. Should repeat next year. *work very hard. He is*
                         not always prepared.

<u>Citizenship</u>

__1. His/Her co-operative attitude and fine citizenship contribute much to the good order and progress of class.
__2. He/She respects authority.
__3. He/She frequently lacks courtesy and self-control.

110

Commendation

___1. He/She shows initiative skill, and thoroughness and applies knowledge gained to new situations.
___2. He/She begins and completes work on time. *?*
___3. He/She takes part in discussions and is helpful to the group.
___4. He/She follows directions carefully. *? Wes needs to take*
___5. He/She shows an improvement in effort. *? more care in his work.*

Probable Reason for Low Mark

___1. He/She failed to have the necessary equipment and materials.
___2. He/She failed to hand in assignments.
_✓_3. He/She frequently came to class poorly prepared.
_✓_4. He/She failed to complete the required work.

> Parents' Comments: I feel a little patience on your part and a lot of understanding for Wesley would be a great help. He does his homework and tries very hard. I feel Wesley is a little nervous but will give his all to do his best. I feel he is giving as much to your class as he can and you being his teacher should expect no more or less than that. All the red pencil markings on the front is a little upsetting for a 10th grader and for me to see. He is not in grade school. If he is a problem and not respectful, I could well understand this ridiculous amount of ???? question marks, etc., but Wesley did not do so badly last year and works as hard this year.
> Maybe going a little easier would help. Thank you and have a Merry Christmas.
>
> Mrs. G.

Wesley's mother mentions doing all right in French *the year before* with another teacher. This never impressed me because it was another year. A grade for the previous year does not automatically carry over to the next. Wesley was graded on *work,* not ability.

Early in the year, the English Department, at my request, tested and diagnosed Wesley as a poor reader with learning problems. I received permission from his parents for his "special help." His grades in French were poor from day one. I arranged for help to be given Wesley by our special help teacher. I suggested at the beginning of the year, as Wesley noted, that he

111

should return to French II. It was the choice of the family that he remain in French III. Every interim report I asked the parents to come and see me. The mother's reaction on the November student evaluation was that I should have more patience.

This student was hyperactive to the point of being disruptive occasionally. I was extremely tolerant with him because I had learned that he had been sent away to private schools where he had had great difficulty. His problem was never adequately addressed until I found him help. I suggested he be put on pass/fail and was liberal in what I called a pass for him; that is, for him I lowered the fail line from 70 to 60.

His parents continued to deal with me through the principal and refused to come to see me in spite of my three requests for a conference.

The memos were sent after several visits and discussion with the counselor. Teachers do not like to write, nor will they write too much criticism—even the truth. They are obliged to be specific, and bluntly so, only after much discussion. When the crisis arrives, parents and students are consulted and warned—orally, long before the paper appears.

After Wesley received an "F" the third quarter, he burst out with vulgar language one day. I wrote a private note to his parents and told them to come and see me. I would not tolerate vulgarity from their son. They were there at once. It was late April; the school year was almost over.

By now I had conferred many times with the learning disabilities teacher and had learned that Wesley was making progress in his ability to "see" how a word was written in English. I would give him as much help as I could in French. My concern was that he be given academic help in order to prevent his increasing frustration with learning.

When the parents came, I calmly told them of all my findings. I knew that they were also aware of these things. I told them that

I suspected that Wesley had learning difficulties at a very early age and that was why he had been sent to a series of private schools. They admitted I was right. I brought out all the reports and memos for them to review. I did not ask them why they had not come to see me as I had repeatedly requested. It was my turn to ask for patience from them for their son. The pressure from them was too great, and their son needed help and understanding in dealing with the academic world. He needed more than pep talks. Failing French was really not important, I told them.

These people were extremely affluent. Their social circle included the White House. Their other children were intelligent (as was Wesley) and without academic problems. This one child was a problem they did not want to entertain.

They went away feeling relieved, I think. My records prevented any noisy outburst of blame for me for not having done enough. Parents will sometimes use the not-too-subtle approach of going through the principal in order to threaten a teacher. Good records prevent problems. But, more important, in my opinion, good records will help students and parents face reality and stop any effort to shift the blame for poor performance to the teacher, the usual scapegoat in a confrontation. *Note:* Wesley eventually improved in his ability to learn in other areas. He had great difficulty, but from this year on he received *special* help.

Teachers must constantly bear in mind that often the son or daughter is an extension of the ego of one or sometimes both parents, or the parents are simply frustrated and do not know what to do. Wesley had never been diagnosed as dyslexic before this year. He was intelligent.

In any interview, a teacher should be the first to speak, voicing concern for the student's welfare and expressing some positive aspect of the personality. I could always begin by telling the parent I had become very fond of his or her child and also express my belief that the intelligence of this son or daughter was equal to the

113

task. After all, we use only 10 percent of our intellectual endowment and very often try to get by with even less than that. I would always conclude by saying that grades were based solely on the quality of work done, never on charming personality or great intellect. However, if the student having difficulty was not richly endowed, I would counsel that hard repetitive work was the only solution for success.

John

> Mon cher ami,   January 4, 1974
>
> Je suis actuellement dans ma classe préférée. The preceding statement is completely false. I hate this class. This crazy teacher named Nelson forced us to write it. I have nothing to say to you frogs over there. I never did like French people after I lived in Versailles for two years. Don't respond because I don't have the time to read it. This school is driving me out of my mind or crazy. France would not be a bad place if it weren't for the French.
>
> John D.

The class was corresponding with a class in Bordeaux, France. John did not have the faintest idea that I would read every note written by every student before I mailed them off to the teacher in Bordeaux.

I called John in the next day to talk to me. He came and was most uncomfortable and immediately said, "Madame, I didn't mean it."

"What," I asked, "about you, John? You are free to express your feelings about me. What you think of me does not bother me. I called you in to tell you that I have no intention of including your insulting letter with the others I am sending to the French teacher. I feel deeply sorry for you, John, and trust that your nasty and prejudiced disposition might improve. If not, you will be miserable and make the people who love you miserable as well. I have learned to love you."

114

John expected an angry Madame Nelson and was mute except for repeating, "I didn't mean it." John was not old enough nor well adjusted enough (he was using drugs regularly) to understand how or why his "crazy" teacher could be fond of him. He was too angry with the world, too angry with people. I did not know why. I never could have admitted to him or any student that I secretly enjoyed being a little "crazy" and unexplainable.

John was unusually cooperative the remainder of the year.

"Never explain," my father used to say. "Your friends don't need it and your enemies won't believe it!"

Charles

Charles was a "problem" almost everywhere in school that year. He was passing his art class, but otherwise the academic situation was more than dreary. It was zero credit.

After going over the schedule with Charles's guidance counselor, I decided to recommend that Charles drop French. Perhaps he could be saved in classes where he needed the credit. The parents refused. Charles was obliged to continue in French.

Charles lived in his own fantasy world. His eyes were as glassy as his ears. I'm sure all he heard was noise around him, except when he was literally jolted into awareness. (I pleaded for help for this student.)

I never ignored him but never embarrassed him. Several times a week I would tap him on the shoulder as I passed and say, "Faites attention, Charles. Rêvez chez vous." (Pay attention, Charles. Dream at home.)

One day after class as the students left for lunch, I suddenly saw the art work that decorated the floor in front of Charles's desk. "I hate French" with fine scrolls all around it was carefully written with black art pencil on the floor. "How had he done it?" I asked myself. Another teacher would soon be entering that classroom and I was always careful to leave the classroom clean and

115

orderly. I was about to wipe it up myself with tissue and glass cleaner, but stopped and asked myself, "What can I do to answer an obvious cry for help from one of my students who feels imprisoned?" I hurried to the office of the vice-principal, a very understanding man.

"Monsieur K., Charles has decorated the floor in front of his desk with an elaborate announcement which reads, 'I hate French,' " I said, then continued without giving Monsieur K. an opportunity to reply. I told him that Charles must be sent back to my room the next period to scrub that off the floor. He agreed to call Charles in and talk to him.

Charles came and Mr. K. told him why I was there. "Oh, Madame, I didn't know I was doing it. I'm sorry," was Charles's defense.

"I believe you, Charles," I was able to tell him, "but you understand that you must clean that floor."

"Oh, yes. Oh, yes." And away he went to clean the floor.

Monsieur K. and I regarded each other for a minute and then I told him of my efforts to lighten Charles's academic burden and the resultant failure.

"I have not given Charles enough attention," I told Monsieur K. "Failing or not, he needs as much attention as the others. I promise you Charles won't be back because of my class," I said.

The students in this class soon became aware that Charles was receiving a great deal of attention from Madame. Three remained after class one day to ask me why. "Charles lives in a dream world but must be helped to understand and face reality. He needs to be valued and to have someone pay attention to him," I told them.

"But he's failing. He won't work," they protested.

"True," I said, "but he still needs attention. I must show him I love him. What is more important to Charles right now? Passing French or learning that the world is real and that I care about him?" My inquisitive trio left the room, their questions answered.

In the months ahead I was warmed and encouraged by the caring behavior of three formerly curious students when they interacted with Charles. Their Gospel of Caring gradually spread to other members. Before the year was out, my three self-appointed helpers would occasionally remind me that Charles needed some more "attention" from me.

I would like to write that Charles ceased his dreaming, started to study, and passed brilliantly. I cannot; Charles failed the year in French. But there was more to the story. The next fall, two days before the arrival of the students, Charles was waiting for me outside the records room.

"Guess what, Madame," he began. "I am going to take French all over again with you."

I was stunned, but quickly recovered and said, "Now, Charles, you know me. You will have to work. I don't give grades; you have to earn them."

"I know, I know."

Charles moved, however. His military father was transferred to Florida. The last day before he left he stopped by to talk and asked a question. "Why do your students come back to see you, Madame, after they have graduated from high school?"

"I don't know, Charles. I have never asked them. I am always happy to see them. Have you any ideas on that?"

He hesitated, then said, "I think it's because they respect you. Well, goodbye, Madame."

I hugged him and then watched him as he started for the stairs. He turned and called back, "I'll be back to see you, Madame."

Somehow I did not feel I failed with Charles.

Bill

Bill was the unanimous choice of the foreign language department for the outstanding student of the year. At midyear he was a third-year "A" student of Russian and an "A" student in fourth-year advanced placement French with me. He had been accepted at a university. He had no more worries—just breeze through the last half of the year, he thought. Then he found sex and drugs and everything started to unravel.

He started to fail simple grammatical tests which were little more than review. He did the oral and written report of the literary work he had chosen for the third quarter and emerged with a very low "B–." His work continued to deteriorate in French. I checked with my colleague to see how Bill was working in Russian. He wasn't. The same behavior (no work) prevailed in all academic areas. All of Bill's teachers felt completely helpless. Reporting to the parents what was happening did not help. Bill was eighteen and thought he was in total control.

The last quarter he was late with his oral and written report on the book he had chosen to read. He said he was not going to do it. I asked him to stop by to see me after school. He did.

"Bill," I told him, "you shall do the final report. Do you understand? It is overdue, but you will be given a failing grade in this class if it is not done. You are late, but I shall allow you two weeks to do it. However, you shall do ten pages instead of the usual three or four."

He agreed.

Two weeks later, Bill appeared with seven pages, not the assigned ten. I read the report. It was excellently done. "Bill," I began, "these seven pages do not fulfill our contract. I never accord a perfect 100 percent on a report or a speech, but this is excellent. Would you be content with ten points per page?"

"Oh, yes," he responded.

"Agreed. Your grade will be 70 percent three times." (Reports received three grades.)

Bill finished the year with an average for the year of 86.6 percent. As was my custom, I calculated the year's average for each student and gave it to all of them on my note paper before the final grades were officially recorded. They could come to me and correct any errors they thought I might have made. They were to keep their own records throughout the year. Bill came to see me and asked what his grade would be. (Eighty-seven percent was the lowest grade for a "B" in our school, and 86.6 was not 87. It isn't on a paycheck or a tax bill either.) I asked Bill what he thought he deserved.

"Well, you always give a few points to the next number, Madame."

"Yes, I do, Bill. Do you think I should stretch things for you, Bill?" He hesitated. "Go home," I said, "and come back on Monday and tell me if I should *give* you something—and whether you deserve it."

Bill came back Monday after school. He seemed surer of himself than he had been since he started his academic slide. "No, Madame," he said. "I don't think I deserve a stretched grade."

"I agree, Bill. Your grade is a 'C' for the year. But you have done something difficult, Bill, which deserves admiration. You have been honest with yourself and me. I won't worry about you anymore. The grade is much less important than learning to take a look at yourself—an honest look. God bless you."

Whether Bill expected a stretched grade because he was honest, I do not know, nor would I guess. But there was no protest from him or his parents over the final grade of "C."

Sadly, the foreign language department could not award Bill the accolade of outstanding foreign language student of the year, which he had earned at midyear. We were obliged to choose someone who had stayed the course and run the entire race.

Terry

Terry was beginning to use marijuana. He had not quite become a daily user but was using it on weekends. How did I know? The physical signs of the habitual user had not yet appeared, but Terry was beginning to let his homework slide. He was extremely able, and I told him just that. I also added that I loved him and his poor work was making me unhappy.

He promised better work.

By midyear, the downward trend in all his classes had not been checked. Then Terry cut my class and forged my name as well as another teacher's name to two passes. The full-time guidance counselor had accepted my note without question, but checked with Mr. C.

To: Madame Nelson and Chief of Guidance

Date: 10 Oct. 1971

From: S. C., Vice-Principal

Subject: Terry K.

Cut *French class* and forged a pass to guidance having Mr. C's name signed to the pass. Terry said he had to study for an exam.

Action taken: Mrs. Nelson called the family. No other cuts have been recorded since the last office confrontation. Terry has been told he owes Madame Nelson at least two days' detention; one for the class cut and one for the forged note.

Madame Nelson will notify Terry of the day he is supposed to show up for detention (at Madame Nelson's convenience). Terry was admonished by the office for the cut and for the forged note.

Terry served his detention. I called home after this and insisted that both parents come to see me. Terry's mother told me that her husband was too busy to come. I replied that I would meet them at school at 6:00 A.M. if necessary, but I wanted to talk to both of them.

They came at 7:00 A.M. one morning. The father resented being there and showed his anger by pacing up and down in my classroom lighting one cigarette after another and launching a tirade against his son, accusing him of ingratitude without cause. He complained of his son's increasing use of marijuana and his wayward friends. Puffing his cigarette, his free arm waving, he finally exploded, "I wash my hands of him completely!"

Terry's intimidated mother sat quietly during her husband's long, angry outburst. Her agony showed in her eyes and trembling lips.

I sat and listened until this suffering man had exhausted his ire, then I stood up and asked him to sit down please. (A woman who is five foot three and weighs only a hundred pounds has a great psychological advantage when she stands and her audience is seated—and suffering.)

"You *cannot* wash your hands of your son, sir. He is your legal and moral responsibility. Terry tells me that you are 'always hassling' him about his marijuana smoking," I told him. "While you have been here only about ten minutes, you have lighted five cigarettes and have made my room almost untenable for me since I am allergic to smoke. Your cigarette smoking is just as bad a habit as Terry's marijuana, he thinks. I regret to say that I agree with him."

"He is your son and I know you love him or you would not have come. You want to help him, both of you. I do too. I love your son. That is why I insisted that you come. May I suggest that we develop a plan; you at home (perhaps with a more united front for you, his parents), and I here at school will encourage and help more. I shall get some peer help for Terry as well. Perhaps you could make a contract with him to give up cigarettes if he gives up marijuana."

The father was speechless. The mother promised they would encourage and help. The father made no promises. He had tried to impress me with how important he was (he guarded the President of the United States). I had told him Terry came first. He had vented his anger; I had not run for cover. He complained about Terry's using an illegal drug, and I told him his legal drug habit was as bad and perhaps worse. The poor man. I felt downright sorry for him as he left. He was accustomed to having people scurry out of the way at his orders but he was utterly failing as a father.

I turned Terry over to a budding female tyrant in his class and charged her with seeing that Terry did his weekly dialogue or speech. She wrote the dialogues, always writing a dramatic part for herself. She made Terry her servant, a complaining wall at her French château. Her repertoire was extensive. She was in love with French history and loved to play royalty.

Karen drilled Terry like a master sergeant and, in a sense, replaced a demanding teacher and a complaining father. I don't know what her threats were. She was larger than he and probably promised to break a bone or two! He produced and never cut the class again. She saved him. He emerged with a "D" for the year.

Evidently there was no contract with his father and Terry continued to cut other classes and to smoke his marijuana.

To: Madame Nelson   Date: 3/29/72
            All teachers of Terry

From: S. C., Vice-Principal

Subject: Terry K.

Parent conference held for continued truancy in various classes. Terry was suspended effective today for three days. Upon readmittance, the teachers have been asked to encourage Terry to attend and to complete all assigned work in order to finish strongly this school year.

The suspension was imposed because Terry chose not to attend classes on numerous occasions and previous admonitions [all oral until now] mandated attendance.

Letter drafted to acknowledge the suspension.

(Madame Nelson noted he had not cut her class again!!)

I was not invited to parent conference because Terry was not truant in my class again.

Karen, his "godot," finished her university studies with a Ph.D. in French literature. Terry became a traffic controller at National Airport after high school and was occasionally obliged—and delighted—to use his French.

Ginny

Ginny had the sunniest disposition. Her peers liked her. She appeared to have many close friends and was accepted in any peer dialogue group. Her happy smile and cooperative attitude made her an asset to the classroom community. Her behavior was exemplary.

Ginny spent three years with me at levels II, III, and V. She prepared her homework, was rarely absent, and never cut class. The first two years her grade was "C." This never gave me concern for I valued a "C" student as much as those who received "A" or "B." I reserved my worrying concern for those who earned "D" or "F" as a result of indifference and no work.

Ginny worked; indeed, she was intellectually curious and industrious and I knew it. Her apparent inability to earn a better grade aroused in me a desire to learn why her industry brought less than brilliant results. I had remarked many times that some students made progress more slowly than others, but I had contented myself by rationalizing that some of us appear to be born more intelligent than others, always feeling guilty with this banal explanation.

Note: I did not accept the theory of the "gift" of tongues or language, except in a special spiritual climate. The Bible notes this gift and on rare occasions I had seen and heard people clearly and brilliantly pronounce a sermon in a foreign tongue when they did not know the language well.

The great work of the world was and is done by people who are "C" students but by dint of persistence and the passion to do well many moved themselves into the great achiever's class.

The uneven results of the industry of many students finally moved me to a search for a better answer than intelligence. I had begun testing all my students with the Pimsleur Aptitude Test, which gives many clues to the possible difficulties students experience but I had noted that the desire to learn could not be adequately measured, nor could the results of extraordinary diligence.

Ginny was a senior in level V when I decided to search the student records, noting the results of tests and academic progress on all my students from their entry in school. It was tedious work, but in Ginny's case it gave me insight into a longstanding problem. Her records indicated great difficulty when she began to learn to read. Her verbal score in all the succeeding years was dismally low in the standardized tests. Ginny had a richer vocabulary in French than in English.

I compared Ginny's score on the Pimsleur test the first time she took it to the second time as a French V student. Her aptitude had increased.

In the two previous years Ginny had spent with me, I had noted that she had suffered a severe asthma attack about three weeks after school began and was absent several days. What had triggered the attack? I used to wonder. Ginny returned to school both years still wheezing a little but determined to hurry to make up her work in spite of the drowsiness her allergy medication produced. After my search of the records, I asked Ginny to come to see me after school. I told her that I had something I wanted to tell her. She was tense, wondering what could possibly be the cause of a conference with me.

"Ginny," I began, "I have discovered why you suffer an extreme attack of asthma every year about the third week of school."

Her eyes widened in wonder. She remembered that I told my students every year that I was clairvoyant but I had yet to prove it precisely except in vague instances.

"Ginny, my dear," I continued, "you count the books you must read, the papers you must write between September and June, and you are so overwhelmed that you think you won't be able to endure it all."

Ginny's eyelids were squeezed tightly shut; huge tears rolled down her cheeks. "Oh, Madame," she whispered, "if you only knew."

"I do now, Ginny. But I have a program to propose that will help change all that if you will cooperate," I said.

Ginny cooperate? She would have stood on her head if I had asked that of her.

I suggested that she buy a large artist's sketch notebook— about 15" x 18". She was to cover the page with two lists of words that gave her trouble with spelling or whose meaning she did not know, hang that page in a conspicuous place where she ate her meals, and practice spelling and using each word in a sentence. Each week she would begin another page, and she would continue this process throughout the year. Why place the lists where she ate her meals? Eating is pleasurable; one is less tense and worried. Learning should be associated with an idea of pleasure.

Ginny told me that day that she wanted to go to college. I urged her to go. I asked her, however, to remember that she might be obliged to go over a page, a problem, or the like, more than once—perhaps many times, until she knew the meaning or the solution. I told her that the number of times it took to grasp and comprehend what she wanted to learn had very little to do with intelligence, in my opinion. It took two magic ingredients: desire and persistence.

Ginny completed French V with a B average. She was proud of herself and I was as happy as she.

The year Ginny had spent with me in French III she had made me a miniskirt. This particularly revealing mode of feminine fashion had burst upon the scene—bringing consternation to women whose legs were more attractive if covered. I was conspicuous among my peers by refusing to raise my skirts above the knee. Some of my students later told me that those years they secretly hoped that *some day* Madame might be in fashion either by my raising my skirt or by the return of fashion to the length I found acceptable for me and for them. I had raised my eyebrows at some skirt lengths and always inquired if the student were dressed for a fencing lesson.

I wore Ginny's miniskirt only one day—with black tights. I created such a disturbing sensation that even the principals commented on the unexpected fashion show in the foreign language area. The next day my skirt length returned to below the knee and stayed there. But Ginny knew I loved her or I would not have appeared in her miniskirt.

What happened to Ginny? She finished her undergraduate work with a 4.0 average, applied to three medical schools and was accepted at all three of them.

Her senior year of medical school she called to tell me that she would be going to London to spend two months in a hospital there and hoped to get to France before returning home. I encouraged her to go. She did. When she returned she called me to report: "Madame, I went to Paris and I understood everyone and everyone understood me." The sound of her voice reflected her feeling of exultation.

Today Ginny is married, has recently had her first child, and is a practicing physician in Minnesota.

I am certain that were I to meet Ginny today we would be able to communicate in French. What Ginny learned, she learned very well indeed. Her senior year as a French V student, Ginny placed third in the state of Virginia in the National French Contest, much to the surprise of her guidance counselor who came to me to express her doubts.

Dyslexia has only recently been adequately diagnosed. Today, I fear, some students may be tagged too early as learning disabled when all they may need is more personal and loving attention.

Paradis Terrestre
L'Antre de la Vieille
Dragonne

"Madame, vous êtes sûre que vous n'avez pas une araignée au plafond?"

Peut-être que vous l'avez dit.

8

Athletic French: An Experiment

The title may arouse a thoughtful and puzzled look. That is what I, as well as others, called it the year I decided to tackle the "Great Experiment."

Twelve of my French IV students told me near the end of the year that they would not be taking French V their senior year if I did not teach it. At first, I ignored them, thinking they were indirectly trying to pay me a compliment. They were indeed serious when they showed me their schedules for the following year. I could not persuade them otherwise.

A short time previously, the athletic coach had asked me if I could do something about seeing that his athletes be given a chance to fill the entrance requirement of Virginia colleges for two years of a foreign language. I had assured him that all students in the school would be welcomed in the foreign language department, but we did not approve of nor did we accord grades merely for "bench warming."

A wild idea gradually took shape in my brain—combine twelve highly motivated honor students at fifth level with twelve first-year students. I had witnessed peer teaching over the years in all my classes and at all levels in the dialogue groupings. In fact, I was outspoken in my belief that the biblical parable of the talents and the admonition to care about "neighbors" should be in force in all of us. We owed something to members of the society of church, city, and nation we chose to call our own. We were constantly in debt to others and our God for everything, including the air we breathe. If talents were not used, they were lost. I am sure that not all my students shared my belief but they all quickly learned that peer cooperation was necessary in classes with me. I refused to tolerate student mockery of each other. After being obliged to face their peers in speech and dialogue situations, they learned to value the support of their audience that I always described as their kind, tolerant, and supportive allies.

The wild idea germinated and gradually took root after I discussed it with the prospective French V students. They looked doubtful but gravely considered it and agreed. I told them the success of this venture would, of course, depend upon them. I expressed my belief that it could be done, but only they could assure that we would achieve our goal.

The athletic coaches were cooperative, the administration was receptive but doubtful, and my colleagues in the foreign language department gave me very low marks for my wild idea but remained curious. We were all doing as many innovative things as possible to improve the learning of foreign language and to encourage continued study.

The chief of guidance agreed that students who would not be cooperative in this experiment in peer learning and teaching would be removed from the class and sent to the regular French V class taught by another teacher. The French I students would remain. The French V students understood that and agreed.

We began the year with twelve French V students and twelve French I. Of the French I students, four were white male athletes, four were black male athletes, and four were girls—not athletes, just pretty. I explained my plans carefully the first two days:

1. Original dialogue writing would begin early the second month.
2. Each French V student was assigned a French I classmate as

his or her special responsibility. Their charges would be changed on a regular basis once a month.

3. French V students were charged with taking part in and supervising all dialogues, which were to be performed every two weeks or oftener if possible.

4. French V students were to sit beside French I students in simple quizzes and oral verb drills, all participating in oral work at the same time.

5. French V students were expected to behave responsibly when they were assigned to the independent listening and comprehension work.

   (A student, an electrical genius, had constructed two small switch boxes connected to a tape recorder. As many as six earphones could be plugged into each switch box at the same time. Thus, on one side of the room French V students could be engaged in listening and/or writing exercises when I was working across the room with the French I students. I had an extra small room just off mine but never sent the French I students to work alone.)

6. The French V students were to receive one or two grades each quarter, one grade for the quality of supervision and the teaching of their charges, and the other for encouraging and tutoring (free of charge) outside of class.

7. French V students would move ahead responsibly in the Advanced Placement program outlined for all those preparing for the Advanced Placement test. This would be done without constant cajoling and reminding from me. The class was not directed toward the Advanced Placement test; however, the students would be expected to do the reading.

8. All athletes would be graded on a pass/fail basis unless they chose otherwise.

The program began, or I should say, I thought it did. However, the clanking noises of movement in brains and bodies were

not evident to my ears and eyes. It soon became apparent that my "senior helpers" had reverted to adolescent-type behavior of "me first, let Joe Doakes do his own thing," and the promises of co-operation were forgotten. "Senior-itis" had set in the first week instead of the next April. And I detected another subtle and more deadly disease—intellectual snobisme. After all, they were the elite of the school. Not one was a sweating team athlete. These students played tennis, swam, bowled, and the like. They had already earned and established their reputation as scholars and "brains."

Privately pleading with these twelve "retired" peer teachers, I continued to hope through the third week. My wild idea slowly gathered storm clouds of hurricane dimensions and I debated whether to retreat to the cellar of defeat or brave the fray and fight to "save the house."

The Thursday evening of the third week I called the school to report myself ill. I was ill indeed. Physically and emotionally spent, I retreated to my bed to think, to analyze, and to implore our Divine Creator for help to wade out of this swamp of despair. Exaggeration? By no means! Self-doubt is an endemic and sometimes overpowering, crippling disease with schoolteachers who take their charge seriously. It has driven many able teachers from the classroom. Administrators, students, and parents rarely comprehend or even acknowledge this devastating illness—unless, of course, they have experienced it themselves.

By Sunday evening, that imperative haunting voice that has often asked me embarrassing questions was hard at work goading me and digging me out: "Coward! Are you going to let a pack of adolescent, rebel snobs beat you to a pulp? Are you going to let those poor, lethargic athletes 'warm the bench' all year?" Then came the final straw; an appeal to my pride: "Your reputation is at stake, you weak-kneed, lily-livered quitter!"

I got out of bed, strapped on my pistols, put on my John

Wayne hat, and marched into the classroom Monday morning. Adolescents were no match for my conscience.

Athletic French class began with my voice booming, "I've tried everything else; now bow your head!" (Not "heads"; we have only one each in French—usually!) In French, slow and measured, I prayed mightily for divine help to teach these young people the meaning of and the necessity for caring and doing for each other during the year we were to spend together. I asked for inspiration to devise any techniques necessary for them to experience success in this experiment and joy in the work. I sat down.

The silence in the room was heavy. The stillness seemed to smother all of us, pressing our heart and halting our breath for an instant. Suddenly, pell-mell, the French I students rushed across the room to their stunned peers.

"What did she say?" they all asked their recovering teachers. The exchange and the mixture of French and English words warmed and stirred the stillness of the room. That day the class became a community united, no longer divided. The barricades came down between the elite forces and those who didn't know much and who just waited for the final bell to ring in their classes.

We had verb drill that day with seniors seated beside their charges leading out, pronouncing vigorously everything we did. Within two weeks they were writing dialogues with their charges, copying sentences in French, and taking notes. Grammatical explanations were made to the beginners by their peer teachers who sometimes paused and asked me questions when they were uncertain.

"To teach is to learn." That old adage of the pedagogic profession took on meaning for those seniors, several of whom, I learned later, went into teaching.

Verb quizzes were given on two levels the same day at the same time. One sentence was dictated for level I and one sen-

134

tence for level V until the four or five sentences were completed for each group (see chapter 11). For the week of trial verb quizzes, the peer tutors sat beside their student learners and helped orally and also taught the correct spelling.

The level I students gradually began to distinguish between verbs, subjects, objects, and the other parts of speech, a skill that had eluded most of them even in English. When level V students were giving oral reports, doing a dictation, or examining an advanced grammatical principle, the level I students were listening to and writing material I had put on tape for them. Both groups remained in the same room.

Caution: Do not expect even the most responsible high school students to remain diligently at work unless you supervise them, that is, watch them. I tried it with the seniors. They were sent to an adjoining room that led to my classroom one day and spent their time quietly making and flying paper airplanes out the window. This unusual activity was spotted by a vice-principal who came to my door with the astonishing news. I told him that there must be some mistake. My students didn't do things like that. Alas! It was true. I discovered it when I walked into the next room. The peer "teacher" who was leading this aerial experiment never had the time to take French during his four years of university, but he did not forget it, he told me. He was an engineer and wrote to me often after leaving school.

When he graduated from the university, he joined the Peace Corps and was sent to Upper Volta, Africa, where he was obliged to speak French for his two years there. He loved it. In my opinion, it was fit punishment for his slight lapse from being responsible. Needless to say, the two groups in my French class were kept within eye and arm reach throughout the year after flying airplanes out the window.

The seniors took an interest in their charges in and out of the classroom. The "Big Shots" greeted their classmates everywhere—in French. They cheered our eight athletes at football and basketball games because they were personally interested in them.

That year I went to the games occasionally, an activity that had never interested me before. The second football game of the year was well underway when my husband and I arrived. Our team was losing. I went to the barrier at the edge of the field at time-out and called to a student.

"Send M. W., R. H., and M. R. to me," I told him. "I want to talk to them."

They came and I told them I would give them an automatic 95 extra grade if they won the game. They won! The poor opposing team did not know what had struck them. The principal was jubilant and called to me, "Madame, you brought us good luck."

The miracle of receiving a 95 in Madame's grade book was a transfusion that brought results. I decorated them the next day with cardboard medals with the legend "Champions," which is the same in French as in English. Our team won the regional that year. They were indeed champion players.

Did that French class make a difference? The answer can only be found in that mysterious academic hinterland of *unmeasurables*.

Do not conclude that these out-of-class activities were unimportant to what we did in the classroom. The building of the ego for our athletes was a necessary step early in the year, I believed, in order to arouse any discernible academic movement. Tying them emotionally to their senior peers, to the teacher, and to the class was vital in order to carry them through the year. The whole school soon identified these eight athletes with an unusual class where some of the elite of the school were their classmates. This gave these young men an importance in the academic area they had never before experienced.

Making the class feel united did not solve all our emotional and academic problems. By the end of the fifth week, a few others had to be resolved with individual students.

One senior student of brilliant potential, but completely selfish attitude about cooperation and tutorial responsibility, was moved out of the class to the regular French V class. He protested, but my agreement with the guidance director and the announced and known rules for membership in the class quickly ended the problem.

The four black athletes decided they would test me about the truancy rules I established for all my classes. They all cut the same day. I immediately notified the football coach. They appeared together the next day after a thorough reading of the "Nelson law" from the coach and then one from me.

The black athletes were having grades stretched (gifts really) in some of their academic classes. I called them in together and put them on notice: "Gentlemen, there is something you should know about me. I won't give you one extra point just because you are black. Do you understand?" The four met my stern gaze and considered a moment. Then they broke into smiles. "That is the way we want it." "Good," I said. "It takes a smart athlete to play good football and basketball. If you are intelligent enough for that, you have all you need to do well here—if you try. I promise you that I shall go the extra mile to help you succeed here."

All French I students, the eight athletes and the four pretty girls, were tested and evaluated by the English Department at my request by the end of the fifth week. In addition, I had tested them with the Pimsleur Aptitude Test. The results of these tests were delivered to the vice-principal for instruction, the guidance counselor, and the director of guidance. One black athlete and one white athlete were evaluated as academically gifted. All others showed above average in academic potential on all our tests.

I announced the following to the whole class: "All our tests show that all French I students have superior academic possibilities; two can be classified as gifted; therefore, you are all capable of what I shall be expecting of you. Your grade, of course, will be based upon your work, not on your potential."

There never was any talk of bias or racial prejudice. This was important since there had been accusations made in other academic areas. The school was predominantly white, but many of our best athletes were black. This class helped give our athletes a different image and outlook.

The year had its usual ups and downs in academic performance with the twelve French I students. They were not highly motivated to work, but their self-esteem was immeasurably improved as a result of being in this experimental class.

Two of the athletes failed the class. One of the white students simply could not shake his ingrained proclivity for bench warming. He refused to work. He was able to survive in all his other classes by simply being physically present; his heart and thoughts were usually elsewhere—perhaps on the basketball court. His eyes were constantly glassy with his dreamy stare. His coach protested to me that his star player never cut class and was always there. I countered that I refused to accord a body a grade. Grades were the result of activities of the mind.

I talked with the principal and told him that if the "F" in French meant that the star player could not play basketball, then the student should be removed from French and put in Sandbox II—my favorite term for a pretend class. Unfortunately every school has a few. The "star" went elsewhere to shine.

As spring approached, the call of the bursting buds and fresh air outdoors proved too great a temptation for one of the black athletes. He started to cut class. In the fall, M. R. had been so dedicated to being present every day (after the one cut) that he even came to class the day after breaking his leg at the football practice. His doctor told him he did not have to go to school the next day. "Oh, yes, I do!" my convinced disciple declared. He came and I decorated him with a cardboard medal for valor. The football coach told me the story the day after. We both rejoiced.

When M. R. started to cut class in the spring, both the coach and I pursued him relentlessly for a month. However, football season was over and fall was too far away to figure strongly in the uncertain goal structure of this student. Glands and habit won the day.

The French V students survived the year creditably with grades of "A" or "B," which they had richly earned. We all, students and I, looked forward to the end of the year with a mixture of relief and sadness. We were proud of what we had accomplished together and sensed somehow that the close feeling of being part of something special in human relations might never again be so intensely experienced.

Two days before journey's end, the students contrived to have me called out of the room just as class began. I returned to find them all lined up in the middle of the room, the table spread with treats and a silver tray to present to me. On the edge of that tray they had scratched into the silver all the names of the survivors, including the black athlete who was sometimes tempted to take a stroll instead of report for class.

That day I did not pray; I wept unashamedly. Never in my life had I been so "pushed to the wall" as I had been the first few months. But never again did I feel as much pride in the accomplishments of courageous students. It was an experiment I would never again repeat—owing to the difficulty in finding willing level V students as well as the enormous teacher workload—but the joy and satisfaction of having done it has never left me.

The next year, seniors gone, the French I students were placed in French II regular classes. My incurable truant was the only one missing. One other black athlete was obliged to go to another high school as a result of boundary changes. He was enrolled in

French II but spent the first month pleading to be allowed to come back to our school. Unsuccessful, he spent his year in French plaguing his teacher with his tales of how Madame did things. The other two black athletes and two white players came back to me in a regular French II class and survived. My girls were divided; two with me and two elsewhere.

The players in our school were indeed accepted at the university level. The athlete at the other school joined the navy and used his French.

Memory plays tricks on us. Oddly enough, the problems have receded when I think of this class. I remember the tremendous triumphs of the athletes, especially of the four blacks.

One day that year I invited a black gentleman who had served two years in the Peace Corps in French-speaking Central Africa to come to tell us his experiences. He was accompanied by a black lady from Haiti, a native French speaker. They were a sensation. Our returned Peace Corps worker recounted how he "sweated" over learning French to prepare for and to do his work in Africa. He admitted that he had been an indifferent student in high school. His conclusion: "Not working in high school was my biggest mistake." The class was impressed, especially the black students and no doubt my paper airplane engineer. Four years later he too was in Africa.

I sometimes wonder what stories the senior tutors and their French I responsibilities are telling of this special year in their life.

Memory is the pickpocket of the brain—suddenly stealing a corner of the mind, transporting it to another time and place, leaving the body to function on "automatic pilot." Present reality ceases to exist. Great emotion experienced in the past, and suddenly remembered, allows the thief easy access to the brain. This imperfectly describes how I feel when I think of this class more than anything I have written. I am grateful to the two students who did write to me. They have filled me with the certainty that others remember the class and learned from the experience.

April 20, 1979
Alexandria, VA

Chère Mme. Nelson,

I have been meaning to write to you for a long time. I was in summer school all last summer and could not make it to your retirement party. Please accept my very best wishes (rather belated) for your new pursuits.

I'm sure you are probably busier now than when you taught at Fort Hunt, if I know you. I do hope, however, that you are really doing some things that you like to do; you deserve some things for yourself. You always gave so much of yourself to others.

I know people have told you this before, but I need to let you know how much you meant to me. I will never forget you as my teacher or as a terrific human being. You taught us all more than our French lessons; you helped us believe in ourselves. I never cease to remember that last class we had (5th and 1st year). It is impossible to correct eighteen years of failure in one year, but I know that we *all* came away from that class with a better sense of ourselves and an understanding of others. I consider myself very lucky to have had you as my teacher.

I am graduating from University of North Carolina at Chapel Hill this May 13. I will receive my B.S. in Nursing. It has been a lot of work and I am ready to leave Chapel Hill for bigger things. I have just been accepted into Columbia University's MBA/MPH program. I will get a Master's in Business Administration and also a Master's in Health Administration. It is a long program (two years of class work and a one-year paid residency in a hospital), but I am really looking forward to the challenge. It is going to be great living in New York City, quite a switch from North Carolina.

Well, I hope you are doing well and pursuing things of interest to you. Best wishes to you and your family.

Sincerely,
Barbara H.

My note: Barbara was one of the level V students. This letter arrived four years after the year of the Athletic French experiment. The other member of that memorable class who wrote was the one who later went to Africa with the Peace Corps. He wrote from Africa (see "Retired Pay," chapter 17).

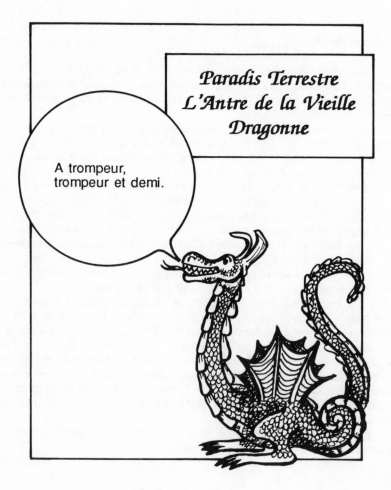

9

Cheating

An Aberration or a Habit?

Teachers must be alert constantly to cheating in their classrooms. They concern themselves with the construction of tests that will be valid measures of what has been taught and learned; therefore they must concern themselves with possible cheating.

Teachers who do not take testing seriously waver in their system of values and cheat their students of the opportunity of measuring themselves and their efforts. Honesty, therefore, must be taught by teachers, whether they see symptoms of dishonesty in their charges or not. The hard lesson is that students who cheat on a test cheat themselves more than anyone else. Once their dishonesty is known or observed, they can no longer be trusted.

I always announced and explained these principles the first week of school:

1. You are all honest until I learn that you cheat.
2. Should you be tempted to cheat on a test, try to remember these things:
   a. You cheat yourself most of all.
   b. You are dishonest and not to be trusted.
   c. Once you have lost my trust, it will be difficult to regain it.
   d. Should I be asked to write a recommendation for you for a job or for college entrance, I will not lie for you.
   e. You will be tested many times here and everywhere else as

143

long as you live. Strive to be honest always with yourself and others.

This appeal to be honest always impressed my students. They knew how I felt and what I thought about learning to be honest.

Honesty must be taught and learned; it is not an instinctive habit. Fear governs too much and influences behavior as soon as a child learns to seek and desire approval. Sometimes honesty is taught and emphasized in the home; sometimes it is neglected. However, this does not excuse teachers from the moral responsibility of teaching students to be responsible. *Honesty is the basic ingredient of responsibility.* Honest self-evaluation is a result.

Constant preaching does not advance the cause but *constant vigilance* does. Some basic invariable rules:

1. Never walk out of the room during any test. That is unfair to students.
2. Never pick up a paper of a student you think is cheating. You might be wrong.
3. Never openly accuse a student of cheating regardless of solid evidence. There are other ways. *Your role is to teach.*
4. Arrange your students' desks so that they are in a semicircle. Cheating is extremely difficult and you are able to survey the room quickly with this arrangement. You can survey the room at a glance.
5. Move your students often.

I allowed my students to sit where they chose the first two weeks, but I explained that I would ask them to move to another seat now and then and to be prepared to move without protest.

Those first two weeks students reveal themselves to you if you are a careful observer. You will be able to determine who is highly motivated and who is not. The peer leaders will emerge quickly. You will notice who is the favored friend of each student. You will also be able to spot the loners and the rejected. Make your mental notes and remember. Write it down in *code* if

144

your memory requires that.

Begin your testing by giving practice tests—no grades. Allow the students to grade their own papers. You will have corrected everything on the board. Pick up the tests with the grades the students have given themselves. Examine them carefully.

Rules of Testing

Establish testing rules such as those listed below:

1. Have everything written in pencil so that an error can be erased if students want to change an answer.
2. Correct everything in red ink. Errors then are not erased, but circled and corrected below or above the error.
3. Insist that students do class correcting with a red pen as soon as they have time to provide themselves with one. (I always kept a supply of red pens on hand.)
4. After the first two weeks, students should never correct their own papers. (I picked up the tests and redistributed them myself. I never gave them to the friendly neighbors of the student or to their buddies. I gathered papers from one side of the room and began the redistribution on the other.)
5. Students should write their student *number* in the upper right-hand corner, noting period and date. They should *never* write their names on a test to be corrected in class.
6. Students who are to correct the test write their names in the bottom right corner.
7. Never vary the system. A consistent *system* saves time.
8. Number tests and bring them back, sometimes with order of questions changed. This can accomplish two things: measure progress and discover cheating. This is true of any kind of exam.

Observe these policies when someone is obviously cheating:

1. Move the *person from whom the student is cheating or the student who is helping another cheat.*

2. *Say nothing*. Just ask the student to move even in the middle of a test.

3. *Do not openly accuse*. The wandering eye might be the result of profound thinking. Try to remember what you do when you are thinking and trying to remember.

There is no damage quite so great as that which results from an *unfair accusation*. The student and the parents will never forgive you. Students have often come in to see me after having been moved during a test. Their question was: "Madame, did you think I was cheating?" I could always reply, "Certainly not, my dear. I know you would never cheat." I never told them that I avoided moving the cheater. I waited for another day to do some changing with the cheater.

Those who were tempted to cheat soon learned that my confidence in them was worth something. This confidence built trustworthiness in them. A student who persists in cheating can be helped to change. I allowed them to cheat once. When I saw their excellent grade, I would always write on their papers in French, "Bravo! I knew you could do it. I am proud of you." Then I was always certain to bring that test back. In the meantime, I would move the cheater to a place between two students who were struggling. The second grade—always lower, of course—would be the valid grade, but the student would receive credit for both. Then I would call the student in for a conference. I would point out the difference in grades, showing the student that I had numbered the test and that it had reappeared, perhaps with the questions in different order. Then I would ask something like, "Were you ill the day you took this test the second time?" The student usually did not have an answer. I would continue, "You had to be ill or upset. I know that you know these things. You proved that on the first test. Now, my dear, I can only expect excellent work of you. I know you can do it."

There is no answer to a teacher so convinced of the student's ability, except to work and prove the teacher correct. Such a teacher has gently and subtly put the students on notice without accusation. Cheating will be difficult for them in the future.

Demanding that a student confess will bring alienation. Do not try it. All you want is work and progress in all your students. If tests are frequent enough, a cheated grade will not weigh very much. If tests are varied enough cheaters will give themselves away by being correct on one test and incorrect on another like it.

Any teacher who wishes to humiliate a student is a vindictive person, uncaring about the tender ego of the student. Face-saving is not unique to the Orientals. If a cheater does confess, forgive at once and assure that student that you know that it will never happen again. *Praise for such a confession. Do not condemn.* Treat your students with dignity and respect. Treat them as your intellectual equals and as the responsible adults you want them to become. They will endeavor and desire to justify your faith in them. However, be vigilant—gently vigilant—but not a *vigilante*.

Warning: If you are not vigilant and regularly wink at open, deliberate cheating, your students will not respect you, nor will they respect the curriculum you teach. They will justifiably consider you stupid. Equally damaging results of regular cheating in a class will be the lack of cohesion and peer support. There will be no sense of community, which is absolutely necessary for students to enjoy the learning experience.

I learned the hard way my first year of teaching. I was not vigilant, but rather suffered the illusion that cheating would not even occur. I discovered that the most charming young man in one of my classes was a confirmed cheater. However, I learned that fact after I had questioned myself about the lack of cohesion in the class and the obvious lack of respect of the students for me. That day I moved the cheater to the front seat. The class climate improved but never equalled that of my other four classes. I had confronted the cheater. *He lost face and I almost lost the respect of that class*—all serious errors I resolved never to make again. The students had thought I knew the cheating was taking place. I had to learn that some students do try to cheat and that *adolescents never betray their peers.*

Trust your students but respect them by making cheating impossible, or, at the least, very difficult and not worth the effort. Make your testing so varied that students are never able to profit from a cheat sheet. They will repay you with trust and respect, which are absolutely necessary for the learning climate to be peaceful and productive.

10

Truth and Consequences

Adolescents are interesting creatures to teach. I told students that I love to teach their age group because they were "becoming"—older and wiser, or younger and sillier. Growth and change in this age are always dramatic, even in six months. At the beginning of the year a boy may be looking me in the eye, no taller than I. By Easter he might be looking down at me with his pants reaching barely to his ankles. The same dramatic change is often evident in the girls. They may begin the year with no makeup and no perfume. At year's end the reverse is true. Their physical changes announce they are young women and young men—no longer children.

The wise approach for a teacher is to treat them as adults from the day they walk through your door and *to expect responsible adult behavior* of them—which means they must be prepared to suffer consequences of irresponsible behavior. They will sometimes feel lost as a result of this adult treatment, but it is my experience that they will run harder to meet your goals and learn to set their own.

Try it. They like it. You will love them more. How you treat them and what you are will be remembered long after what you taught will have grown dim in their memory. Your students quickly discover what you *are*. If you are without faith, without hope for them, you will not need to tell them. They will know what you think and how you value them before you admit these emotions and thoughts to yourself. Therefore, have faith in them. Never allow them to cease hoping for themselves because you never will. Therefore, insist that they accomplish something and that they obey the rules you make for your class.

Try to remember that learning to set goals, working to achieve them, and finally being able to honestly evaluate our efforts are the marks of maturity. It is a never-ending process and a great adventure. Learning to accept the consequences of promises not kept and goals not obtained is as important as dreaming and making glorious plans and building "nos châteaux en Espagne" (our castles in Spain). It is the finished product that counts.

Help your students to understand this concept by doing for yourself what you expect of your students. Savor the doing. The only hope is hope itself and accomplishing what we set as goals.

I have written that I expected and required that students learn to evaluate themselves by examining what they were, or were not, doing and their solutions for solving any problems. The notes that follow, written by my students, should demonstrate just what some of them thought. My explanatory notes are interspersed here and there. As students became accustomed to writing these evaluations and confessions, they became more analytical and objective about judging their own work and behavior. They learned to accept consequences. It was a growth experience for them and for me. They taught me much about their personality and kept me constantly aware that these young people were not yet adults but "becoming."

These notes were written by every student at the end of every quarter. The end-of-the-year note evaluated their work for the year and was done before I gave them their final grade. This is a small sample of the notes every student was asked to write:

1. Why he/she was absent (as a result of a cut).
2. Why speech or dialogue was not given.

152

3. His/her own analysis of the work done and the grade he/she thought should be accorded because it was *earned* (at the end of every quarter and the end of the year).
4. What could be done to improve poor performance.
5. Goals they would set and strive to attain after a conference with me about work or behavior.

From the Students

(Mistakes in English and French are those of the students. My notes are in italics.)

I, Danny Favreau, skipped class on Friday, Oct. 10, 1975, for the first and last time.

Danny F.

He never skipped again.

* * *

Madame Nelson, I think I should probably get a "D" for the year. Though my grades hardly show it, I feel I have learned too much to fail the course for the year.

I deserved the grade that I received. I didn't study as much as I should have and didn't come for help when needed. I plan to come during break and spend extra time studying.

Maggie L.

* * *

Je crois que j'ai mérité. Parce que je n'ai pas fait mon mieux toute le temps, mais j'ai essayé un peu du temps et je pense que j'ai passé mon examen de final (j'espère).

Suzi M.

Je n'ai pas fait de mon mieux tout le temps. J'ai réussi à mon examen final. J'ai essayé de temps en temps, pas toujours.

* * *

I don't know my speech and I did not write it 3 times.

Evan O.

Same student 4 times and many more during the year.

I was not prepared to do my image today.

Evan O.

* * *

I have not copied over any of my verb quizzes even though Madame Nelson has reminded me to do so. I intend to copy these verb quizzes over by Thursday and if they are not done by then, I will come Friday to finish copying them over.

Evan O.

* * *

The first thing that I will do is catch up in the work that I am behind in. I will study all the things that I have not done well in. I will end this quarter with good grades and I will start the next quarter with a fresh beginning. I will do my homework all the time and I will learn the discours. I will work to please Madame Nelson and myself. I will also try to find the joy in working.

Evan O.

The above is a contract written by student after a chat with me. My invariable question: What do you contract to do to change your grade and do the work of this class? Evan never kept his promise. He failed French deliberately to show his father that he hated French. I called the mother several times but the poor woman could only wring her hands and tell me of the conflict between father and son. I think he wanted to keep his promises to me, but vengeance upon a stern father had greater appeal.

* * *

I am not prepared for today's speech, Jeanne d'Arc.

Eric S.

* * *

I am not prepared to do my speeches today.

Adrienne B.

The speeches had to be made in class, not after school. Few were absent on speech day.

* * *

Goals: (1) No more talking in the class to the surrounding girls around me.   (2) Coming to break with very few exceptions.   (3) Studying for one hour each night.   (4) Pay attention during class.   (5) Coming prepared to class.

David D.

* * *

Madame Nelson, J'ai écrit mon image, mais je ne le sais pas trés bien. Je n'ai pas l'air heureuse cet après midi-Je ferai deux images la semaine prochaine.

Chris W.

No, she did not. That was not permitted. When present, students spoke or received a zero.

* * *

I don't have my speech ready for French class today.

James C.

* * *

I'm sorry Madame, but I don't know it.

Clare C.

* * *

I didn't copy my speech and I don't know it.

Clare C.

* * *

Madame Nelson, I came to school with a cheat-sheet with my speech on it. But after a lot of thinking, I said to myself, no way. I threw it away. I would rather get a zero than use a cheat-sheet in your class. I'm sorry I ever thought of it. I'm just cheating myself. P.S. I really wrote the speech 3 times, but I can't find it. I did my speech last week.

Clare C.

* * *

Do I use my time wisely? NO! On weekends I won't use my time as freely. I will spend one night doing homework of all my classes. The other night will be for French to review verbs. Every other day I will learn 10 new vocabulary words. To test myself on the weekend, I will also read aloud from French books and learn the vocabulary. I will come for extra help each Tuesday and Thursday regularly and during break. I will write and start learning my speeches on the weekends.

Clare C.

Clare was a brilliant young lady but refused to work. I alerted the mother early in the year. Clare was not working anywhere. She led a grasshopper existence only; she "sang and danced" all year.

* * *

I'm going to try to get a "B" next time. I will study more.

David Q.

He did.

* * *

I didn't do my speech or copy it.

Bronwen A.

* * *

I'm not prepared today.

Sybil W.

* * *

I was not prepared to do my image today.

Sybil W.

A pattern is being set with Sybil and must be changed. Parents should be called. [I always telephoned the parents of a student who regularly came unprepared.]

* * *

I will copy over my verb quizzes and not let them wait 'till the last minutes. I will know my speeches and come to class whether I'm sick or not. I need to study more for verb quizzes.

Beth E.

* * *

The reason I didn't go to school was because I didn't want to. I walked to a friend's house and then we went to McDonalds and then we walked around. In the future, I will not skip class and I will try my hardest to do well.

Tririe B.

Tririe cut class and received a zero, the usual "gift" I had for such behavior.

* * *

I got the grade I got because of not studying enough. I will try to understand and study a whole lot more next quarter.

Lynda D.

* * *

This next quarter I will try to keep up the good work I have done in the first quarter. If I get anything less than what I previously got, you have a right to be disappointed.

Beth C.

A very able student.

* * *

I don't always study. I make dumb mistakes on quizzes and tests. I am not always prepared. Sometimes I don't listen in class. I tried to make up the 0 on the dialogue last week but you weren't here. I plan to study more this quarter. I'll try not to make dumb errors. I will be prepared to the class. I will make up my 0's.

Sandra O.

* * *

This grading period I did not review for examens as often as possible. Also, I didn't always finish my homework. Occasionally my pronunciation was poor on discourse. This fourth grading period I will put forth extra effort to accomplish better grades and do my best.

Ellen W.

* * *

I got an "F" this quarter because I didn't try as hard. I was a little lost at the beginning of the year and got more and more lost as time went by. I've come in a couple times at break, but it doesn't seem to help. I can't *concentrate*. I've got a tutor now and it really is helping. She's going over the tenses and I'm understanding much better. I should be getting better grades on verb quizzes. I haven't gone over all of them yet. She had gone over things that we were tested on, and I worked hard and studied hard, but still failed with 30's or 50's. It doesn't help much. But I really hope and am gonna try harder to bring my grade back up to a D, maybe a C. But I don't want to fail and don't intend to. I'm going to keep the tutor and study one half hour every night.

Sandra G.

Records should be examined to see if student has learning difficulties elsewhere. I must pay attention to Sandra's friends. Who are they?

* * *

I believe I should get a "C" because I have not cut class in 18 weeks. I always have my work in if you look in your grade book the really only thing I did bad was as you say that I *disturb* the class. Next nine weeks I will do probably the same. But I will study more for the tests and will not disturb the classroom like I did the last nine weeks.

Steve G.

This student was hyperactive and had a learning problem. He struggled valiantly and calmed greatly before the year was over.

* * *

I received the grade I did because I wasn't working hard enough on things I didn't understand. In the future I will, when something new is introduced that I don't understand, stay after or come for break.

Elizabeth B.

* * *

The reason why I got this grade in French is because I didn't study hard enough. What I am going to do this last quarter is study.

Sybil W.

Here is Sybil again. She waited too long and did not pass.

* * *

159

I got this grade because I have 4 other classes that have homework and I don't have enough time to do all the studying I need because I don't get home from *soccer until 5:00 P.M.* I am also very lazy.

Caroline B.

An honor student not content with a "B."

* * *

I plan to study more although I don't like French and I was forced into it and I can't work *too* well when I hate it. I also plan to write my verb quizzes 10 times and do them when they are due. And I'll always come for extra help.

Gretchen S.

Students who are forced too much by parents often rebel. Look for early symptoms.

* * *

I received the grade I did because I had (and have) trouble under-standing and remembering the rules for much of the grammar we have done this 9 weeks. I'm sure that if I study really well and get some help from a tutor this 9 weeks, I can bring my grade back up to a "B."

Mary Beth K.

* * *

Je crois que j'améliore parce que, J'ai repété beaucoup de fois. Aussi j'ai préparé chaque fois.

Wesley G.

Learning disability; unable to read English but how he struggled!

* * *

I earned the grade that I did by not making up missed speeches and failing too many tests. Next quarter I will try not to be absent as much and will try to earn a better grade.

Suzi M.

* * *

I am going to get a "B" if not an "A." I'm not going to have any of this "C" garbage. I'll study my verbs longer. I'm glad we're going to go more into vocabulary. I think I might do better at that. I will try, Madame.

Jane S.

She set goals, but not high enough.

* * *

[Same student, later in the year]
I got the grade probably because I was lazy. I could have worked harder, but with all due respect, it was not all my fault. When I worked hard I also fell on my face. Elaine and I spent an hour writing our dialogue and you called it garbage. I was absent the next day so we changed what you had changed. Asked a former French student to correct it, put it on correctly and then you gave us both 70's. What can I do?

Jane S.

Jane came in to see me. She was angry with herself. I never called a dialogue "garbage." Admitting to laziness is very difficult. We prefer blaming others.

* * *

I think I should get a "C" because I worked harder than all of these other people who got a "D." I have a 69 average. I didn't have any zeros through the 9 weeks. I am getting a "B" next time because I am sick of this stuff.

Luke M.

Luke did better. He came through with a low "D." Sixty-nine was an "F" in our system, I gave him a point.

161

* * *

I received the grade that I did because I have to have something explained to me before I can understand it and make it stick in my head. Last quarter we zoomed by and I couldn't keep up like many students I know. This quarter I will try to understand the work better and I hope I can bring up my grade.

Jill B.

"Zoom" is not the word. We plowed the same furrow many times. This dear girl was a dreamer; concentrating on listening too difficult a task, but vital in foreign language.

* * *

The reason I got the low "B" I got was for several different things. I didn't study every night. I didn't have a good attitude toward this class and I didn't try my best. I plan to get an "A" the last nine weeks.

Tom C.

Good student. Evaluated himself well.

* * *

I am unprepared for my French speech. I did not know it.

Jennifer T.

* * *

When I first came in the class, I was confused and that mixed with laziness doesn't work very well. I never knew that there was a speech every friday. The first Friday I was told about it but didn't do it but the second Friday I didn't ever hear anything about it and was surprised when everyone showed up with one. Maybe I wasn't listening. The other I just didn't do. After that was a skit and when I asked around about getting in a group, nobody needed anyone else and everyone was already in a group. I'm not blaming anyone but if there is anyone to blame, it should be me.

Aitz L.

This was a first-class dreamer with eyes wide open, seeing nothing, and plugged ears as well! I had to become her seeing-eye dog and unplug her ears. She improved and was placed in a group.

* * *

Dear Mme. Nelson,

I did something terrible in class and I feel very guilty. Would you please tear up my dictation for today. I'm sure you know why. I'm very sorry, truly I am and if you have lost all confidence in me, I can understand. I wrote this to apologize and if you want I'll not go to your class again.

I'm asking you for another chance. If you can find it in your heart to forgive and forget, it'll never happen again! I want an "A" in your class and I swear I'll work for it! Please help me!

Diane

What an extraordinary young lady. I never worried about her again.

* * *

I got a lower grade this quarter because I missed too many days and I didn't make up all my work. I feel that if I am here every day this quarter I can get an "A" again.

Alan D.

Students who have learned to set goals and keep promises are invariably good learners.

* * *

Je ne sais pas mon discours du 23 janvier. [I do not know my speech.]

The only thing one can say and be *truthful* about it in this situation is I'll try, memorize speeches, study, and try for an "A."

1. I will come 3 times a week during the break.

2. I'll come 1 time a week after school.

Swosnar

He did. He worked hard to recover from this zero.

* * *

I didn't finish it! [her speech].

Adrienne S.

What was not finished *on speech day was not counted.*

* * *

I got my grade because I didn't study enough but I never came into class and didn't know my discours, dialogue, etc, except one time when I tried, when I was sick. I'm going to try to get a "B" next time.

David P.

Good student; soon became responsible.

* * *

I could have gotten an "A" this quarter. When I got my billet doux, I had a 91 average and now I have a 90 average. There were several tests I didn't study for and my grades reflected this. My oral grades should have been 95 but I came to class unprepared too often and I talk during class.

I really wanted an "A" this quarter, but I defeated myself. I will get an "A" next quarter.

Allison I.

Excellent students can always evaluate themselves honestly.

* * *

Je pense que je recevrais un "P" pour l'année. Les premiers trois quartiers J'ai failli rater mais je pensais à mes autres classes. J'ai reçu un A dans presque toutes mes classes sauf le français. Le dernier neuf semaines étaient trop difficile pour [*sic*] moi. J'ai passé [*sic*] environ six examens finales [*sic*] seulement en français, et je croix que je les ai bien faits. J'étais très inquiète que vous nous avez [*sic*] donné les examens finales [*sic*] qui sont examens surpris. Et vous nous avez seulement donner [*sic*] dix à trente minutes pour un examen de trois à six pages.

L'année prochaine j'irai à l'Universite de Richmond. J'espère que j'étudierai encore des langues étrangères.

Susan P.

She did study foreign languages. This student never really challenged herself. Her IQ was the highest in her class. P = Pass and must be 70 = D. A pass is not calculated on grade point average. Her language ability was extraordinary.

* * *

Je crois que j'ai merité un "A" dans votre classe de français. Au commencement de cette classe, j'ai étudié peu mais j'ai voulu apprendre beaucoup de la langue, alors j'ai commencé à mieux travailler pour toute l'année. Je veux bien rester avec vous pour pleusieurs années, mais vous ne serez pas ici l'année prochaine. J'adore la langue française et je veux apprendre autant d'elle que possible.

Je veux Mme. Nelson pour français 5 l'année prochaine.

Chris W.

* * *

Je crois que j'ai mérité un "A" pour ma note finale. Voici les raisons:

1. Je faisais de mon mieux cette année, et je faisais un effort.
2. J'améliorai la qualité de mon travail.
3. Je parlais toujours en class, en me servant du vocabulaire.

L'année prochaine, je vais m'inscrire à l'Université de Virginie. J'espère devenir un professeur, et plus tard un counselor de guidance au lycée. Je veux continuer la danse et la musique aussi.

Melissa B.

She did. Brilliant student.

165

* * *

J'espère recevoir 94, 94, 94 pour ces neuf semaines; mes discours et mon reportage n'ont pas été si mal. Je parle couramment pendent les heures de discussions. Mes opinions sont plus ou moins utiles.

Chang N.

* * *

Je mérite un "D" en français parce que je n'ai pas étudié toujours, et je n'ai pas essayé. Mais j'étudierai l'année prochaine, et je mériterai un "B" si vous m'aurez aidée. Je vous aime Madame (Merci). Ne nous partez pas! [*sic*] [Author's note: She meant, "Don't leave us."]
L'année prochain [*sic*] mes classes sont:
1. Anglais—Mr. Rose
2. Orchestra—Mrs. Schwaner
3-4. Clerk-typist—Mrs. Blake
5. French 3—Madame Nelson
6. U.S./V.A. History—Mr. Combs

June R.

* * *

I think I've worked a little bit harder this semester. I know I could *of* done better though. I've done all the work and tried on them. Except for re-copying the verb quizzes. But I think I deserve a low "C." I will be taking Mr. Ahern for French next year.

Patricia C.

Notice the use of "of" as part of the verb. This student does not yet know verbal structure in English.

* * *

Je crois que je mérite un "B." Pas plus. Mon moyen n'est pas si bon mais à-vrai dire j'ai fait un effort. Toute cette année j'ai eu un tas de classes à faire. Je crois que mes verbes ont amélioré. Mais en somme j'ai fait un effort. Dans la classe c'était moi parmi deux ou peut-être quatre étudients qui ont parlé tout le temps que vous avez demandé.

Au sujet de l'année prochaine, j'irai à St. John's College à Annapolis. Pour les deux premiers ans, Je n'aurai pas de cours en français mais je vais lire beaucoup de livres en français et aussi je vais parler chaque jour avec les "juniors" et les "seniors" qui le suivront.

Alex C.

* * *

With rare exceptions, by the end of the year the students had learned to evaluate themselves well and honestly. If there was too much of a difference in what they thought they had done and what they actually had done, I asked them to come to see me so we could discuss the problem together. Rarely did I have a student incapable of seeing the consequences of his or her lack of effort and of recognizing the quality of the work done. In my opinion, this evaluation of self was as important as the French.

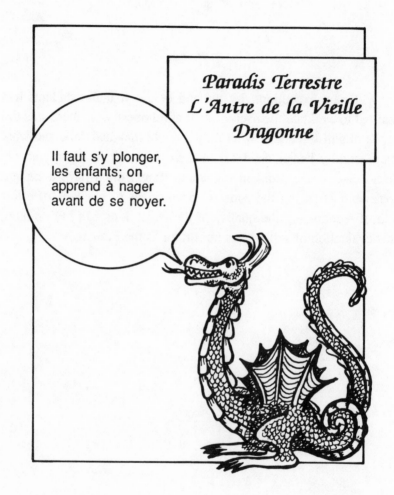

11

The Verb Quiz
A Once-a-Week Special Technique

Order out of Confusion

The first year of my teaching I slavishly followed my text in the teaching of verbs. I knew that the verb was the heart of all oral and written expression; but aside from teaching the language of language, how was I to teach verbs? As other teachers and the texts?

They taught verbal structure by giving written quizzes with directions to put the listed verbs of the test in the present future, imperative, and other verb tenses. Students obliged like monkeys—pushing buttons marked red, green, or blue—they did it by sight. The students were able to do this, but I observed that at the end of the year they walked out of classrooms in a state of semi-confusion, often complete confusion, when they *heard* verbs used in tenses other than the present.

Living only in the present is the cultural or perhaps genetic tendency of youth in their thought processes, but I knew that students had to surmount that barrier between present and past—remote and near—and future, and surmount it the first year.

The all-written method of teaching verbs did not work and I knew it. This method is still perpetuated in high school texts and in university classes. One summer I enrolled in a graduate class

169

in the United States in advanced grammar and composition, and what did I find—written verb quizzes with the directions to put the verbs in this or that tense. What a joke! In my classes in France, I was obliged to recognize orally and to write verbs in all tenses as a result of regular dictations. There was no written sheet of paper with directions to put verbs in any tense. Recognition came through my ears. Believe me, I learned to spell as well as comprehend where I was in the time frame of the dictation, and quickly. I did not remain in the limbo of the present very long. I used the same technique of dictation with my students the first year, but progress was too slow for my taste. Verbs and their tenses had to be taught more quickly and more efficiently in order to resolve this constant confusion in my students when they were obliged to scratch comprehension even out of the written page. Their eyes and their ears had to be taught to coordinate their efforts. Verbs in speech do not arrive in the tight restricted bundles of tenses as presented in texts. Verbs have to be taught in the context of a sentence, not a verb list, or confusion will continue to reign.

My students wanted to talk and I wanted them to be able to talk and understand me and each other. They had to understand and talk better than Miss Piggy, who speaks French but understands only herself. *Exposing* my students to the verbal structure would not produce anything but momentary illness (fear). I wanted to vaccinate them early against the disease of confusion when they heard, spoke, or wrote. They had to learn to recognize all spoken tenses of verbs early. Thus, the oral and written verb quiz was born, thrived, and became a weekly ritual. The day for the verb quiz was changed from Friday to Monday for reasons already explained in the preface and chapter 5. Tenses had to be contrasted.

Confusion in my students rapidly fled. It flew away, took wing from the classroom, and verbal order installed itself in its place in the thinking of my students. Fear is a specter that haunts all of us at times. The weekly verb quiz soon established itself as the most useful technique in my bag of "tricks." My students were no longer deceived by their ears; their eyesight improved for they more quickly perceived the meaning of the written page as well.

Knowing the entire verbal picture of the verbal structure takes the fear out of learning to use and recognize verb tenses. This *knowing* proceeds gradually and surely if begun early. Writing the entire scheme of tense and structure and reciting it orally will give students a sense of relief if it is done early the first year in any language. Foreign language texts do not do this in the United States. Their authors seem to like to make everybody guess. How would you like to guess what is around a curve if you are driving at night on an unknown road without markers? What does one do in safari country when lions or an immovable rhino or hippo might be lurking out of sight. One proceeds cautiously, hesitatingly. Is that the way we want our students to plunge into the foreign language we teach? Plunging into some texts is like jumping into a swiftly moving stream swarming with crocodiles. Our poor students too often are gobbled up by frustration, drowned by fear. Sometimes they are fortunate enough to scramble out, but too often they flee this confusion in terror. Having a map of the route to be followed, names of villages along the journey, and sign markers on each curve always gives confidence to a traveler beginning a voyage into an unknown land. Try to remember that you, the teachers, are the guides into this foreign country of sound and symbol. Don't keep your destination secret. Give your students signposts ahead by describing the whole journey briefly and early. Tell them that the swiftly moving rivers are all filled with beasts that they will domesticate with ease. They will meet new things they know dimly, not because of warnings of difficulty, but as a result of your assurance and early explanations that will help them enjoy the voyage. They will learn to deal with new situations without fear and resistance and make sense out of tense.

My Rules for the Verb Quiz

1. *Every verb exam was dictated.* The students wrote what they heard.
2. *A complete sentence was always dictated so that comprehension—useful comprehension—was in the context of the spoken or even of the literary language.* The everyday speech of a people is not always the literary language of the written idiom. However, the written or literary text must be understood orally as well as the everyday means of communication. Otherwise we could not read newspaper articles, stories, or poems aloud to each other or to students in the classroom. French people could not any more understand their classic theater (Molière, Racine, Corneille) of the Golden Age. English-speaking people could not understand the Bible or Shakespeare. Therefore, the language tenses we class as literary in French must be taught orally as well as those we use in everyday speech. Our students would not even understand a conference at the Sorbonne without this literary baggage.
3. *At least three sentences, usually four or five, were dictated for every exam.* These sentences thus allowed me to employ at least three or four tenses and usually more if the sentence was a compound of two or more clauses. I began at level one with four simple sentences and very early included compound sentences as soon as relative pronouns, clauses with the conjunctions *if, when, as soon as,* and the like, were introduced. The agreement of past participles soon became a part of these first dictated verb quiz sentences. There is almost no end of grammatical principles, idioms, or agreement of adjectives that can

be introduced, reviewed, and practiced in a quiz. Practice and review are vital in order to make language habitual in the thought process. The verbs to be conjugated were dictated rapidly in the infinitive form. Dictating *slowly* in areas that students already know breeds sloppy listening. Any *new regular verb* that I wanted to add to their vocabulary was written first in its infinitive form on the blackboard. Vocabulary building using regular verbs was a weekly technique.

4. *The verb quiz was timed after my students had been taught how to take this test.* This teaching usually took two quizzes. After giving an untimed first quiz, I warned the students that the second quiz would be timed in order to measure how long they required. I had a timer with a bell that began to tick as soon as I had finished the dictation of the quiz. Allowing about ten minutes, I set the timer back an extra minute or two if the students did not seem to be finished. Thus, by the third week the students had learned how to take a timed quiz.

I found by testing various time spans that a quiz allowing twenty minutes produced much poorer results than a ten-minute quiz for the same amount of territory covered. Remember that first reflection is usually correct. Students had the time to go back and change correct answers to incorrect answers when they spent twenty minutes. A demonstration of the difference between the results of a ten- and twenty-minute quiz will convince doubters if the twenty-minute quiz is used unannounced after the students are accustomed to ten-minute quizzes. Extra time on a quiz also gave some students the time to cast a surreptitious glance at a neighbor's paper. Try not to tempt students. Gradually the time for a verb quiz can be reduced to only five to eight minutes.

5. *When the bell rang, I quickly picked up all quizzes myself.* I tried to allow stragglers an extra minute, but I observed the entire class closely, moving about quietly to observe how well

students were working and finishing. Sometimes I set the timer back a minute or two before the bell to allow them time to finish, but not always. Be reasonable. After I had picked up the quizzes beginning on one side of the room and finishing on the opposite side, I redistributed the quizzes, being careful to distance a quiz from the owner. The students who received the quizzes for correction wrote their names on the bottom right corner of the page in red ink or red pencil and wrote all corrections in red above any error. The student doing the correction *never crossed out the error* (see chapter 2).

6. *Send students to the blackboard to write the sentences in the quiz* (one student for each sentence). All go to the blackboard at the same time in order that the entire quiz may be written quickly to save time. I can hear teachers asking how this can be done. Very easily. I asked that two long blackboards be installed in my room—one on each of the two facing walls of my room. When I made this request of my superiors, I promised them that I would save them the cost of a mountain of paper that they allocated to me. Every year each teacher can draw on a paper allotment whose cost in the aggregate is enormous. Ask to see a school's paper budget for one year. Multiply that item by the number of schools in your system and you will cease wondering about the gobbling of our forests and the floating of school bonds. I asked for this information and almost floated into space. Asking for an additional blackboard was a simple matter for me. I was not surprised when the extra blackboard was installed forthwith, and colleagues wondered how I got it. I wasn't even noisy—just positive. The blackboard is the cheapest and most useful visual aid any teacher has. It does not have to be picked up by garbage collectors, recycled, or burned. It is cheaper than computers and never goes "down." A slate blackboard is more durable than the school where it is hung and will be useful when the wall

collapses. It destroys no forest in its making, creates no pollution except dust in the classroom. My portable vacuum cleaner regularly disposed of the weekly accumulation of dust created by my industrious students and me. Vive le tableau noir!

Since all the sentences were on the blackboard, correction proceeded at a rapid pace. I asked the students to speak the sentences and the verb conjugations as we went through each one. Oral drill became an easy exercise into which students were enticed without their becoming aware that they were engaged in oral acrobatics. They are doing some correcting—thinking—in the process. Drill was more meaningful. They were hearing and seeing and writing at the same time—powerful combinations for learning. This is an ancient technique that Americans have forgotten or discarded.

After a verb quiz and its speedy correction, there is usually time for something else to add to the learning of verbs, to answer the "why" questions of verbal structure. A good grade on a verb quiz and a passing grade on speeches and dialogues usually salvaged even the stragglers and the strugglers. As an added incentive to reviewing and learning the verbal structure, I raised the grade on a quiz if the students would copy that quiz three times *without error.* If errors were made, the grade was not raised. Student assistants often helped me by going over these recopied quizzes. That helped the assistants if they were studying French, which was usually the case, and it helped me. Going over a stack of recopied quizzes did not take much time as long as the students copied as I instructed. The three copies were lined up one after the other.

7. *The verb quiz was always given on Monday* (see preface).

Madame Nelson's Verb Book

This notebook of verb quizzes for all levels was separate from my log book, which contained copies of all other exams as they were given and all the papers I gave to my students throughout the year. The verb book was a notebook containing nothing but verb exams that were always dictated.

There were no answers to any of the quizzes in my verb book. There were occasional notes to myself that were in a code to me: (1) levels of difficulty I, II, III, IV, V; (2) sometimes an "X" meaning that this quiz was used for testing comprehension of certain sounds and combinations of sounds; and (3) "XX," which meant extremely useful for a grammatical principle that was a barrier between English and French.

Repetition is the essence of language acquisition and ease with verbal structure. My verb book was mute evidence of the various ways I found to repeat in verb quizzes what I wanted my students to learn. I never tired of this technique because it produced dramatic results when I made it oral *and* written.

My verb book took on a life of its own and became a precious road map for me to help students over language road blocks in comprehension and structure. It was known to all my students. They knew of the tradition of the verb quiz.

One year my verb book disappeared. It developed legs. After frantic searching, I concluded that it was gone forever. I told my students. They were as stunned as I. Not for one minute did I entertain the notion that a student of mine had taken the book. I told my students that. They knew there were no answers to anything in my verb book, but whoever took the book didn't reckon with the desire of my students to come to my aid, nor did the culprit take into account what was in my head as a result of years of effort in constructing the book. Since it was not unusual for me to have taught four students of the same family, I discovered that verb quizzes had been passed "down the line." One young lady produced an entire notebook of her three sisters' careful filing of all the verb quizzes over a period of four years. With old quizzes produced by many students and with what was in my head, the verb book was soon reconstructed.

On more than one occasion my students came to my aid. They recruited their parents to help run the testing center for the National French Contest. They learned their verbs and used them as students, and then they returned from college to tell me that the oral and written verb quiz given on a regular basis was the most valuable of any technique I used. It helped me to know that my students prized *what* I was doing and *how* I taught.

The following sample quizzes can only give a small example of what my verb book contained. Every quiz bears a number in my book. Someday I may publish it, but tapes will necessarily accompany it.

The student number, period, level, and date must all be together in the above order in the top right corner of the page. If the information is in a different place, I insist that the student redo this section. The grade is added at the top of the page after grading.

Each verb in the sentence must be correct in every respect. The verb is what we are examining. Each infinitive must be conjugated correctly, even including any agreement of a past participle if a past participle is involved. There is no partial credit.

Count the number of verbs involved, including the verb or verbs in the sentence, and divide the total into one hundred in order to know how much each verb will count.

One point is subtracted for each spelling mistake for other words in the sentence. These do not add to the total but will be subtracted if there are errors. Correct spelling should be expected in known words. *Note: In some verb quizzes there may be thirty-five verbs. Count three for each verb and use one hundred six as a perfect score.*

177

Sample Quiz   *(Grade added)*

Student Number_____
Period_____
French (I, II, III, etc.)_____
Date_____

(The italicized is dictated.)

1. *Je ne veux plus rien faire.*
   pouvoir   Je ne peux plus rien faire
   faire   Je ne fais plus rien
   voir   Je ne vois plus rien
   aller   Je ne vais plus + là (warn students)

2. *Ils finissent leur travail à l'heure.*
   vouloir   Ils veulent
   comprendre Ils comprennent
   parler   Ils parlent
   être   Ils sont

   Note: Students who write nonsense after the conjugated verb are not
   paying attention to meaning. Mark this as a serious error.

3. *Ils vont partir bientôt.* (futur proche, not présent)
   guérir   Ils vont guérir
   apprendre   Ils vont apprendre
   obéir   Ils vont obéir
   mourir   Ils vont mourir

4. *Vous parlez français couramment.*
   finir   Vous finissez
   aller   Vous allez
   voir   Vous voyez
   pouvoir   Vous pouvez

[Signature of student correcting quiz]

178

The verb quizzes that follow may be used at any level as review after the material has been taught and tested initially. The number of each verb quiz comes from my verb book. (There are about 150 verb quizzes in my verb book.) There are examples for every level of French. The verb quizzes are used to teach, practice, and reinforce the concepts used in class. Remember, the foundation of learning a language is constant repetition and review.

In my classes there was no credit given for writing correctly known words that had been repeated many times, but if careless mistakes were made in these words the student suffered a one-point loss. Therefore, carelessness sometimes could bring more than a five-point loss if that was the value of the verb.

Verb Quiz 1

(The number of each verb quiz comes from my verb book. There are examples for every level of French. I have not always marked the level where I used them for a grade. They were used to teach and to practice often.)

1. Elle est morte il y a un an.
   devenir
   naître
   tomber
   venir
   faire

2. Ils sont nés en France.
   arriver
   sortir
   recevoir
   faire
   mettre

3. Elle est sortie tout à l'heure.
   connaître
   dire
   apprendre

se laver
s'habiller
pouvoir
tenir
vouloir
comprendre
descendre
vouloir
pouvoir
savoir
comprendre [repeated]
descendre [repeated]
retourner
rester

4. Il descend l'escalier.   (perfect score 106,
   venir   each verb counts 3)
   recevoir
   être
   avoir
   mettre

Note: The *italicized* verbs listed in number three were repeated. This was not an accident but a test to see if students were listening.

Verb Quiz 2

1. Qu'il apprenne ses devoirs!
   savoir
   faire
   pouvoir
   être
   avoir

2. Il m'obéit en tout.
   ouvrir
   connaître
   recevoir
   mettre

3. Il fera de son mieux demain, j'en suis certaine.
   voir
   pouvoir

    savoir
    avoir

4. Ils comprennent leurs leçons.
    vouloir
    pouvoir
    savoir
    aller

5. Je veux parler français.   (perfect score 100,
    savoir   each verb counts 3)
    venir
    aller
    être
    comprendre
    mettre

Verb Quiz 3

1. Ils savent nager.
    vouloir
    pouvoir
    aller
    faire
    avoir
    être
    vouloir
    pouvoir

2. Elle a pu faire ses devoirs de bonne heure.
    aller
    venir
    savoir
    être
    sortir
    écrire
    parler

3. Il viendra demain.
    être
    avoir
    aller

faire
pouvoir
savoir
venir

4. Je mettais mon chapeau souvent cet hiver-là avant de sortir.
être
vouloir
faire
venir
aller

5. Ils vont partir demain. (futur proche, not présent)
finir   (perfect score 109,
mourir   each verb counts 3)
descendre
comprendre

Verb Quiz 4

1. Ils apprennent à lire.
vouloir
pouvoir
aller
faire
avoir
être
vouloir
pouvoir

2. Elles ont pu faire leurs devoirs.
aller
venir
savoir
être
sortir
écrire
parler

3. Il voudra mieux parler.
être
avoir
aller

faire
pouvoir
savoir
venir

4. Ils savaient leurs leçons l'année passée.
être
vouloir
faire
venir
aller

5. Il va partir demain.   (perfect score 106,
finir   each verb counts 3)
mourir
descendre
comprendre

Verb Quiz 5

1. J'étais fatigué(e) ce jour-là.
savoir
avoir
lire
dire
s'asseoir
craindre

2. Nous avons eu de la chance.
venir
aller
pouvoir
vouloir
se reposer

3. Ecrivez vos devoirs vite.
être
avoir
savoir
faire

4. Ils veulent partir de bonne heure.
pouvoir
faire

aller
avoir

5. Il vaudra mieux savoir tout cela.
   venir
   mourir
   voir
   envoyer

6. Elle est ravie que vous fassiez vos devoirs.
   pouvoir   (perfect score 115,
   savoir   each verb counts 3)
   faire
   aller

Verb Quiz 6

1. Ils viennent de sortir. (passé récent)
   mourir
   apprendre
   s'asseoir
   finir

2. Il fallut qu'on parlât français.
   partir
   s'asseoir
   craindre
   finir

3. Je veux qu'on m'écoute attentivement.
   pouvoir
   savoir
   aller
   avoir

4. Où que vous alliez faites de votre mieux.
   vouloir
   voir
   craindre
   sortir

5. Vas-tu étudier ce soir?
   se laver
   s'habiller

s'asseoir
s'arrêter

6. Donne-moi tes livres.   (perfect score 100,
   partir   each verb counts 2)
   faire
   parler
   finir

Verb Quiz 23

1. Elle est ravie que vous soyez venu(e)(s)(es) à l'heure.
   pouvoir
   savoir
   faire
   aller
   devenir

2. Ils allèrent à la campagne cet été-là.
   partir
   écrire
   mentir
   mordre
   naître
   mourir
   savoir
   s'asseoir
   mettre

3. Il donna un livre à son ami.
   mettre
   connaître
   prendre
   pendre
   vouloir

4. J'allais en France souvent lorsque j'étais petite.
   mettre
   savoir
   être
   choisir
   punir
   vouloir
   s'asseoir

5. Ils se connurent il y a longtemps.
   sortir   (perfect score 104,
   venir   each verb counts 2)
   devenir
   tenir
   vouloir
   voir
   s'asseoir

Verb Quiz 25

1. Je suis contente qu'on parle si bien.
   savoir
   pouvoir
   s'asseoir
   craindre
   faire
   vouloir

2. Je vais quitter cette boîte à deux heures pile. (futur proche)
   s'endormir
   partir
   se méfier
   se fier

3. Elles viennent de se marier. (passé récent)
   sortir
   mourir
   tomber
   finir
   s'asseoir
   se faire

4. Va-t-en!
   finir
   partir
   sortir
   s'asseoir

5. Il parla doucement.
   voir
   venir
   mettre

battre
bâtir

6. Il fallut qu'on partît seul.   (perfect score 100,
   tomber   each verb counts 2)
   écouter
   sortir
   s'asseoir

Verb Quiz 26

1. Le maître est triste qu'il ne soit pas là.
   finir
   écrire
   vendre
   faire
   avoir

2. N'en achète plus.
   crier
   finir
   descendre
   aller

3. Il fit une promenade dans le bois.
   aller
   venir
   être
   avoir

4. Elles sont invitées à visiter une fabrique.
   mettre   (perfect score 100,
   recevoir   each verb counts 3)
   comprendre
   voir
   lire

Note: (1) Sentence 4 will test the passive; (2) sentence 2 tests the imperative and the rule of dropping the *s* for verbs of the *er* group; (3) sentence 1 tests the subjunctive and the present; and (4) sentence 3 tests the passé simple.

Verb Quiz 27

1. Je la conduisis au poste d'essence.
   nager
   finir
   ranger
   attendre
   s'asseoir

2. Elle en était rentrée de bonne heure.
   retourner
   s'habiller
   s'étonner
   vivre
   habiter

3. Elle craint qu'il ne pleuve demain.
   aller
   vouloir
   devoir
   savoir
   mourir
   éteindre

4. La jeune fille qui *vous* attendait est ma soeur.
   recevoir   (perfect score 100,
   voir   each verb counts 3)
   croire
   manger
   commencer

Note: Sentence 4 will test comprehension quickly. Will the student conclude that vous is the subject or the object?

Verb Quiz 28

1. Ils apprennent à lire de très bonne heure.
   pouvoir
   savoir
   connaître
   mettre
   devoir

2. Ils finissent leurs devoirs.
   parler
   écouter
   étudier
   obéir
   choisir

3. Elle arrive seule.
   apprendre
   comprendre
   prendre
   entendre

4. Ils peuvent faire leurs devoirs.
   faire
   être
   avoir
   dire

5. Ils ont fini leur travail.
   vouloir
   pouvoir
   apprendre
   savoir
   mettre
   lire
   dire

6. Je veux qu'on fasse un bon travail.
   savoir   (perfect score 100,
   pouvoir   each verb counts 2)
   avoir
   être
   partir
   rester
   mourir
   dire

Verb Quiz 29

1. Ils vont à l'école ensemble.
   pouvoir
   savoir
   vouloir
   faire

2. Elle est allée à l'école seule.
   partir
   sortir
   venir
   parler
   se plaire (plu—past participle is invariable. There is no e.)

3. Ils sont morts hier.
   partir
   vouloir
   ouvrir
   savoir
   prendre

4. Vous parlez bien le français.
   être   (perfect score 104,
   avoir   each verb counts 4)
   partir
   finir
   se reposer
   s'habiller
   se réveiller
   se plaire

Verb Quiz 30

1. Elles sont parties pour la France.
   retourner
   venir
   devenir
   entrer
   apprendre

2. Ils savent nager.
   vouloir
   pouvoir
   apprendre
   faire
   partir

3. Elle a écrit une lettre à son papa.
   sortir
   aller
   mourir

   arriver
   descendre

4. M. Parker allait souvent en France quand il était petit.
   vouloir   (perfect score 100,
   partir   each verb counts 3)
   finir
   écrire
   parler
   s'asseoir

Note: Test 30a differs from 30 in sentence 3 with its plural subject. This is excellent for a retest to see if students *always* listen for meaning and to check on any possible cheating. This sentence is a powerful contrast of verbs conjugated with *avoir* or *être* in compound tenses.

Verb Quiz 30a

1. Elles sont parties pour la France.
   retourner
   venir
   devenir
   entrer
   apprendre

2. Ils savent nager.
   vouloir
   pouvoir
   apprendre
   faire
   partir

3. Elles ont écrit des lettres à leur papa.
   sortir
   aller
   mourir
   arriver
   descendre

4. M. Parker allait souvent en France quand il était petit.
   vouloir   (perfect score 100,
   partir   each verb counts 3)
   finir
   écrire

parler
s'asseoir

Verb Quiz 31

1. Elle était fatiguée.
   mourir
   finir
   pouvoir
   vouloir

2. Ils étaient partis pour la France.
   demander
   retourner
   mourir
   naître
   parler

3. Elle a très bien parlé de son devoir.
   sortir   (Devoir in the singular
   manger   means duty—honorable
   écouter   duty—not homework)
   écrire
   devenir

4. Ils finissent de bonne heure.
   pouvoir   (perfect score 100,
   vouloir   each verb counts 4)
   savoir
   prendre
   comprendre
   partir

Note: Quiz 31a differs in sentence 1 by having a plural subject and in sentence 2 by the change from a masculine to a feminine subject. Students must use great caution. This test will indicate whether an early class has warned a later class. Give test 31 and not 31a if you suspect this.

Verb Quiz 31a

1. Elles étaient fatiguées.
   mourir
   pouvoir
   vouloir

2. Elles étaient parties pour la France.
   demander
   retourner
   mourir
   naître
   parler

3. Elle a très bien parlé de son devoir.
   sortir
   manger
   écouter
   écrire
   devenir

4. Ils finissent de bonne heure.
   pouvoir   (perfect score 100,
   vouloir   each verb counts 4)
   savoir
   prendre
   comprendre
   partir

Verb Quiz 33

1. Elles étaient parties avant moi.
   mourir
   venir
   sortir
   travailler
   se laver
   se lever

2. Elles étaient fatiguées hier.
   pouvoir
   vouloir
   avoir
   être
   battre

3. Nous avons bien fait nos devoirs.
   écrire
   sortir
   retourner
   se laver

se plaire
mettre

4. Ils apprennent à lire le français.
savoir
pouvoir
vouloir
dire

5. Je finirai avant midi.
parler
étudier
écouter
partir
avoir
être
savoir
pouvoir
voir

6. Il se peut qu'on parle mieux le français que l'anglais.
savoir   (This dependent clause
pouvoir   is subjunctive)
être   (perfect score 100,
avoir   each verb counts 2)

Note: Test 33a differs from this test in sentence 4. If I suspected cheating I did this often, but warned my students to trust their ears.

Verb Quiz 33a

1. Elles étaient parties avant moi.
mourir
venir
sortir
travailler
se laver
se lever

2. Elles étaient fatiguées hier.
pouvoir
vouloir
avoir

être
battre

3. Nous avons bien fait nos devoirs.
   écrire
   sortir
   retourner
   se laver
   se plaire
   mettre

4. Ils savent jouer à la balle.
   savoir
   pouvoir
   vouloir
   dire

5. Je finirai avant midi.
   parler
   étudier
   écouter
   partir
   avoir
   être
   savoir
   pouvoir
   voir

6. Il se peut qu'on parle mieux le français que l'anglais.
   savoir   (Another dependent
   pouvoir   subjunctive clause)
   être   (perfect score 100,
   avoir   each verb counts 2)

Verb Quiz 34

1. Elles avaient longtemps étudié.
   partir
   sortir
   tomber
   revenir

2. Je finirai avant midi.
   sortir
   partir
   entendre
   avoir

3. Elles ont écrit la leçon.
   rester
   descendre
   mourir
   étudier

4. Ils prennent leur petit déjeuner à huit heures.
   pouvoir
   savoir
   comprendre
   vouloir

5. Nous faisons toujours notre leçon.
   être   (perfect score 100,
   avoir   each verb counts 4)
   comprendre
   mettre

Verb Quiz 35

1. Ils parleront français bientôt.
   écrire
   partir
   être
   avoir
   pouvoir
   savoir
   voir
   faire

2. Elle s'est lavé la tête. (Warning: This sentence has a direct object. Thus, no extra e on lavé. The other verbs have the extra e.)
   se lever
   s'habiller
   se reposer
   s'arrêter

3. J'etais parti(e) avant midi.
   travailler
   chanter
   oublier
   se laver

4. Tu n'as pas compris cette leçon.
   dire
   lire
   vouloir
   entrer

5. Écoutez-moi.
   finir   (perfect score 100,
   partir   each verb counts 3)
   descendre
   manger

Note: Quiz 35a which follows differs from this test only in sentence 2 which tests the accord of the past participle.

Verb Quiz 35a

1. Ils parleront français bientôt.
   écrire
   partir
   être
   avoir
   pouvoir
   savoir
   voir
   faire

2. Elles se sont lavées.
   se lever
   s'habiller

se reposer
s'arrêter

3. J'étais parti(e) avant midi.
   travailler
   chanter
   oublier
   se laver

4. Tu n'as pas compris cette leçon.
   dire
   lire
   vouloir
   entrer

5. Écoutez-moi.
   finir   (perfect score 100,
   partir   each verb counts 3)
   descendre
   manger

Verb Quiz 36

1. Lave-toi.
   écrire
   écouter
   descendre
   finir

2. Nous nous sommes levés(es) de bonne heure.
   s'arrêter
   se laver
   se reposer
   travailler

3. Lorsque j'étais petite j'allais souvent en France.
   s'arrêter
   s'habiller
   se reposer
   se réveiller

4. Je ferai toujours de mon mieux.
   aller
   avoir

finir
voir

5. Nous étions sortis(es) sans elles.
   mourir   (perfect score 100,
   descendre   each verb counts 4)
   étudier
   prendre

12

Hélas le Subjonctif

The title of this chapter will confuse monolingual Americans.
Most will simply skip this chapter without a second glance, thinking that the subjunctive concerns them not at all.

Does the subjunctive tense exist in English? Is it ever used in
speaking or writing? The answer to both questions is yes, of
course. But who uses it? Anyone who speaks passable English,
everyone who speaks *good* English, everyone who reads the Bible
in the King James version and employs the language as it is used
there, and everyone who reads and understands good literature.
Listen to the oft-repeated Lord's prayer:

> Our Father which *art* in Heaven,
> Hallowed *be* thy name.
> Thy kingdom *come*
> Thy will *be* done
> In earth as it *is* in Heaven.
> *Give* us this day our daily bread
> And *forgive* us our debts, as we *forgive* our debtors.
> And *lead* us not into temptation,
> But *deliver* us from evil:
> For thine *is* the Kingdom,
> And the power, and the glory, for ever.
> Amen.

The first three verbs, *be, come,* and *be,* are in the subjunctive mood. *Give, forgive, lead,* and *deliver* are in the imperative mood. *Is* is in the present indicative mood (so is *art,* of course, but we no longer use "thee" or "thou" in speaking except to God).

Listen to Moses: "Ye shall not add unto the word which I command you, neither shall ye diminish ought from it, that ye *may keep* the commandments of the Lord your God" (Deut. 4:2). "And thou shalt do that which is right and good in the sight of the Lord: that it *may be* well with thee, and that thou *mayest go* in and possess the good land which the Lord sware unto thy fathers" (Deut. 6:18). (The italicized verbs are in the subjunctive mood.)

What does all this have to do with learning a language or even speaking acceptable English? A good deal if we are to teach students correct speech and also to write well. It is absolutely vital that a student *understand* this well if a foreign language is being learned.

Please notice the verb *understand* in the preceding sentence. We would ordinarily say, "He understands this well," in the present indicative. The *understand* above has no *s* because the principal clause, *it is absolutely vital,* announces necessity, but the uncertainty of the outcome of the subordinate clause requires the subjunctive form: *understand.* We do not know if he will understand, thus the uncertainty of outcome regardless of how vital we think this *may be* (more subjunctive). Subjunctive is also required after some verbs of thought and desire.

I used to ask my students to tell me which verb was correct in this sentence:

> *are*
> It is important (vital/necessary) that you ___ there.
> *be*

Most of them usually replied "that you *be* there." My next question was, "Then the verb *to be* is conjugated as follows?"

I *be*	We *be*
You *be*	You *be*
He (she, one) *be*	They *be*

They invariably laughed and protested that no, *to be* is:

I *am*	We *are*
You *are*	You *are*
He (she, one) *is*	They *are*

Well, well, well! The subjunctive exists in English and there it is for the verb *to be*. In English we sometimes add two other markers to announce uncertainty of action: *may* and *might*. With this kind of an explanation, my students readily accepted the idea and the necessity of learning to understand and to use the subjunctive. Any prayer requires the subjunctive in a subordinate clause. Typical prayer: "Our Father, help us that we *might* be faithful and obedient."

The only difficulties I observed in the teaching of the subjunctive to American students arose from the teachers of foreign language—and the texts. Some teachers taught, and still teach, foreign language in English. Some know how to speak the foreign language they are teaching. Some do not. Some foreign-born teachers who speak their native language very well teach in English since Americans are viewed as linguistically ignorant around the world and therefore incapable of learning another language.

Some teachers managed very well in French except when they should have used the subjunctive. I have known some who actually spoke the subjunctive badly and even deformed French at levels I and II in order to avoid it. American texts did not deal with it early enough, and the teachers wished to avoid it because they erroneously considered the subjunctive difficult for themselves and for their students. It is not. Teachers must never avoid the subjunctive. The ear is the best teacher for students. Students should hear it from their teachers daily at the first level. Teachers who do not know this mood well should force themselves to learn it.

When to begin: The first day

How: By correctly speaking the language to your students.

Why: One cannot avoid the subjunctive in everyday language if a teacher speaks good French, Spanish, English—any language. The students will quickly become accustomed to hearing and understanding the sound of the subjunctive. It is vital that you *do* not corrupt the language in order to avoid it. *Do* is subjunctive but is the same as the present indicative here.

When to explain the subjunctive: Before the end of the first month. Let your students be aware of what they are hearing. You need not expect them to completely absorb it, but hearing will help.

What is the subjunctive: A concept of time and action linked to uncertainty of results of that action. It is widely and often used in all European tongues and usually in a subordinate clause.

1. There are *only nine verbs in the French language with irregular radicals. Note:* The radical of the three italicized verbs is the same as *nous* and *vous* of the imperfect. These are:

avoir	savoir	*valoir*
être	pouvoir	*vouloir*
aller	faire	falloir

(All are part of your core group.)

avoir = to have

que j'aie	que nous ayons
que tu aies	que vous ayez
qu'il (elle, on) ait	qu'ils (elles) aient

The *que* is used here to announce that these clauses are subordinate to a principal clause *spoken* or *assumed.*

être = to be

que je sois	que nous soyons
que tu sois	que vous soyez
qu'il (elle, on) soit	qu'ils (elles) soient

Note: Students will hear these two verbs from you at once and often as well as the other seven.

2. Only these two (*avoir* and *être*) have irregular *endings. All other verbs* of the language have the *same endings* for the subjunctive: *e, es, e, ions, iez, ent.*

je	e	nous	ions
tu	es	vous	iez
il	e	ils	ent

3. All other verbs take their radical from the third person plural of the present tense: *they.*
4. *Remember:* If you are dealing with an *irregular* verb, *nous* (we) and *vous* (you) of the subjunctive are the same as *nous* and *vous* of the imperfect except *savoir, pouvoir, faire, avoir,* and *être.* For example:

Ils doiv [radical] ent: present, third person plural.

que je *doive*	que nous *devions*
que tu *doives*	que vous *deviez*
qu'il (elle, on) *doive*	(same as imperfect)
	qu'ils (elles) *doivent*

Ils comprenn [radical] ent: present, third person plural.

que je comprenne	que nous compren*ions*
	que vous compren*iez*
	(the same as the
qu tu comprennes	imperfect)
qui'il (elle, on) comprenne	qu'ils (elles) comprennent

The rules of the formation of the subjonctif are quickly learned as well as the irregular verbs.

Radicals of six of these irregular verbs vary a little; three do not: *savoir, pouvoir,* and *faire.*

avoir	savoir	vouloir
être	pouvoir	valoir
aller	faire	falloir

(Endings are regular except for *avoir* and *être*.)

Only *savoir, pouvoir,* and *faire* have the same radical for all persons. All endings are regular.

savoir—sach
pouvoir—puiss
faire—fass

Falloir, of course, has only the third person singular to be learned.

Qu'il faille; *never* qu'on and *never* qu'elle.

5. I made these charts early in the year and gave them to students for their notebook.

Learning to Use the Subjunctive

Students learn usage by *constant oral drill* a few minutes each day; explanations alone will not teach.

Procedure: Draw up a list that includes almost all of the occasions when the subjunctive is required in most of the everyday situations and in literature (see Aperçu in this chapter).

1. The following list should be typed and given to students as the learning of subjunctive use begins—certainly before the end of the first year or earlier. My students received them by Noël of the first year, sometimes before.

2. Go down the list carefully in oral drill using the nine irregular verbs named frequently. Their usage is a frequent everyday affair in spoken French.

3. Gradually require that the students accept the pattern of thought involved by not consulting the two typed sheets of the beginning process during drill.

4. A sentence carrying the subjunctive should appear early on a verb quiz as an extra practice sentence with no penalty for errors. The students will thus become accustomed to subjunctive patterns of thought and its sound. *The first trials should always be with the nine verbs with irregular radicals where one can hear the subjunctive and the rule of the formation of the subjunctive can be employed with other verbs, regular or irregular.* Regular review on verb quizzes reinforces the subjunctive early.

For example, the italicized is dictated on a verb quiz:

Il faut que vous fassiez vos devoirs.

Present			Subjunctive	
aller	il va	he goes	que vous alliez	that you may go
partir	il part	he leaves	que vous partiez	that you may leave
avoir	il a	he has	que vous ayez	that you may have
être	il est	he is	que vous soyez	that you may be

5. Contrasts are powerful in helping students learn the basic principles and absorb the rules that govern verb structure.

6. There is no substitute for choral drill that will fix the learning process in a student's brain. *Do not forget! The sense of hearing is the most powerful sense we possess. Bombard their ears with the daily sound of French. Insist that they open the mouth and repeat.* Thus, they hear themselves and each other.

7. Oral drill and choral drill should never be neglected on the subjunctive, even at advanced levels. Begin the subjunctive before the end of the first year. You need not grade this. Remember that *your goals* are (a) *comprehension* and (b) *speech.*

Verb quizzes for all tenses will be found in chapter 11, "The Verb Quiz."

The thought process in learning the subjunctive is the only barrier to transference from English to French or any other European language. Therefore, oral drill, not verb sheets, I found, was the only method upon which I could rely. The drill had to be the complete structure of a sentence with the subjunctive in it and not just repeating aloud a verb list of the subjunctive.

Thus: (in oral drill)

> Je me réjouis que vous soyez préparés aujourd'hui.
> Je suis contente que vous soyez préparés aujourd'hui.
> J'ordonne que vous soyez préparés.

All the students had to do was to associate the idea of *Je me réjouis, Je suis contente,* and *J'ordonne* with the verb in the subordinate for *vous* as subject. I announced the necessary verb in the infinitive after I stopped using the practice sheets.

Un Aperçu

(This is given to students for their notebooks and used for oral drill.)

1. Après certaines conjonctions, parmi les plus communes:

   Conjonctions

pour que	pourvu que
afin que	à condition que
de peur que (ne)	jusqu' à ce que
avant que (ne)	au cas que
de crainte que (ne)	malgré que
en attendant que	non que
sans que	soit que . . . *soit que*
à moins que (ne)	de sorte que
quoique	de façon que
bien que	de manière que

   Prépositions

pour	de crainte de
afin de	sans
de peur de	employer avec l'infinitif
avant de	

2. Après des verbes de volonté:

vouloir	approuver	admettre
désirer	commander	défendre
souhaiter	permettre	empêcher
aimer	ordonner	nier
aimer mieux	demander	démentir
préférer	exiger	

3. Après des verbes de sentiment, d'émotion, et de doute:

regretter	être satisfait (e)	être étonné (e)
craindre (ne)	être triste	être surpris (e)
avoir peur (ne)	être désolé (e)	s'étonner
être content (e)	être fâché (e)	être fier (fière)
être heureux (euse)	se plaindre	(Prononcez le "r" in
être enchanté (e)	se fâcher	both words)
être joyeux (euse)	être inquiet	avoir honte
se réjouir	être inquiète	douter (mais se douter
		prend l'indicatif)

4. Après certaines expressions impersonnelles:

il faut	il se peut	il est étonnant

il est nécessaire	il suffit	il est étrange
il est important	il est temps	il est douteux
il importe	il convient	il est *h*onteux
il vaut mieux	il est convenable	il est heureux
il est préférable	c'est dommage	il semble
il est peu probable	(mais l'indicatif après il est probable)	

il me semble
il te semble
il nous semble   Take l'indicatif
il vous semble
il lui semble
il leur semble

Note: All these are followed by *que,* of course, when you practice.
H in honte and honteux is *aspirate;* therefore no liaison.

5. *Notez bien:* Employez l'indicatif après:

il est vrai que   *Mais, quand ces expressions sont négatives ou*
il est sûr que   *interrogatives, employez le subjonctif:* Il
il est certain que   n'est pas vrai qu'il vienne. Est-il vrai qu'il
il est évident que   vienne? *Mais notez bien: quand ces expressions*
il est probable que   *sont négatives et interrogatives employez*
il paraît que   *l'indicatif.* N'est-il pas vrai qu'il sait tout?
Trouver
Penser
Croire
Expérer
Compter

6. Après certaines expressions indéfinies (proposition = clause):

qui . . . que   quel . . . que
quoi. . . que   où   . . . que

7. Dans une proposition (clause) relative qui indique une chose
   cherchée, desirée, mais pas trouvée: Je cherche une maison
   qui ait cinq chambres.

8. Dans une proposition relative après un negatif ou un interroga-

tif: Il n'y a pas de college à Lyon qui admette des externes.

9. Dans une proposition relative après *premier, dernier, seul,* ou un superlatif quand il s'agit *d'une opinion* et *pas d'un fait;*
C'est le meilleur homme que je connaisse.

These previous pages of explanation should be given to students for their notebook and regularly reviewed aloud. Use them for oral drills.

Do not keep the "how" and "why" of the subjonctif secret. Point out that it is part of English as well as French.

Repeat these examples now and then. Then conjugate the verb "to be" in the present in English—many times if necessary.

Ask students if it goes like this:

I be	we be
you be	you be
he be	they be

They quickly realize that the verb "to be" in the present is:

I am	we are
thou art	you are
she, one, he is	they are

Remember that "may" and "might" announce the English subjunctive. These explanations were always revelations to my students. These *repeated explanations and examples* helped my students cross the barriers of the language.

The subjunctive is not difficult to teach. If we know it well and use it correctly, our students will *imitate us.*

Let us be good models. C'est simple comme bonjour. (It is as simple as hello.)

Our students will copy our attitude as well as how and what we say. If we view the subjunctive as difficult, I promise you that our students will do the same and only half learn it. Something half-learned is soon lost. Bonne chance!

211

13

Le Passé Simple

American textbooks for French do not use or deal with the passé simple (past definite) early enough, in my view. They tip-toe into it backwards. Simple short stories are altered and "simplified" for American students. The opinion of textbook authors of the ability of students in this country is evidently very low indeed.

One summer I was enrolled in a graduate class of grammar and composition at one of our excellent universities well known for its foreign language faculty. My classmates were all French majors, many of them teachers. One day everyone had come early for class; we were going to have a verb exam and they were studying. I was not studying verbs but reading. Two students turned to me and said, "If only there were some rules to follow to form the passé simple."

"But there are," was my reply. All the others looked up and almost in chorus said, "What are they?"

I told them I would be happy to *show* them and tell them. (The "show and tell" syndrome is deeply embedded in my teaching techniques.) I went to the board and constructed the charts and told them the rules as I moved along. We had enough time before class for me to finish my charting and explanation. I was still standing at the board when the professor walked in.

"What are you doing?" he asked me. I told him that I had just explained the formation of the passé simple and given the class the rules. He replied that there weren't any rules. I said there were indeed rules that could guide a student quickly through this maze.

"Explain them," he demanded. The second explanation for the students cleared up their questions, they told me later. The professor's comment after I had finished: "It won't work." My response was, "But it does."

We all proceeded to take the verb quiz the professor gave us. Two days later our papers were handed back, and wonder of wonders, every student received an "A." Some had perfect papers. The passé simple was taken care of with no faux pas. After the third week of almost perfect verb quiz grades, our professor suddenly announced the regular verb quizzes would be discontinued. We all knew why. Everyone was getting a perfect score on the verb quiz. In a letter to me, months before I enrolled in the class, the professor wrote that a weekly verb quiz was absolutely necessary since he found that students did not know verbs. The professor (Ph.D. plus postdoctoral work) never admitted to me that my system worked. He knew that I had spent several years in French schools (he had not) and that I did not have a Ph.D. The students thanked me privately, but the professor never said a word.

I had learned the basics of the rules of the passé simple from a remarkable French professor in France. She had not, however, done any analysis of the innumerable verbs whose radicals did not arise from the past participle of the verb. I always felt that there had to be a pattern somewhere for the majority of these verbs.

After I had eliminated the verbs whose past participles ended in *é, u,* or *s,* I was left with many verbs whose past participles ended in *t.* I then eliminated the one of these I knew was irregular in the passé simple (mourir), and I then began to see a consistent pattern in the others. Since the third person plural of the

present is the radical for the subjunctive in verbs except nine, I wondered if the same radical would work for these verbs whose past participle ends in *t*. It worked like a charm. Thus were born Nelson's rules for the passé simple. My students regularly returned from universities to tell me they could gloat a little about their knowledge of the passé simple rules. The verbal structure of French posed no problem for them after level II.

It is strange to me that authors of Spanish textbooks in all nations including the United States introduce and quickly teach the pretérito–passé simple–past definite. Do students who study Spanish have larger intellects than those who study French? According to some "experts" who do not speak French or Spanish, the latter is supposed to be easier to learn. (I do not think so.) Why, then, is the pretérito–passé simple introduced early? Because authors are obliged to do this. Spanish speakers *must* use it to speak the language. A definite time marker—ayer, anoche— requires the use of the pretérito-passé simple. There are other situations as well. This is not true in French. However, the knowledge of the passé simple is required if a student is to understand a newspaper, a fable, or a short story. This understanding unlocks the written page.

The passé simple was once used regularly for speech. One still must understand it orally if the classic theater is understood. A lecture (conference) on history or anything else would defeat a listener if the passé simple were unknown. Then why not teach this important tense early? Our students want to know why the French do not usually say: "I went to France," "I wrote the letter," or "he did the work." They will quickly discern that a translation in a text is not structurally correct, that, for example, "J'ai fini" means "I have finished" and not "I finished." They will quickly accept the passé simple as a literary tense and learn it.

My students were introduced to the passé simple through the written page. They copied short historical sketches the *first year* and *memorized* them for a Friday speech. They thus learned quickly the principal irregular verbs for which there is no rule for formation: *naître* = to be born; *mourir* = to die; *faire* = to do, to make; *être* = to be; *voir* = to see; *venir* = to come; *tenir* = to hold; and *devenir* = to become.

Can you imagine six to ten lines recounting the story of Louis XIV, Napoleon, Henri IV without these verbs? In addition to learning these highly irregular verbs of the passé simple, they learned how they sounded; they also learned their numbers. Memorizing this stuff fixed it in their brains. I never had to waste time on drilling numbers. Memorizing dates did the trick. They learned history as well.

Verbs in the passé simple appeared on verb quizzes for practice the first year and for a grade at level II.

Teaching the passé simple should be considered a *necessary* part of the French curriculum *in the second year.* Poetry, literature, newspapers, classic theater cannot be understood without it. *It must be learned early in order to introduce literature that is not mangled by simplifying it.*

There is a pattern to the verbal structure in the passé simple that is easily learned. Fewer irregularities appear than in the present tense. Copying brief paragraphs will teach the irregular verbs as well as the regular in the first year.

Madame Nelson's Rules

1. The radical is found in the past participle with some exceptions.

2. All verbs ending in *er* carry the endings *ai, as, a, âmes, âtes, èrent. There are no exceptions here!* Even *aller* behaves regularly.

3. Regular verbs ending in *ir* and *re* have the same endings—*is, is, it, îmes, îtes, irent.*

217

Thus, a chart would be:

er *verbs*	ir *and* re *verbs*
allé [radical]	(same endings for both groups)
parlé [radical]	fini [radical] entendu [radical]

Endings	*Endings*
all/é [radical]	drop *é, i,* and *u* fin/i entend/u

Verbs with *ir* and *re* endings have the *same* endings:

er *verb endings*		ir *and* re *endings*	
je—ai	nous—âmes	je—is	nous—îmes
tu—as	vous—âtes	tu—is	vous—îtes
il, elle, on—a	ils, elles—èrent	il, elle, on—it	ils, elles—irent

4. What does one do with irregular verbs? Use the past participle as the radical and *use your head.*

Past Participles

to perceive --------- apercevoir	aperçu	j'aperçus
to appear ----------- apparaître	apparu	j'apparus
to have ------------- avoir	eu	j'eus
to drink ------------- boire	bu	je bus
to know (as a result of seeing) -------- connaître	connu	je connus
to run --------------- courir	couru	je courus
to gather ------------cueillir	cueilli	je cuellis
to owe -------------- devoir	dû	je dus (The u loses its accent in devoir when the *u* is followed by another letter.)
to sleep ------------- dormir	dormi	je dormis
to be necessary ---- falloir	fallu	il fallut
to flee ---------------fuir	fui	je fuis
to read -------------- lire	lu	je lus
to lie (to tell a lie) ---------------- mentir	menti	je mentis
to put --------------- mettre	mis	je mis
to appear ----------- paraître	paru	je parus

218

to leave ------------- partir	parti	je partis
to permit ----------- permettre	permis	je permis
to please ------------plaire	plu	je plus à Jean—I pleased John
to rain -------------- pleuvoir	plu	il plut—it rained
to be able to ------- pouvoir	pu	je pus—I was able to
to promise --------- promettre	promis	je promis
to receive ---------- recevoir	reçu	je reçus
to laugh ------------ rire	ri	je ris
to know (as a result of learning) ------ savoir	su	je sus
to seat oneself (to sit down) ------------- s'asseoir	assis	je m'assis
to serve ------------- servir	servi	je servis
to silence oneself - se taire	tu	je me tus
to be worth -------- valoir	valu	je valus
to live -------------- vivre	vécu	je vécus
to want to --------- vouloir	voulu	je voulus

5. Dire—dit—*Je dis, tu dis, il dit* (to say, to tell).

These three persons are the same as present tense as with all regular ir verbs. But *nous dîmes, vous dîtes, ils dirent. Note:* The accent on *vous dîtes* makes the passé simple. *Vous dites* (no accent) is présent.

6. The ending for *all verbs except the* er *group* have the same final consonants *s, s, t, mes, tes, rent.*

7. The ending for third person plural is always *rent* for *every* verb, regular or irregular.

8. There is a small group of verbs of high usage that have irregular radicals: to be: *être—je fus, tu fus, il fut, nous fûmes, vous fûtes, ils furent;* to do, to make: *faire—je fis, tu fis, il fit, nous fîmes, vous fîtes, ils firent.*

être = to be		*faire = to do, to make*	
je fus	nous fûmes	je fis	nous fîmes
tu fus	vous fûtes	tu fis	vous fîtes
il fut	ils furent	il fit	ils firent

These two verbs should be learned together. Which has *i* in the infinitive? *Faire*. It is then easy to remember and to distinguish from *être*, which has no *i*. Other highly irregular verbs which have no rule:

to die --------------	mourir	je mourus
to be born ---------	naître	je naquis
to see --------------	voir	je vis

Family of verbs ending in *enir*

to become ---------	devenir	je devins
to come back -----	revenir	je revins
to hold -------------	tenir	je tins
to come -----------	venir	je vins

9. Verbs whose past participle ends in *t* (with the exception of *dire* and *mourir*) use the radical of the third person plural of the present and add the logical endings *is, is, it, îmes, îtes, irent*, as do all regular *ir* and *re* verbs.

to write—écrire
ils écriv/ent
écrit—past participle
j'écrivis—nous écrivîmes
tu écrivis—vous écrivîtes
il écrivit—ils écrivirent

to fear—craindre
ils craign/ent
craint—past participle
je craignis—nous craignîmes
tu craignis—vous craignîtes
il craignit—ils craignirent

to conduct—conduire
ils conduis/ent
conduit—past participle
je conduisis—nous conduisîmes
tu conduisis—vous conduisîtes
il conduisit—ils conduisirent

to open—ouvrir
ils ouvr/ent
ouvert—past participle
j'ouvris—nous ouvrîmes
tu ouvris—vous ouvrîtes
il ouvrit—ils ouvrirent

The following verbs belong to the same group and any other verb whose infinitive ends in *eindre, aindre* or *oindre:*

Infinitive	Past Participle	Present	Passé Simple
atteindre	atteint	ils atteign/ent	j'atteignis
éteindre	éteint	ils éteign/ent	j'éteignis
peindre	peint	ils peign/ent	je peignis
teindre	teint	ils teign/ent	je teignis

Note: Or any verb conjugated like these six:

	Past participle		
construire	construit	ils construis/ent	je construisis
couvrir	couvert	ils couvr/ent	je couvris
découvrir	découvert	ils découvr/ent	je découvris
détruire	détruit	ils détruis/ent	je détruisis
offrir	offert	ils offr/ent	j'offris
souffrir	souffert	ils souffr/ent	je souffris

The passé simple should be taught in the dictated verb quiz in conjunction with other tenses. If taught orally, it will be remembered. Remember, the *ear* is mightier than the *eye*. The passé simple is simple indeed. If the passé simple is copied and memorized for speeches, the students quickly learn to use it. They reinforce themselves and each other on speech day. A newspaper will have meaning the first year.

14

De la Prononciation

Many teachers concern themselves too much with accents, forgetting that we all have our own accent, unique to each one of us in our own tongue. I have heard teachers complain that they were unable to teach their students to roll the *r.* The rolling of the *r* has different emphasis in various regions in France and Spain.

Our emphasis should be on comprehensible pronunciation. The *r* can remain unrolled if we can teach our students to comprehend speakers from many regions and to make themselves understood. They must be understood anywhere in the world in any milieu of the society of the language in question. This understanding and making oneself understood underline the absolute *necessity for foreign language teachers to study and travel in the country whose language or languages they teach.* Foreign language teachers are sometimes obliged to teach more than one language.

Foreign language teachers, therefore, must be good imitators. They also should be able to spot a regional accent when they hear one and point this out to their students. In addition to regional accents there exists class pronunciation in all countries, even in the United States. However, this diversity of accents and pronunciation is beginning to disappear somewhat as a result of the use of television around the world. When I listen to the news on

American television, I am filled with despair, not by accents but by pronunciation, grammatical corruption of sentence structure, and the outright fabrication of words that do not exist and for which there are understandable and meaningful words already in the tongue. *Irregardless* is one that fills me with trembling. When someone would use that word in the presence of an acquaintance of mine, he would put his finger up and quietly say, "No, no, the word is *dis*irregardless." He of course was being half-humorous and half-serious—by subtly cancelling out the "ir" with a "dis," and therefore returning the term to its original meaning. *Enthused,* although being accepted into the language, gives me problems. It is simply not good form and is avoided by careful writers and speakers. What is wrong with using the correct adjective, *enthusiastic?*

The point I am making is that language teachers, including those who teach English, *should know well the language they teach* and choose the most widely accepted usage in the society their language represents. We should do everything possible to avoid teaching isolated regional peculiarities but concentrate on good speech at the educated level. We are, or should be, engaged in education or the improvement in our means of communicating the spoken and the written word.

Too many of my French Canadian friends were made miserable when they lived in France. They were considered and treated as foreigners and not politely. If their teachers in Canada had emphasized and taught the differences between French as spoken in Canada and the French spoken in France, they would have been more at home. They would have understood and better imitated metropolitan French.

It is not just accent that is involved when people cannot understand and communicate. The pronunciation is usually at fault. Foreign language teachers must be aware of this. *Understandable pronunciation can and must be taught.*

For foreign language teachers who have never studied in the country whose language they teach, I hope that this book may encourage them to repair this lack. It is my belief that this part of their education should be a requirement. Mere sightseeing is a poor second measure. There is no substitute for living with the people whose language we teach. I regularly returned to France to do a stage pedagogique after the initial three years of study. I always returned more French than American and my students regularly expected the latest report on what was going on. I talked to all the local people I met on every visit. Taxicab drivers especially are a wonderful fountain of the latest—from politics to fashions to the current (always deplorable in their view) behavior of young people. Old friends welcomed me and invited others to meet me. One dear friend gave a reception for me one year and told me she would invite one American. The "American" turned out to be the French-born (and still French) wife of an American colonel.

Living a summer in Europe or in the country from which the foreign language originates is an excellent idea and certainly culturally profitable for foreign language teachers. We all return with a better appreciation of the basic qualities all cultures share and a better and closer look at our own.

Alphabet

Many U.S. foreign language texts neglect the teaching of the alphabet and give it little emphasis. I feel this is a mistake. I am not thinking of the international phonetic alphabet for pronunciation, but the alphabet or the sound and name of each letter when one spells a word aloud in French. Teachers will quickly bore their students out of their skulls if they insist that students learn the markings and sounds of the international alphabet. They will gradually pick that up as they begin using a dictionary or note this alphabet if it is written in their text. However, students must be

225

taught how to spell by hearing their teachers and repeating in *chorus*. I began teaching my students the alphabet the first week, then I separated consonants from vowels. Some students could not name the vowels. The first year I learned not to be astonished at anything.

I began by writing the alphabet on the board and naming the letters in French. Students were especially intrigued that *j* and *g* were reversed in their names and that *h, w, x, y,* and *z* had names far removed from their English names. Since the names of the letters do not always indicate their sound in a word, this has to be taught by word examples in the structure of a sentence.

I wrote the alphabet first then wrote the vowels, always adding the half vowel *y*. The students repeated everything in chorus. I then noted the principal diphthongs *ei, au, ou, ai,* and the nasals *en, on, an, in, un*. Thus the following chart:

vowels = voyells		*nasals*	*diphthongs*
a	o	en	ai
e	u	an	au
i	y	in	ei
		un	ou
		on	

h had to be noted since it is never sounded in any of the Latin tongues, but it does affect the pronunciation.
h muet = mute
h aspiré = aspirate
e muet = mute should be noted as well as its effect on the rhythm of the phrase and its effect on pronunciation. When following a consonant, *that consonant must be pronounced.*
é accent aigu = acute accent
ez terminaison = ending
er terminaison = ending
(é, ez, and er have the same sound)

These all carry the same sounds. If pointed out early, the students will readily accept these three as the same in sound. *Caution:* Do not spend long periods drilling these sounds. The correct pronunciation will come quickly and be remembered if they quickly appear in the context of word and sentence. The teacher must be a good model and must oblige students to repeat everything in chorus.

Dictation to Teach Sounds with Meaning

In short dictations, I very early began to teach sound with meaning, always being careful to construct sentences with words that are pronounced alike or slightly changed but that carry a different meaning and spelling. For example:

C'est ma fille; *ses* cheveux *sont* longs.
Mes crayons *sont* bleus, *mais* ses crayons *sont* jaunes.
Son livre est vert et noir.
Mon livre est noir et jaune.
Mes livres ne *sont* pas dans le sac, *mais* dans ma serviette.
Ces livres-ci *sont* à lui.
Je *mets mes* gants avant de partir, *mais* lui, il *met ses* gants dans sa poche.

The above italicized words have the same sound of at least one other word but differ in spelling and meaning. If teachers have forgotten how they learned the foreign language they teach, the sound traps for beginners will have been forgotten as well. When I began asking students why they had written *cette à lui* instead of *c'est à lui,* I quickly realized that I had to begin the contrasting of sound earlier with words of different meaning regardless of where the text began the presentation of possessive and demonstrative adjectives. For example: I began first year with *avoir* and *être* always, but with them I taught the possessive adjectives.

Possessive Adjectives

ma, mon, mes	notre, nos
ta, ton, tes	votre, vos
sa, son, ses	leur, leurs

I gave them the whole picture in short dictated sentences. The demonstrative adjectives were given the same time as the above:

> ce, ces
> cet, ces
> cette, ces

Thus students will not continue to write *cette à lui,* which makes no sense, but *c'est à lui,* although they sound alike.

Teaching the possessive adjectives with être especially, will eliminate confusion in such a sentence:

> *Sont livre est sur la table.*

This makes no sense. They will know that *sont* is part of the verb *être* and *son* means his or her. Only contrasts in dictation will do this. English has its sound traps. Try to imagine how a Latin speaker will deal with *ill, hill, hell,* and *heel* when *h* is never sounded for them.

It took me some time to eliminate the spare-parts approach that I found in American texts and to construct *sound contrasts* in short dictated sentences to teach sound with meaning. I began to analyze how I had been taught, for I did not remember any confusion with sound. I had been taught by contrasts.

A verb that requires short dictations to firmly defog comprehension is the verb *mettre.* It should always be taught in conjunction with *mais = but* and *mes = my* possessive adjective as in this sentence already written above:

Je *mets mes* gants avant de partir, *mais*, lui, il *met* ses gants dans sa poche. (All italicized words carry the same sound.)

These short dictations should be immediately written on the blackboard and repeated many times, and they should be kept in the students' notebook.

Throughout a student's study, even at advanced levels, dictations should be used to check and to teach oral comprehension as well as to teach students to write sense and to spell phonetically. Yes, French is a phonetic language—much more so than English.

Refining Pronunciation

Early in the year of level one, I copied two fables from La Fontaine, *L'ivrogne et sa femme* and *La jeune veuve* (The drunk and his wife and The young widow). My students and I regularly went over these two fables until they were memorized. The stories are both amusing and the students enjoyed them. In these two fables there is every imaginable sound and pronunciation with the exceptions I have already noted. As the students learned each fable, they began to correct each other and themselves. The refining of their pronunciation continued rapidly. Occasionally I would dictate parts of these fables to help refine spelling as the students related sound with written phonetics.

In addition to the two fables, I gave them two pages with the basics of French phonetics that every class at every level received at the beginning of the year. These pages provided quick and easily understood examples of the "how" of the sounds of French. They were carried in the students' notebook and produced if I found there was any doubt about how a new word was pronounced. These pages follow.

Correcting and refining the pronunciation of students deserves attention at all levels, but students should have some ready reference in order to help themselves. Every new word should not be a mystery until it is pronounced by the teacher. *If students are not quickly taught to help themselves, they have not been taught much.*

Tapes with different voices reciting the same thing will speed the learning of pronunciation and its refinement, as well as the ability to recognize accents. Comprehension of different voices and accents will improve gradually. One of the most able and most learned of my language teachers in France was an aged lady who had false teeth. These encumbrances clicked as she spoke and the noise at first disturbed me. In later years I remembered this fine teacher who taught me so much and was filled with gratitude even for the clicking of her teeth. I learned to deal with sound distractions and to recognize regional accents quickly.

After learning a fable, the student begins to correct himself. Notice the phonetic value of the fable: (to be memorized)

L'ivrogne et sa femme
Chacun a son défaut où toujours il revient:
    Honte ni peur n'y remédie.
  Sur ce propos, d'un conte il me souvient:
    Je ne dis rien que je n'appuie
  De quelque exemple.
          Un suppôt de Bacchus
Altérait sa santé, son esprit et sa bourse.
Telles gens n'ont pas fait la moitié de leur course
    Qu'ils sont au bout de leurs écus.
Un jour que celui-ci, plein du jus de la treille,
Avait laissé ses *sens* au fond d'une bouteille,
    [final *s* is pronounced in this word]
Sa femme l'enferma dans un certain tombeau.
    Là les vapeurs du vin nouveau
Cuvèrent à loisir. A son reveil il *trouve*
L'attirail de la mort à l'entour de son corps,
    Un luminaire, un drap des morts.
"Oh! dit-il, qu'est ceci? Ma femme est-elle veuve?"
Là-dessus, son épouse, en habit d'Alecton,
Masquée et de sa voix contrefaisant le ton,
Vient au prétendu mort, approche de sa bière,
Lui présente un chaudeau propre pour Lucifer.
L'époux *allors* ne doute en aucune manière [today's spelling is alors]
    Qu'il ne soit citoyen d'enfer.
"Quelle personne es-tu? dit-il à ce fantôme
    —La cellerière du royaume
De Satan, reprit-elle; et je porte à manger
    A ceux qu'enclôt la tombe noire."

Le mari repart sans songer:
"Tu ne leur portes point à boire?"

* * *

La jeune veuve

La perte d'un époux ne va point sans soupirs:
On fait beaucoup de bruit, et puis on se console.
Sur les ailes du Temps la tristesse s'envole:
      Le Temps ramène les plaisirs.
      Entre la veuve d'une année
      Et la veuve d'une journée
La différence est grande: on ne croirait jamais
      Que ce fût la même personne.
L'une fait fuir les gens, et l'autre a mille attraits:
Aux soupirs vrais ou faux celle-là s'abandonne;
C'est toujours même note et pareil entretien.
      On dit qu'on est inconsolable:
      On le dit; mais il n'en est rien,
      Comme on verra par cette fable,
      Ou plutôt par la vérité.

      L'epoux d'une jeune beauté
Partait pour l'autre monde. A ses côtés sa femme
Lui criait: "Attends-moi, je te suis; et mon âme,
Aussi bien que la tienne, est prête à s'envoler."
      Le mari fit seul le voyage.
La belle avait un père, homme prudent et sage;
      Il laissa le torrent couler.
      A la fin, pour la consoler:
"Ma fille, lui dit-il, c'est trop verser de larmes:
Qu'a besoin le défunt que vous noyiez vos charmes?
Puisqu'il est des vivants, ne songez plus aux morts.
      Je ne dis pas que tout à l'heure
      Une condition meilleure
      Change en des noces ces transports;
Mais après certain temps, souffrez qu'on vous propose
Un époux beau, bien fait, jeune, et tout autre chose
      Que le défunt.—Ah! dit-elle aussitôt,
      Un cloître est l'époux qu'il me faut."
Le père lui laissa digérer sa disgrâce.
      Un mois de la sorte se passe;
L'autre mois on l'emploie à changer tous les jours

Quelque chose à l'habit, au linge, à la coiffure:
  Le deuil enfin sert de parure,
  En attendant d'autres atours.
  Toute la bande des Amours
Revient au colombier: les jeux, les ris, la danse
  Ont aussi leur tour à la fin;
  On se plonge soir et matin
  Dans la Fontaine de Jouvence.
Le père ne craint plus ce défunt tant chéri;
Mais comme il ne parlait de rien à notre belle:
  "Où donc est le jeune mari
  Que vous m'avez promis?" dit-elle.

Following are more pages for students' notebooks.

De la Prononciation

1. *Où Ou*

un fou	mourir	nous pouvons
le cou	la tour	vous pouvez
la cour	le tour	une foule
le four	nous mourons	vous voulez
Bourges	vous mourez	nous voulons

2. *Heure*

leur	je demeure	soeur
je meurs	acteur	éditeur
tu meurs	menteur	facteur
ils meurent	coeur	

3. *Peu*

eu	tu peux	mieux
un feu	il peut	eux
je peux	ils peuvent	

4. *Envoyer*

royaume	nous croyons	employer
royal	vous croyez	coudoyer
vous voyez	moyen	foudroyer
nous voyons		

5. *Sound alike*

et	ai (ending; same as é)
é	ais, ait (endings; same as é in fast speech)
ez	
er	

6. Nasal Sound

in, im, ein, ain, aim, as endings are pronounced the same way—when followed by une consonne *the same* way. Add an *e* muet (or any other vowel)—they are no longer nasals and change sound.

vin	fin	éteindre
simple	enfin	se plaindre
vain	interet	feindre
pain	interesser	ainsi
plein	important	Berlin

7. Not Nasal

Ein, am, an, ain, on, en, im, in + voyelle are no longer nasal. The *n* or *m* is pronounced. The *i* in *in, im,* or *imme* has full vowel value. Thus *i* then sounds like *e* in *feel* (English). The diphthongs *eim* and (French diphthong) *ain* become *è* as in *fell* (English) and the *n* is pronounced.

immédiate	bon—bonne	fin—inutile
plein—pleine	don—donner	an—année
main—maine	en—ennemi	Use contrasts.

8. *on*

ils sont	nom	ils font
son	bon	dont
ils ont		

9. *Marseille*   *Versailles*

These combinations, *eil, eille, ail, aille,* if preceded by a consonant or a vowel, always are pronounced as Mar*seille* or Ver*sailles.*

eil—terminaison m.
eille—terminaison f.

une treille
un appareil
une bouteille
la veille de Noël
une v*i*eille femme
un v*i*eil homme
[give first *i* its
full vowel value—*e*
as in *feel*]
pareil
un embouteillage
surveiller (verbe)
un conseil (nom)
conseiller (verbe)
v*i*eillir (verbe)
[*i* here has its full
value as in the
adjectives above]

ail—terminaison m.
aille—terminaison f.

la volaille
travailler (verbe)
un travail
une trouvaille
un détail
une muraille
qu'il aille   [*aller* in
que tu ailles   the sub-
que j'aille   junctive]
qu'il faille   [*falloir* in the
                     subjunctive]

Caution:
ail + voyelle = elle
in other words,
aile = elle [same sound]
[sound the l]

10. Un *s* entre deux voyelles est un *z* (hard).
    poser   se reposer
    conduisez   baiser
    viser

11. Deux *ss* entre deux voyelles est doux (soft).
    pousser   nous connaissons
    la mousse   vous connaissez
    ramasser   ils connaissent

12. Un *s* entre une voyelle et une consonne est doux (soft).
    ainsi
    un escalier
    un escarpement

13. C followed by *a, o, u,* ou une consonne is hard unless soft-ened by une cédille.

    Cannes   clair
    car   confort
    vécu

C softened by addition d'une cédille:

je reçois

tu reçois

il reçoit

ils reçoivent

reçu

[no need for cédille]

nous recevons

vous recevez

14. *G* followed by *a, o, u,* ou une consonne is hard as in *great. G* followed by *i* or *e* or *y* is *soft* as in *edge.*

gare	grand	guide	manger
gomme	Gringoire		gymnaste

15. The *g* is softened by adding *e* and must be added in verbes having a *ger* ending before *a, o, u.* (It is not necessary to add *e* for an ending beginning with *e* or *i.*)

(Imparfait)

je mangeais

tu mangeais

il mangeait

nous mangions—not necessary

vous mangiez—not necessary

ils mangeaient

16. *Gn* is sounded like *canyon* except for about five words—even the French forget these rare exceptions. One example: *stagnant* (hard *g*, not as in *canyon*).

la campagne

la montagne

ils plaignent

signer

[as in *canyon*]

17. On doit prononcer une consonne devant un *e* muet.

mort—silent *t*

morte—*t* must be pronounced

18. *Et* on ne prononce *jamais* le *t* de ce mot. *Jamais!!!* Never, *never* pronounce the *t* of the word *et = and.*

19. *Moi (oi* as *w* in *water)*

toi

une fois

une foire

un poire

je vois

je dois

une foi	voilà	je crois
un foie	voici	un roi

20. *Au*

aux	faux	des maux
le royaume	fausse	maudire
la chaume	une faute	autrefois
augmenter	un défaut	

21. *Am, em, an, en* + consonne se prononcent de la même façon.

antérieur	envoyer
antan	exemple
ambitieux	employer
ambulant	enfin

22. Le tréma—the double point ¨. Double point qu'on met hori-
zontalement sur les voyelles e, i, u, pour indiquer que la voyelle
qui précede doit être prononcée séparément, comme dans cigu-ë,
na-ïf, la perestro-ïka.

This is a brief picture of pronunciation rules. However brief it
may be, we should not fall into the trap of considering how students pronounce a word a matter of no consequence. They can
easily be misunderstood. Thus, misunderstandings result in no
communication, which is the goal of speech.

Communication is the number one priority of all language,
oral or written. *Fluency,* or ease of communication, is the next
priority—ability to *converse, read,* and *write* in an effortless manner. The written word must not be forgotten in a single-minded
pursuit of ease of speaking about the weather, restaurant talk, and
the like. Pronunciation can be refined as students learn to read
and write, as well as when they are talking to others. The whole
picture must be kept in view constantly.

Paradis Terrestre
L'Antre de la Vieille
Dragonne

Il vaut mieux faire
envie que pitié.
On est souvent puni
par où l'on a péché.

15

Grammar—"Teach It"

The languages spoken by the world are battered by natural enemies in every culture. The airwaves that once carried only
seeds, spores, and volcanic dust now have additional baggage.
Sound waves, once unheard except for the wind, rain, and thunder, carry demolition squads that squat on the antennas of every
home with radio and television. The chief of squad number one
is Ignorance; his chief of staff is Invented Jargon. They sneak into our ears and thinking, destroying the language we speak. The
total destruction of speech and thought patterns will eventually
undermine any culture, any language, by cutting us off from our
past, our ability to read records. Our only weapons are vigilance
and hard-nosed teaching of our language.

I am reminded of the story of an Italian general posted to
NATO who told my husband and me of his total confusion when
he was sent to a conference, which was conducted in English,
covering highly secret matters. The American general conducting
the meeting announced some necessary beginning procedures and
then concluded they would then "send up the balloon." Our Italian friend, who was a pilot, stood up and said, "I thought this conference was to deal with airplanes and missiles. What have we to
do with balloons?" He then told us how incensed he was by the
jargon and the slang spoken by the American military. He spoke

several languages besides his native Italian, but he had not learned the English that was coming out of the mouths of even the command level of American forces in Europe. He never ceased expressing his shock to us years after. He had been obliged to be able to speak English and French for his posting to NATO. These were not the requirements of American officers who at least should have been required to speak understandable English.

The American people do not yet see the need to speak, read, and write correct English. They are even less able to see the need of understanding and speaking a language other than their own.

Recently I listened to a college graduate supposedly prepared to teach English say: "Me and my husband did this." I hoped that the first time was a mistake. No. She did it again. A native French friend was seated next to me. She poked me in the ribs and whispered in French, "I hope that she isn't teaching English now." Until we monitor our demolition squads and insist that our young be taught well in English *and* another foreign language, our nation and the passing on of our culture and our linguistic past will be at risk. We must change our careless ways and weigh more carefully the importance of our language. It is a treasure that allows us to use our past in order to prepare our future. The preservation of this gold mine of learning should dominate our thoughts in all teaching situations.

The winds of change regularly sweep through the halls of academe whispering or sometimes howling, "Change! A new method has been discovered." Change means progress to Americans; there seems to be no other way for too many. The whisperers or the howlers can always count on the herd instinct in Americans to follow if the cry is insistent enough and if it promises ten easy lessons to perfection—especially in a foreign language or even dealing with our own language. Intelligent teachers will stop, look, and listen. Then they will continue with tried and true methods. Change does not always mean progress forward. Too often it means loss.

We are a nation hooked on the alluring advertisements that promise instant gratification in beauty, weight reduction, pleasure, and the like. In academe it has been the new math, no grammar, no phonetics, no writing, just printing. They have to sneak up on a child to teach him cursive. It has to be all fun and games. I started grammar school with a teacher who taught me how to write and the necessity of practicing. I taught high school students who could print only and who did not know a pronoun from a verb. The structure of an English sentence was as alien as Sanskrit. Ponder these gems:

1. He drove he and Laura to the airport.
2. The director called Anna and I in for a chat.

and contemplate this one taken from a book on counseling written by a Ph.D:

3. He wanted he and her to examine the same report.

In sentence 3 the second *he* represented the subject. This sentence needs to be rewritten entirely. The writer had evidently forgotten the reflexive pronoun, *himself,* and had substituted the pronoun *he* that can be used only as a subject. Could this have been a typographical error? I doubt it. I regularly hear these horrors out of the mouths of people with advanced degrees.

Use such grammatical horrors as the three in the above sentences to analyze subject and object pronouns. Teach your students to hear the stupidities by saying the sentence without *Laura* and *Anna* and *her.* Even the worst speakers of English will substitute *him* in sentence 1 and *me* in sentence 2. In sentence 3 they will recognize that there are reflexive pronouns in English, and they will accept them in French and transfer something they see readily in English to the foreign language they are learning. They will

241

recognize the necessity for clarity and restatement of a thought.

Teachers of English and teachers of foreign language must teach grammar. I care not at all for "fashion" in teaching. Teachers must take a sentence apart and do some analysis. Structure must be taught. Depending upon analogy alone in an English or a foreign language class is to risk total defeat. Even the most apt and able students must understand how to analyze a sentence in order to help themselves and to learn how to use the language to create word images. Do not expect imitation and oral repetition to do all of this. Sometimes the models of the language (the teachers) need some more study, too.

There is no transference from English to French unless students are taught grammar. At the least, a foreign language teacher may be a key figure in helping to dam the tide of language pollution that regularly spews from the television channels. Ask your students to listen intently to news broadcasts and to pay special attention to sports newscasters, the coaches, and the players they interview. Contrasts can be profoundly shocking. They provide opportunities for quick analysis and transfer to French.

Grammar requires constant attention. Here are some areas for constant review:

1. *Interrogative pronouns should be used the first day.* Have a short dialogue written on the board; all questions and answers. Start with the subject and object pronoun for *what*.

What are you doing? (*Qu'est-ce que* vous faites?)—Object
What is going on [happening]? (*Qu'est-ce qui* se passe?)—Subject

Both of the above examples must be translated as *what* in English, but notice the difference in sound and spelling in the French. Translation should often be more exact in order to establish a manner of thinking. Texts usually translate too loosely.

Every grammar quiz should have examples of the interrogative pronouns as well as other grammatical principles. Do not compartmentalize grammar. You are teaching communication, oral and written, that is used *daily*.

2. *Object pronouns should be introduced to students at the outset.* Unfortunately, such pronouns are presented in bits and parts in American texts. They are begun when students understand only the present tense of a verb. I found this approach was wasteful of time and confusing to students. Since I began the teaching of verb tenses by contrasting the present tense with passé composé (past indefinite), I also taught the placement of object pronouns at the same time. The students then had a total picture. Learning came as a result of practical use beginning the first week and continuing throughout every year of study.

Students can never be taught to read and understand dialogues and simple stories without being aware of object pronouns and their placement. American texts postpone this until the last half of the first year. The placement of object pronouns changes spelling and sound in foreign language. The very thought is rearranged.

The following is the chart I used from the beginning. It remained on the board for the first few weeks and was regularly redrawn for review. The object pronouns are listed in the order they are placed before the verb.

The objects of column 1 and column 3 *cannot be used together* before a verb, that is, in the same sentence. Something else must be done. The pronouns of column 1 influence the past participle only when *they are direct objects,* that is, when there is no preposition involved. *Two pronouns* from this column (1) cannot be placed before a verb at the same time.

me	=	me, myself, or to or for me or myself.
te	=	thee, thyself, or to or for thyself or thee.
se	=	himself, herself, oneself, itself, or to or for himself, herself, oneself, itself (never *him* or *her*).
nous	=	us, ourselves, or to or for ourselves or us.
vous	=	you, yourself, yourselves, or to or for yourself or yourselves or you.
se	=	themselves or to or for themselves (never them).

Order of Placement of Pronoun Objects before Verbs

me te se	le la	lui	y	en
nous vous se	les	leur	y	(de) en
May be *direct* or *indirect* objects. When indirect, the prepositions *à* or *pour* are involved; no agreement of past participle.	Always *direct;* no preposition; for people or things.	Always *indirect.* Prepositions *à* or *pour;* used for people.	Always *indirect.* Prepositions *à* and all prepositions of place: *en, dans, devant,* etc.; used only for places or things, *never for people.*	*Indirect for things;* used for people in groups. The preposition *de* is involved or understood Required in partitive construction.

3. *The teaching of agreement of past participles with a preceding direct object must be begun at the same time as the lesson on their placement.* The acquisition of the principles of the placement of object pronouns and the agreement of past participles are *formidable barriers* between the structure of English and French. *Constant attention* to these barriers will bring early and rewarding results in comprehension of the oral and the written word. Examples should appear on every test and quiz a teacher gives. They should be often reinforced on a verb quiz after the first month at level one and at all subsequent levels as well.

The text will not present them early enough to allow a student to acquire them the first year. Ignore the texts and teach the language. When the students reach the unit or chapter where object pronouns and agreement of past participles are presented as grammatical principles, they will feel comfortable and recognize them as old friends.

A text should not be increasingly difficult, but increasingly simple as the students progress. Why? Because we should give them the "Big Picture" early, after which we work on the barriers daily in oral and written work.

Here are some basic rules of agreement of past participles that may help you. There are many exceptions to the general rule and many verbs whose past participles are invariable. For complete information, consult *Dictionnaire des Difficultés de la Langue Française*, par Adolphe V. Thomas (see Reference Guides in this chapter for a complete reference to this dictionary). The following rules are used by permission of this publisher.

1. Participe passé employé sans auxiliaire.
   a. Le participe passé employé sans auxiliaire s'accorde comme un simple adjectif (avec le nom ou le pronom auquel il se rapporte): Une feuille jaunie. Des bijoux cachés. Une page vite lue. Assise à l'ombre, elle lisait. Grisée d'air pur, survolant la plaine alourdie de chaleur, l'alouette chante à plein gosier. Frappées par cette nouvelle imprevue, elles tombèrent évanouies.

Cas Particuliers

   b. *Sont invariables et considerés comme formes figées les participes approuvé, lu et vu lorsqu'ils sont employés seuls.*
   c. Sont également invariables les participes suivants lorsqu'ils sont placés immédiatement avant le nom précédé ou non d'un article ou d'un déterminatif: *approuvé, attendu, certifié, communiqué, entendu, excepté, ôté, ouï, passé, lu, reçu, supposé, vu* (v. ces mots à leur ordre alphabétique): Attendu les événements. Nous vous remettons la totalité de votre commande, excepté les denrées perissables. Passé trois semaines, j'aviserai le propriétaire.
   A cette liste, on ajoutera les locutions et expressions suivantes, dans lesquelles entre un participe: *non compris, y compris, étant donné, excepté que,* etc. (v. ces mots): Il y avait douze présents, non compris les femmes. Etant donné les circonstances, on lui pardonnera sa faute.
   d. Si ces participes *sont placés après le nom auquel ils se rapportent, ils reprennent leur fonction d'adjectifs et s'accordent:* Les événements attendus se présentèrent ce jour-là. Les denrées perissables ex-

ceptées, nous vous remettons la totalité de votre commande. Il y a trois semaines passées, j'avisai le propriétaire. Il y avait douze présénts, les femmes non comprises. Les épreuves ci-incluses sont celles de votre dernier papier.

2. Participe passé des verbes conjugués avec l'auxiliare "être."

Le participe passé des verbes conjugués avec être s'accorde en genre et en nombre avec le sujet du verbe: Les feuilles sont jaunies. Les bijoux ont été cachés. Plusieurs pages avaient été lues. Vous êtes trempés de sueur.

a. *A noter que cette règle n'est pas applicable aux participes passés des verbes pronominaux dans lesquels le pronom réfléchi a la fonction de complément d'attribution, parce que, dans la conjugaison de ces verbes, être est mis généralement pour avoir:* Elles se sont accordées sur ce point (c'est-à-dire elles ont accordé elles). Elles se sont accordé un répit (elles ont accordé un répit à elles). *[My note: This verbal trap should be taught when pronoun objects are begun. American texts overlook this too often. It is not a difficult concept. Teach it early.]*

b. *Voir aussi, plus loin, participe passé des verbes pronominaux et participe passé des verbes impersonnels ou des verbes employés impersonnellement.* Si le sujet nous ou vous ne désigne qu'une seule et même personne, le singulier est de rigueur: Nous sommes persuadé (en parlant de soi) de la perfection de cet appareil que nous avons construit de nos propres mains. Vous êtes, monsieur le Président, estimé de tous. Nous, Préfet des Vosges, assuré de l'appui du Conseil général . . .

3. Participe passé des verbes conjugués avec l'auxiliaire "avoir."

a. Le participe passé des verbes conjugués avec avoir s'accorde en genre et en nombre avec le complément d'objet direct lorsque celui-ci précède le participe. Il reste invariable: 1° si le verbe n'a pas de complément d'objet direct; 2° si ce complément suit le participe.

Ainsi, on écrira: Les jouets que nous avons achetés (nous avons acheté quoi? *que,* mis pour jouets: le complément d'objet direct précède le participe passé). Quelles pages avez-vous lues? Les lettres que je vous ai écrites, les avez-vous reçues?

Mais le participe reste invariable dans: Ils ont chanté (pas de complément d'objet direct). Ils ont chanté hier soir (id.) Ils ont chanté sans conviction (id.) De même dans: Nous avons acheté des jouets *(le complément d'objet direct est placé après le participe passé).*

b. *(La recherche du complément "objet direct est indispensable pour déterminer l'accord du participe passé des verbes conjugués avec avoir."* Se rappeler que le complément d'objet direct qui précède le participe passé est le plus souvent l'un des pronoms me, te, se, le, la, l', les, nous, vous, ou encore le pronom relatif que. Il faut donc se rapporter à l'antécédent pour déterminer le genre et le nombre de celui-ci.)

c. Autres exemples avec participe passé précédé d'un complément d'objet direct: Ci-joint la lettre que tu as cherchée. Les épreuves que m'a fournies le photographe. Les ravages qu'ont faits les inondations dans ce pays. C'est une règle que lui avait transmise son père. On les a punis de prison. Quels services il m'a rendus! Que de bons conseils il m'a donnés! Combien de fautes il m'a épargnées! On vous a longtemps cherchées, mesdemoiselles.

En somme, le participe passé conjugué avec avoir s'accorde avec le complément d'objet direct quand, sous la dictée, on connaît ce complément au moment où l'on écrit le participe.

d. *Les verbes intransitifs, transitifs indirects et impersonnels n'ayant pas de complément d'objet direct, leur participe passé reste invariable:* Ces deux films nous ont plu (verbe transitif indirect). Les rivières ont débordé. Les beaux jours ont passé rapidement. Elle a pris les médicaments qu'il a fallu (verbe impersonnel). Les orages qu'il a fait ont gâché les récoltes. La famine qu'il y a eu dans cette région.

e. *Les participes passés couru, coûté, régné, valu, vécu (voir à l'infinitif de ces verbes) sont invariables au sens propre (ces verbes sont intransitifs), mais varient au sens figuré* (ils sont alors transitifs). La pluie n'a cessé de tomber pendant le quart d'heure que nous avons couru (sens propre). Les dangers que nous avons courus (sens figuré). Les trois millions qu'a coûté cette maison. Les mille efforts qu'a coûtés cette épreuve. La somme que cette bague a valu. Les joies que ces vacances m'ont values (m'ont procurées). Les soixante-quinze ans qu il a vécu. Les belles années qu il a vécues.

Pesé est toujours invariable au sens d' "avoir tel ou tel poids": Ce colis ne pèse plus les 5 kilos qu'il a pesé autrefois, mais Votre commande est prête, je l'ai pesée moi-même.

Cas Particuliers

On rencontre parfois l'invariabilité, qui est un reste de l'ancienne grammaire.

f. Participe passé suivi d'un infinitif. L'accord a lieu si le complément d'objet direct, étant placé avant le participe, *fait l'action exprimée par l'infinitif:* La femme que j'ai entendue chanter. Les fruits que j'ai vus tomber. (C'est la femme qui faisait l'action de chanter; ce sont les fruits qui tombaient. On pourrait dire, d'ailleurs: *La femme que j'ai entendue chantant. Les fruits que j'ai vus tombant.)* [My note: Do not use the last two in teaching *except to explain meaning.*]

g. Dans le cas contraire, le participe passé reste invariable: La chanson que j'ai entendu chanter. Les fruits que j'ai vu cueillir. Ces acteurs que j'ai vus jouer, je les ai entendu applaudir. (Ce n'était pas la chanson qui chantait, ni les fruits qui cueillaient, ni les acteurs qui applaudissaient, etc.; et l'on ne pourrait dire: La chanson que j'ai entendu chantant. Les fruits que j'ai vu cueillant. Les acteurs que j'ai entendu applaudissant [mais les spectateurs que j'ai entendus applaudissant].) Je les ai vus piller (pillant). Je les ai vu piller (être pillés). Les conseils que je leur ai entendu donner. La ville que j'ai vu bombarder. Et avec lui ou leur précédant le participe: Cette mélodie, je la lui ai entendu jouer. Les liqueurs que je leur ai vu verser.

Une autre façon de reconnaître l'invariabilité de ce genre de participe passé est de le faire suivre de la préposition *par* introduisant un complément indirect: La chanson que j'ai entendu chanter . . . par ma fiancée. Les fruits que j'ai vu cueillir . . . par le jardinier. Les acteurs que j'ai vu applaudir . . . par les spectateurs.

h. L'infinitif peut être sous-entendu, et alors le participe passé est toujours invariable (il s'agit surtout des participes cru, dû, pensé, permis, pu, voulu): Je lui ai rendu tous les services que j'ai pu, que j'ai dû, que j'ai voulu (sous-entendu lui rendre). Il a commis toutes les erreurs que son ignorance lui a permis (sous-entendu de faire).

i. Le participe passé reste invariable s'il est précédé de *que* et accompagné d'une proposition complétive construite à l'infinitif: J'ai pris la route qu'on m'a assuré être la plus courte. Les histoires qu'on avait cru être fausses. Ceux qu'on avait supposé avoir passé la frontière. Ces hommes qu'on a prétendu être des héros.

j. Le participe passé *fait* suivi d'un infinitif est toujours invariable: Ils ont fait pleurer les enfants. La famille de cette femme l'a fait interner. Elle s'est fait entendre malgré eux.

Voir aussi *laisser* ("Laissé" suivi d'un infinitif).

k. *Lorsqu'une préposition, à ou de (mais généralement à) est intercalée entre le participe et l'infinitif, l'accord se fait si le complément d'objet direct, placé avant, se rapporte au participe* (il faut pouvoir intercaler un complément d'objet direct entre le participe et la préposition): Les couteaux que j'ai portés à repasser (j'ai porté les couteaux à repasser). Ces habits, je les ai donnés à retoucher (j'ai donné ces habits à retoucher). "Quelle peine j'ai eue à le décider." Les gens qu'on a empêchés de partir.

Si le complément se rapporte à l'infinitif, le participe reste invariable: Les contrées qu'ils ont eu à explorer (ils n'ont pas eu ces contrées, ils ont eu à les explorer). Les sommes qu'ils ont eu à verser. Les injures qu'il a eu à subir. Les personnes que j'ai appris à aimer. Pères que les fils ont aidé à venger. Les obstacles qu'on lui a donné à vaincre.

Parfois, la distinction est difficile, et il semble indifférent de faire ou non l'accord: La fable qu'il a eue à réciter (il a eu la fable à réciter) ou La fable qu'il a eu à réciter (il a eu à réciter la fable).

Participes passés invariables:

Sont toujours invariables les participes passés des verbes intransitifs et transitifs indirects (puisque ces verbes ne peuvent avoir de complément d'objet direct) et des verbes impersonnels.

Voici une liste de ces participes passés qui, *employés avec avoir,* sont toujours invariables:

abondé
accédé
afflué
agi
agioté
agonisé
appartenu
avocassé
babillé
badaudé
badiné
baguenaudé
balivterné
banqueté
batifolé
bavardé
beuglé
boité
bondi
bouquiné
boursicoté
bramé
brigandé
brillé
bronché
buvoté
cabriolé
cadré
caracolé
cessé
chancelé
cheminé
circulé
clabaudé
clignoté
coassé
coexisté
coïncidé
commercé
comparu
compati
complu
concouru
condescendu
connivé

contrevenu
contribué
conversé
convolé
coopéré
coqueliné
correspondu
croassé
croûté
culminé
daigné
découché
dégoutté
déjeuné
démérité
démordu
déplu
dérogé
détoné
détonné
devisé
dîné
discordé
discouru
disparu
divagué
dogmatisé
dormi
douté
duré
égoïsé
endêvé
entre-nui
erré
eternué
étincelé
excellé
excipé
faibli
failli
fainéanté
fallu
ferraillé
finassé
flamboyé

flâné
flotté
foisonné
folâtré
folichonné
fourmillé
fraternisé
frémi
frétillé
frissonné
fructifié
geint
gémi
giboyé
godaillé
gravité
grelotté
grimacé
grisonné
grogné
guerroyé
hâblé
henni
herborisé
hésité
influé
insisté
intercédé
jaboté
jailli
jasé
jeûné
joui
jouté
lambiné
langui
larmoyé
lésiné
louvoyé
lui
lutté
maraudé
marché
marmitonné
médit

menti
mésarrivé
mésusé
miaulé
monopolé
mugi
musé
nagé
nasillé
navigué
neigé
niaisé
nigaudé
nui
obtempéré

obvié
officié
opiné
opté
oscillé
pactisé
pâli
paperassé
parlementé
participé
pataugé
pâti
patienté
péché
péri

périclité
péroré
persévéré
persisté
pesté
pétillé
philosophé
piaulé
pindarisé
pionné
piraté
pirouetté
pivoté
pleurniché
plu (plaire)

[My note: Some of these past participles are invariable even with être, *they are always intransitive such as:* se pouvoir, se rire, se plaire, se succéder, se nuire, pouvoir, *etc.]*

plu (pleuvoir)
politiqué
pouffé
pouliné
préexisté
préludé
préopiné
procédé
profité
progressé
prospéré
pu (pouvoir)
pué
pullulé
raccouru
radoté
raffolé
râlé
ramagé
rampé
réagi
récriminé
regimbé
regorgé
rejailli

relui
remédié
renâclé
reparu
reposé (repos)
résidé
résisté
résonné
resplendi
ressemblé
retenti
rétrogradé
ri
ricané
rivalisé
rôdé
ronflé
rougi
roupillé
rugi
ruisselé
rusé
sautillé
scintillé
séjourné

semblé
sévi
siégé
soixanté
sombré
sommeillé
soupé
sourcillé
souri
subsisté
subvenu
succédé
succombé
sué
suffi
surgi
surnagé
survécu
sympathisé
tablé
tâché
tardé
tatillonné
tâtonné
tempêté

temporisé	trépigné	venté
tergiversé	trimé	verbalisé
testé	trinqué	verbiagé
tonné	triomphé	verdoyé
topé	trôné	vétillé
tournoyé	trotté	vibré
toussé	trottiné	viré
transigé	valsé	vivoté
trébuché	valu (avoir valeur)	vogué
tremblé	vaqué	volé (dans l'air)
trembloté	végété	voyagé

4. Participe passé des verbes pronominaux.

a.   Les verbes pronominaux se conjuguent toujours avec être aux temps composés: Je me suis repenti. *Ils se sont lavé les mains mais ils se sont lavés.* Elles se sont battues dans la cour.

Verbes pronominaux proprement dits (ou verbes essentiellement pronominaux). Le participe passé des verbes pronominaux proprement dits (c'est-à-dire de *ceux qui n'existent que sous la forme pronominale,* comme *s'envoler, s'ingénier, se repentir, etc.*) s'accorde en genre et en nombre avec le sujet du verbe: Les serins se sont envolés. Aussi les municipalités se sont-elles ingéniées à en réduire les frais. Elles s'en sont repenties le lendemain. (*Exception: s'arroger,* dont le participe passé s'accorde avec le complément d'objet direct si celui-ci est placé avant, et reste invariable dans le cas contraire: Les droits qu'ils se sont arrogés. Ils se sont arrogé des droits.)

Liste des verbes pronominaux proprement dits: (Their infinitive appears *always* with *se.*)

[My note: The verbs of high usage on this list are in italics and therefore must be taught early.]

s'absenter	*s'ébattre*	*s'éprendre*
s'abstenir	*s'ébrouer*	s'esclaffer
s'accouder	*s'écrier*	*s'évader*
s'accroupir	*s'écrouler*	*s'évanouir*
s'acheminer	*s'efforcer*	s'évertuer
s'adonner	*s'élancer*	s'exclamer
s'agenouiller	*s'emparer*	s'extasier
se blottir	*s'empresser*	*se fier*
se cabrer	*s'enfuir*	se formaliser
se dédire	s'enquérir	se gargariser
se démener	*s'entraider*	se gendarmer
se désister	*s'envoler*	s'immiscer

251

s'infiltrer	se prosterner	*se réfugier*
s'ingénier	se ratatiner	se renfrogner
s'ingérer	*se raviser*	se rengorger
se méfier	*se rebeller*	*se repentir*
se méprendre	se rebéquer	*se soucier*
se moquer	se rebiffer	*se souvenir*
s'obstiner	*se récrier*	*se suicider*
s'opiniâtrer	*se recroqueviller*	se targuer
se parjurer		

Le participe passé des verbes qui ne peuvent avoir de complément d'objet direct reste invariable: Ils se sont ri de ma faiblesse. Ils se sont nui. Elle s'est plu à le tourmenter. Les fêtes se sont succédé jusqu'au lendemain. Que d'hommes se sont craints, déplu, détestés, haïs, menti, trompés, nui! (Ils ont craint eux. . . déplu à eux . . .)

[My note: These verbs can never have a direct object, therefore always intransitive.]

Il en est ainsi de:

se complaire	se nuire	se sourire
se convenir	se parler	se succéder
se déplaire	se plaire	se suffire
s'entre-nuire	se ressembler	se survivre
se mentir	se rire	

5. *Participe passé d'un verbe pronominal suivi d'un infinitif. Le participe passé de ce verbe s'accorde comme le participe passé du verbe simple* (voir plus haut *Participe passé suivi d'un infinitif*): Ils se sont vu jeter à la porte (ce n'est pas eux qui faisaient l'action: ils ont été jetés à la porte par quelqu'un). Ils se sont vus mourir (c'est eux qui mouraient: ils se sont vus mourant). Elle s'est laissé séduire (elle s'est laissée mourir de faim (c'est elle qui mourait).

A noter que le participe passé du verbe faire ou se faire est toujours invariable devant un infinitif: Il les a fait périr. Ils se sont fait entendre malgré lui. Elle s'est fait faire une belle robe.

6. Participe passé des verbes impersonnels ou des verbes employés impersonnellement.

Le participe passé des verbes impersonnels ou des verbes employés inpersonnellement est toujours invariable: Je suis resté chez moi les trois jours *qu'il a plu.* La révolution qu'*il y a eu* dans ce pays a causé bien des malheurs. Les grands froids qu'il a fait cette année. Quelle patience il a fallu pour effectuer ce travail! Il lui est arrivé une fâcheuse histoire.

7. Accord de "laissé" suivi d'un infinitif.

La tendance est pour l'invariabilité du participe passé *laissé* suivi d'un infinitif, que le sens soit actif ou passif: Ils se sont laissé battre. Je les ai laissé faire. Elle s'est laissé aller à la frapper. Toutes les heures que j'ai laissé choir dans l'infini (G. Duhamel, *la Pierre d'Horeb*, 218). Cette "rivière basse" . . . s'est laissé gagner par les arbres fruitiers (D. Faucher, *La France*, I, 460).

Dans ce cas, laissé est considéré comme formant avec l'infinitif une locution verbale. *Toutefois, il n'est pas interdit, il est même conseillé de faire suivre à laissé (pronominal ou non) la règle des autres participes suivis d'un infinitif:* Je les ai laissés s'enfuir. Les enfants se sont laissés tomber (c'est eux qui tombaient). Elle s'est laissée mourir. Elle s'est laissé séduire (ce n'est pas elle qui séduisait, elle était séduite par quelqu'un; invariable) [M. Catel, *Traité du participe passé*, 56]. Comment pouvaient-ils s'être laissé surprendre (ce n'est pas eux qui surprenaient, ils étaient surpris par quelqu'un).

Prépositions: The Unexplainable Idiom of All Languages

I am writing of the preposition after a conjugated verb followed by an infinitive as well as the peculiarity of direct and indirect objects. This preposition barrier, having no set rules to explain and to guide, will not fall because a teacher does not confront it and is unwilling to devise methods to *teach* it. The barrier remains and cannot be easily absorbed in an English-speaking society. Voltaire, after more than two years of his forced exile in England, continued to write and to say, obey *to* someone or something when using English, in spite of his fluency in this tongue.

This roadblock to correct speech and clarity of meaning will shrink to pebble proportion if the teacher will begin the first year and continue with diligence and persistence in teaching it.

What is a teacher to do about prepositions?

1. Go through your text noting all verbs and the prepositions, or lack of same, with *each verbal locution*. The text may never give you any idea of a list. Make one for yourself. A list with an infinitive followed by the correct preposition when an infinitive

follows the conjugated verb is not good enough. Construct sentences. Thus, you have the whole picture again.

2. Construct another list of verbs not followed by a preposition before the infinitive that follows.

3. Write your own oral quick-change drills and regularly have oral drills the last five minutes of class for a week or two. Regularly review these orally at all levels.

4. Construct exams with blanks for the prepositions or their lack. Always correct them orally as well as on the written page.

5. Drill relentlessly all year, every year. Five-minute drills at the end of class are a marvelous exercise. This can be downright invigorating if approached with this attitude: "Do you know whether it is *à* or *de* or nothing?" I shall never forget the answer of Madame Houïs at the Sorbonne when I asked why it must be: "on exige quelque chose de quelqu'un" and not "à quelqu'un." (One requires something of someone.) This is the usual preposition *(à)* when an object of person and an object of thing are involved with the same verb at the same time.

The unsmiling gaze that she leveled at me with the tone (that meant this is the end of the discussion) and her reply, "Parce que" (because) have not dimmed with the years. I, too, learned to say "parce que." It is the only answer to the preposition.

Sample Preposition Test

Donner la préposition convenable, s'il en faut une:

1. Il y a des gens qui n'ont de leur fortune que la crainte _____ la perdre.
2. Pressez le bouton _____ appeler l'hôtesse.
3. Il n'est pas étrange _____ trouver des chameaux dans le désert.
4. _____ vrai dire, je lui en sais bon gré.
5. Sa blessure le faisait cruellement _____ souffrir.
6. Tâchons _____ ne plus le faire.
7. Votre agent de voyage vous aidera _____ organiser des vacances économiques.

8. Qu'il est doux _____ plaindre le sort d'un ennemi quand il n'est plus _____ craindre.
9. Ne vaut-il pas mieux créer que _____ détruire?
10. _____ remplissant la cruche, il l'a renversée.
11. Ce pauvre garcon écrit _____ faire pitié.
12. On n'a pas besoin _____ dormir _____ rêver.
13. Cette compagnie est fière _____ avoir été la première _____ inaugurer ce service.
14. C'est la meilleure route _____ suivre.
15. Elle lui a demandé _____ ne rien laisser en désordre.
16. _____ s' être arrangé les cheveux, elle est partie.
17. Nous allions trop vite _____ pouvoir nous arrêter.
18. Etiez-vous le seul _____ remarquer l'éclipse?
19. Sera-t-il possible _____ forcer cette serrure?
20. Un levier vous permettra _____ régler votre fauteuil de la façon que vous voulez _____ vous reposer le plus agréablement possible.
21. Aurons-nous le plaisir _____ vous voir à la réception?
22. Il est temps _____ commencer _____ réflechir aux responsabilités que nous allons bientôt _____ devoir _____ supporter.
23. Je crois qu'il est assez fort _____ monter les valises.
24. C'est une personne _____ éviter.
25. La politique est l'art _____ empêcher les gens _____ se mêler de ce qui les regarde.
26. Il faut des raisons _____ parler, mais il n'en faut pas _____ se taire.
27. Vous dansez _____ ravir, mademoiselle.
28. Il ne peut guère _____ voir depuis qu'il fait des mots croisés jour et nuit.
29. Nous aimons mieux faire face au danger que _____ ne pas le voir.
30. Je me presse _____ rire de tout, de peur _____ être obligé _____ en pleurer.
31. Je vous dois _____ vous dire la vérité.

Relative Pronouns

Relative pronouns pose few problems *except with* dont. *Do not neglect this when* que *and* qui *are introduced.*

Teach your students that "dont" may be translated as "whose," but the French do not think "whose" but "of whom" or "of which." This will help students recognize that there is the hidden preposition *de* in *dont.*

The Partitive

The partitive always poses problems unless the French *thought pattern* is explained. In France one buys *some* bread (du pain), not all of the bread. Others buy some bread, too, "on achète du pain" (one buys some bread), "on mange du pain" (one eats some bread).

I found it helpful to explain that *un* or *une* do not translate well as *a* or *an*. Help your students to think of *un* or *une, as* "one," a number in a series of many. This will help them to understand the partitive.

You will devise your own methods for teaching grammar. Try to remember that the barriers must receive special and continued emphasis until thought patterns are constructed in the foreign language. Continued use and regular drill throughout the language study will make the language part of your students forever. Do not become weary with repetition. It is the very foundation of language acquisition. Be a good model. Imaginative teachers will devise additional methods to enlarge the above.

Vocabulary

Vocabulary is more easily learned by teaching:

1. *Contrasts*
   mince (thin)   épais (thick)

2. *Related words*
   épouser (to espouse)   époux (husband)   épouse (wife)
   prouver (to prove)   la preuve (proof)
   débiliter   affaiblir (to render feeble)
   (débiliter and affaiblir, synonyms but with nuance of difference)
   débris   morceau, ruine
   décamper   partir

3. *Apparent synonyms*

The following verbs are the same (to know) in English but *not* in French.

savoir (to know)	*connaître* (to know)
(as a result of having	(as a result of having seen
learned something)	someone or something)

Carefully contrast everything, particularly *savoir* and *connaître*, noting the differences.

Contrast these adverbs.
davantage (more)   *plus* (more)

Students can guess the meaning of many words that resemble English. Remember, 40 percent of English originates in French.

Whenever vocabulary is taught, it must be in the context of the sentence structure for it to be fully understood and remembered. The two above examples are especially notable.

Reference Guides

I recommend the following books to help you with style and vocabulary and also to increase your skill and knowledge of the language. These books are readily available in any *large foreign language* bookstore. Some may have to be ordered to be shipped from France.

Bailly, René. *Dictionnaire des synonymes de la langue française.* Paris: Librarie Larousse, 1947.

Blume, Eli. *Workbook in French Three Years.* New York: Amsco School Publications, Inc., regularly revised. (Levels I, II, III, and perhaps Cours Supérieur may be found in a good foreign language bookstore. Otherwise, they must be ordered from the publisher: Amsco School Publications, Inc., 315 Hudson Street, New York, NY 10013.)

Castarede, J. *A Complete Treatise on the Conjugation of French Verbs.* New York: David McKay Company, Inc., 1976.

Grevisse, Maurice. *Le bon usage: Grammaire française avec des remarques sur la langue française d' aujourd' hui.* Gembloux, Belgique [Belgium]: Editions J. Duculot, S.A., 1964.

_____. *Nouveaux exercices français.* Gembloux, Belgique [Belgium]: Editions J. Duculot, S.A., 1969. (There is a new edition.)

_____. *Nouveaux exercices français: Livre du mMaître.* Gembloux, Belgique [Belgium]: Editions J. Duculot, S.A., 1969. (There is a new edition.)

Lasserre, E. *Est-ce à ou de?* Lausanne, Suisse [Switzerland]: Librarie Payot, 1962. (This is a small pocket book.)

Legrand, E. *Méthode de stylistique française.* Paris: J. de Gigord, 1973. (Available from a good foreign language importer of French publications.)

_____. *Stylistique française: Livre du maître.* Paris: J. de Gigord, 1968.

Phyllides, George S. *College Entrance Review in Advanced French.* Cambridge, Massachusetts: Educators Publishing Service, Inc., 1983. (Must be ordered from publisher.)

Thomas, Adolphe V. *Dictionnaire des difficultés de la langue française.* Paris: Librarie Larousse, 1947.

Sample Tests

A.   Ecrire la préposition convenable, s'il en faut une:
1.   C'est impossible _____ comprendre.
2.   Il n'est pas nécessaire _____ fumer.
3.   Pourquoi hésitez-vous _____ me répondre?
4.   Elle a promis _____ ne pas gâter notre plaisir.
5.   _____ vendant les bijoux, il a gagné beacoup d'argent.
6.   Voilà un magasin _____ louer.
7.   Vous avez l'air _____ vous ennuyer.
8.   Je l'ai prié _____ me rendre un service.
9.   _____ réussir, il faut travailler dur.
10.   Il lui a demandé _____ baisser la voix.
11.   Ce savant va _____ étudier les virus des animaux domestiques.
12.   Vous amusez-vous _____ écouter la bonne musique?
13.   S'est-il souvenu _____ lui envoyer la carte?
14.   Je me suis frotté les mains _____ me chauffer.
15.   L'aviateur espérait _____ accomplir la mission avec succès.
16.   Il est bon _____ savoir plusieurs langues.
17.   La pluie m'a empêché _____ partir.
18.   J'essaie _____ travailler dans une pièce tranquille, loin du bruit.
19.   Elle était enchantée _____ faire sa connaissance.
20.   Il vaut mieux _____ prendre le métro.

Add your own sentences using verbs *pouvoir, désirer, faire, préférer, falloir, vouloir, valoir,* and *devoir,* which take no preposition. (*Devoir* takes *de* when it means I owe it to you to do something or "se devoir de faire quelque chose," to owe something to oneself. *Dû* would then be invariable.)

B. Ecrire le pronom qui manque:
1. Qui étudie le russe? Les meilleurs éléves _____ étudient.
2. Etant fatiguée, elle _____ est assise sur le canapé.
3. Est-il content de ces cravates? Oui, il _____ est très content.
4. Où sont les fourchettes? _____ voilà.
5. Je ne vais pas à la campagne aujourd'hui. Il _____ fait trop froid.
6. Ce thé vient-il de Chine? Oui, il _____ vient.
7. Dépêche _____, Bernard, nous devons partir tout de suite.
8. Où vous êtes-vous promené? Je _____ suis promené autour du lac.
9. Vous servez-vous du Guide Michelin? Oui, nous _____ servons.
10. Nous avez-vous reconnus? Non, je ne _____ ai pas reconnus.
11. Donnez-moi du boeuf. Combien _____ voulez-vous?
12. Si vous retrouvez mon crayon, gardez-_____.
13. Seront-ils chez eux ce soir? Oui, ils _____ seront.
14. Est-ce que tu m'appelles, maman? Non, je ne _____ appelle pas.
15. Obéit-il à ses parents? Bien entendu, il _____ obéit.
16. Obéit-il aux règlements? Oui, il _____ obéit.

Brain Teasers

(Consulter les livres indiqués pour trouver le pourquoi de l'accord du participate passé [ou les passages cités dans mon livre].)

[My note: Gens has two genders. This depends upon the placement of the adjective.]

Mon beau village

J'aime ce coin de terre où je suis né; j'aime les visages familiers de ces bonnes gens que j'ai vus, depuis mon enfance, vivre ici cette vie simple qu'ils y ont toujours vécue. Nous sommes, eux et moi, comme d'une même famille. De nombreux événements se sont succédé où nous avons été mêlés et où je retrouve les joies et les malheurs que nous avons éprouvés ensemble.

Des ancêtres communs ont passé là comme nous y passons. Ils se sont survécu en nous; les usages et les traditions que nous sommes plu à suivre, ce sont eux qui nous les ont laissés avec les souvenirs et les croyances qu'ils nous ont légués. Nous labourons les champs qu'ils ont labourés, les maisons qu'ils ont bâties nous abritent; voici les arbres qu'ils ont plantés, voici l'église où ils se sont recueillis, et voici le cimetière où notre piété filiale les a religieusement couchés.

Reprinted by permission of the publisher from Maurice Grevisse, *Nouveaux exercices français* (Gembloux, Belgique [Belgium]: Editions J. Duculot, S.A., 1969), 282.

Why the agreement of the past participle or lack of agreement?

Joies du travail

Sans doute il est des travaux pénibles, mais la joie de la réussite n'a-t-elle pas compensé les douleurs que nos efforts nous ont coûtés et ne nous les a-t-elle pas fait oublier? Le savant se souveint-il encore des dangers qu'il a courus, des difficultés qu'il a rencontrées, des veilles qu'il a passées, lorsque la vérité s'est soudain révélée à son esprit? L'artiste pense-t-il encore aux tourments qu'il a subis, aux dépits que lui ont causés ses échecs, aux angoisses qu'il a eprouvées quand enfin s'est dressée devant lui l'oeuvre qu'il avait rêvée?

Oui, le travail nous rend au centuple les plaisirs que nous lui avons sacrifiés. Lorsque tous ces oisifs qu'on a vus languir d'ennui se seront fait une loi de travailler et qu'ils se seront donné de la peine, ils verront leur ennui se tourner en plaisir.

D'aprés E. Rayot, Leçons de morale pratique

Reprinted by permission of the publisher from Maurice Grevisse, *Nouveaux exercices français* (Gembloux, Belgique [Belgium]: Editions J. Duculot, S.A., 1969), 289.

Why the accord or lack of accord of the past participles?

Caution: This passage tests almost all the rules of the accord of the past participle. It was on an exam I wrote in France.

Les livres sont un capital inestimable. Que de travaux, que de re-cherches n'ont-ils pas coûtés! Ils ont attesté, quand nous les avons interrogés, que les vérités ne se sont fait jour que lentement, que bien souvent les erreurs qu'on a eu (ou eues) à déraciner ont reparu après qu'on les a eu extirpées. Oui, toutes les peines que se sont imposées leurs auteurs pour nous inculquer toutes ces vérités qu'ils ont creusées, rendues lumineuses et offertes à notre soif de savoir, valent bien que nous rendions aux livres, nous aussi, le culte que les esprits d'élite se sont toujours plu à leur rendre.

Dictée que j'ai dû faire en France.

Sentences to Consider on Agreement of Past Participle

1. Vu les difficultés du voyage, nous avons decidé d'ajourner la visite que nous vous avions promise.
2. Autant de démarches nous avons faites, autant de rebuffades nous avons essuyées.
3. Que d'injustices se sont commises que la justice humaine n'a pas punies!
4. Quel est le chasseur qui a tué tous les lièvres qu'il a courus?
5. La gloire est la dette de l'humanité envers le génie, c'est le prix des services qu'elle reconnaît en avoir reçus.
6. Nous avons survécu à trop d'arbres pour ne pas nous être aperçus que les sites meurent comme les hommes.
7. Des années entières s'étaient passées et je les avais vécues comme si mon oncle devait vivre éternellement.
8. Les deux femmes se rapprochaient à nouveau et reprenaient la vieille amitié qu'avaient liée leurs espérances communes.
9. Les visions qui s'étaient succédé pendant mon sommeil m'avaient réduit à un tel désespoir que je pouvais à peine parler.
10. C'était pour Jean, cette réflexion explicative, la seule qu'on eût jamais entendue sortir de sa bouche.
11. Elle s'était arrogé le droit de tout dire.

Reprinted by permission of the publisher from Maurice Grevisse, *Nouveaux exercices français* (Gembloux, Belgique [Belgium]: Editions J. Duculot, S.A., 1969), 288.

Used by permission of Editions Duculot S.A., Rue de la Posterie, Parc Industriel, 5800 Gembloux, Belgique.

16

Administration and Support Personnel

Administrators, Guidance Counselors, Custodial Workers, and Secretaries

Responsibility—Where Is It?

Teachers sometimes complain of all those listed in the title of this chapter, believing smugly that teachers are the *only* important people in the school equation. Some complaints are justified; we are all mortal. But the serious business of educating our young requires cooperation from everyone who is employed in a school system and paid by public funds. We all have a moral unwritten contract to teach in our sphere of responsibility.

All teaching does not transpire in classrooms. Budgets have to be calculated and submitted to those who control the educational purse—budgets for supplies and paper usage down to the last teacher. Costs of building maintenance, including heating, lighting, cleaning, and guarding premises, are mind-boggling in their intricacies. Salaries are simpler to calculate. "American taxpayers will invest $308 billion in education [in 1987–88] and 58 million students will return to public schools and colleges," according to a government report. Education Secretary William Bennett announced to the press that this exceeds the previous-year projection of $278.8 billion in costs. About 3.3 million people will be employed as teachers and another 3.5 million as administrative,

263

professional, and support staff at all levels. The increase in enrollment came from pre-primary and early elementary grades. This increase will gradually be reflected in higher enrollment in the upper levels through the mid-1990s.

Secretary Bennett concluded his remarks that "It's time we started getting a better return on our investment." In 1987–88 a record $4,538 was spent on each student in public and private elementary and secondary schools, which, all told, cost the public funds of states, counties, and cities $184 billion.

Those who are charged with receiving and disbursing these enormous sums (primarily teachers and administrators), even on a single-school basis, should be so conscious of the source of their funds (their own pockets) that waste would be diligently monitored and eliminated. It is easy to measure the amount and quality of the paper used, or the amount of heat and light needed, but it is not easy to measure the benefit that the last recipients, our students, receive from the outlay of public treasure these services require. We can and should at least try to measure the *results* of these millions spent for learning.

In the present media climate (the media can and do create a climate of thought), teachers seem to be the only ones being blamed for the educational mess our nation is in today. They say that it is teachers who are lavishly spending but not giving quality education. I do not agree. There is plenty of blame to go around: from systems overloaded in administrative and professional support personnel (who oftentimes overload classrooms to meet the resulting budget shortfalls), to teachers who don't teach, to custodial personnel who don't clean, to students who won't learn, to parents who think their children should receive grades not earned, to people who are not concerned because they have no children in school, and to the media who rarely find anything good to report. There is egg on the collective face of America and very few have any claim to a halo.

We have deluded ourselves with the idea that learning is nothing but fun and games—ten easy lessons to perfection, no sweat involved. Upon winning World War II, with all our death-creating hardware, servicemen returning by the millions opened our eyes to the lower standard of living of other nations and awakened in us an orgy of national pride in our premier place as a world power. We were the best. No other nation was on top of the mountain. *We became arrogant and intellectually slothful.*

A high school diploma became a *right. The responsibility part was forgotten. Standards were lowered.* This was all part of the societal push to make everyone equal in a society that seemed to have money to throw out the window for machines—in the homes and in the schools. Dress codes were abandoned; behavior deteriorated. The curriculum had to be "relevant," so the curriculum unraveled. Teachers had to "seize the learning moment," so they sometimes presided over "delicious rap sessions," where they let everything "hang out."

I remember listening to some of my colleagues and guidance personnel question the right of parents to know what was going on in and out of the classroom with their sons and daughters. Others gave as their opinion that the responsibility for grades rested solely on the student, not the teacher. And still others denied that either teachers or administrators necessarily had any responsibility to control abuse of drugs by students. The use and abuse of drugs, alcohol, and tobacco was monitored in rising or falling waves of diligence according to the mood. In my opinion this attitude reflects irresponsibility on the part of people who should have been models.

The media cameras hastened to the scene to glorify for our living rooms the "marvelous highs" and "delicious thrills" of "smoke-ins," public disrobing, sex on the grass, and takeovers of public buildings by the rebellious few. This media outpouring led too many of our people to question the very values of the society of man. They were duped by what they saw on the TV screen into believing that all teens were doing what the media cameras pictured.

This was, of course, a distortion. I lived through this dark age in our educational history and saw and fought the virus of irrational irresponsibility. I was not alone. The only forts I was able to hold were my classroom and my home (the home always being the last line of defense in any civilization). I had dedicated colleagues who held their high ground too. When springtime came, a few of us would ask each other: "Are you coming back next year?" Our answer during those trying years was always the same: "I don't know." We hoped for a change in the public permissiveness glorified by the media.

Administrative and guidance personnel received greater battering during this era if their standards remained high. They are always obliged to deal with four separate factions: parents, students, teachers, and their own superiors—not an easy task. A community expects a principal to be a lion in keeping "the lid on things," a lamb when it comes to according good grades, a warrior defending students from any intrusion of police and invasion of privacy, a forgiving savior for disruptive student behavior, and the paragon of gentility when confronted by a noisy protesting parent. Superiors sometimes expect principals to be academic spies on teachers and a financial wizard in calculating costs to the last ream of paper. Teachers expect principals to be staunch defenders regardless of what transpires in the classroom.

Guidance personnel are expected to be highly skilled advisors. They are caught between administrators and teachers, who often erroneously expect them to be the school's discipinarians also—the punishers. Punishment should never figure into the role of guidance counselors; in fact, punishment is utterly antithetical to the role of a guide or counselor.

Well-run schools will have defined the roles of administrators,

guidance personnel, and teachers. Fortunately, there are such schools and they existed even during the darkest years of the national search for self and direction. Islands of excellence continued all over America. Regrettably, they were not the majority. Public opinion has decreed otherwise. *Change* has been the watchword for *better.*

If excellence becomes the norm and not the exception, then the demand and the emotional support must rise and flow from the community into the schools that serve it. School staffs need much more than lots of money, good football teams, and large pep squads; they must also redirect themselves toward good scholarship.

School boards must be elected and terms of members limited. They should have their board of advisors and helpers staffed by those parents whose sons and daughters occupy the classrooms and those whose children are grown. They must bear the burden of employing teachers and administrators and guidance personnel.

The mix of persons at the administrative level must have a preponderance of people with *successful years spent in the classroom.* A Ph.D. does not a good administrator make, nor does a good athletic coach. These qualities do not exclude them either, of course. However, administrators should be, in every respect, superior people who can command respect for what they are without asking for it. They will recognize the necessity of *earning* this respect. They will invariably set the tone of the schools. They will be persuaders and counselors, but they will have high standards for themselves and for all those who are part of the educational process in their schools.

Teachers must give their unvarying support to such people in a task whose dimensions encompass every corner of the school and community. They must recognize the *need of teaching well.*

Guidance personnel must accept the necessity of cooperation with superiors, students, teachers, and parents and accept the heavy responsibility of guiding, *truly* guiding, and counseling all the above. Too often, guidance counselors hear only *complaints* from parents and students. People who occupy these positions must never forget that they rarely if ever hear good reports from parents and students. Therefore, guidance personnel should be obliged to return to the classroom at least part time every other year for up to ten years in order to keep their perspective.

Administrators, too, should *return to the classroom* every three or four years, at no reduction in pay, or at least teach one class every other year. Parents should be invited into the classroom now and then as observers and as teachers (if they have the skills). Any media person filled with teacher-bashing tendencies should be sent to classrooms loaded with every disruptive personality that can be found—and they should be held accountable for what they say and write. They, too, are teachers.

Every school should yearly award an array of medals to administrators, guidance personnel, teachers, cafeteria staff, secretaries, and custodial people. The jury for the awards should come from all of the above groups, the students, and the parents. When peers and colleagues can award each other accolades instead of destructive criticism, an academic climate of peace, respect, and cooperation will prevail and students and parents will inevitably be the beneficiaries. *Those involved in this process will want to excel.*

An acquaintance of mine who was a career Marine officer tells of attempting an experiment along these lines. Having despaired of the tendency in the military of teaching by finding fault, as the operations officer of a battalion landing team that was planning a full-dress practice amphibious assault (ship to shore with air support), he appealed to all the officers of the battalion and all supporting unit officers (which included representatives of all four armed services) to work very closely as a team. There was to be no faultfinding or backbiting. If an officer saw a shortcoming or mistake in the making on the part of another individual, staff, or unit, he was to tactfully and in confidence communicate to the officer responsible what he thought the shortcoming or mistake was. He was to do so as soon as possible with the mind to alleviating problems before they occurred or solving them before they had a serious effect. For the most part, all cooperated as requested with remarkable success.

Everyone engaged in the educational process should expect to be examined for the quality of performance. Teachers must be judged by the performance of their students by testing instruments of national standards. The classroom is the last area and the only area where learning can be partially measured. We must face this inevitable testing. We must be willing to be *accountable* for having taught something that produces results in our charges. I see no other avenue to a renaissance in scholarly discipline in the American public schools. There is no other solution for accounting for and measuring the value received for the public school dollar. But administrators, guidance personnel, and parents should be examined for the quality and quantity of their support for teachers who have the courage to maintain high academic standards for their students. *Cooperation is multilevel and can be nothing else.* American teenagers will automatically groan, complain, and resist higher standards. Progress is never made without resistance. There must be *none* in all those responsible for the educational process. Our charges will supply enough.

However, it is my peculiar belief from my worm's-eye view and experience that resistance to learning is taught and learned at entry levels in our school systems when eager, thirsty learners arrive in the educational mill to encounter classes in free sandbox and mind-numbing dullness, and not enough lengthy frontal attacks on breaking the code of the written language. *Our language must be taught well, early, consistently, and at every level by experts in language teaching.* Parents must teach and encourage the learning of the language by becoming involved themselves in the learning of their children. Family must be an extension of the school and school must be an extension of the family. (I am writing of teaching the native language, not a foreign idiom.) This may seem utopian to some, but I refuse to accept the idea that home and schools cannot fully cooperate. Where I have seen and experienced this total cooperation, I have witnessed miracles of learning and outstanding progress and achievement.

Responsible, discerning administrators I have known have, like the military, decorated their outstanding teachers, and, being intelligent as well as astute, they were able to take the credit for having chosen and supported outstanding and innovative teachers. They practiced what they advocated to their teachers: "Encourage your students." (I have also seen destroyers.)

Responsible guidance counselors who have truly advised and encouraged responsibility in their student charges never made class changes without consulting me and the parents and without seeking a reasonable and beneficial resolution of a problem for a student's welfare. They were not capricious in their judgement but reasoned and persuading. I salute those who behaved so responsibly. Such conditions do not always prevail, but my experience in many instances persuades me that my belief in total cooperation is not utopian. It needs to be tried everywhere.

Teachers who are experts in their field with proved track records need more courage to speak up and resist obvious breaches of professionalism and competence whenever they find it—particularly when it involves the unfair treatment of students or teachers.

One year the usual drive to bring student smoking under control was at high pitch (many years down the road from my legendary visit to the boys' restroom). I decided that the time had come to point out the unfairness and stupidity of this endeavor. I announced to my peers and superiors that I considered this drive against student smoking sheer idiocy since I needed a seeing-eye dog to get through the smoke-filled office of the disciplinary authority and into the equally smoky spaces of many of the offices of the guidance counselors. If they wanted to cut down on smoking, let them set the example. I told them that we occupied public property, which did not accord to teachers or to administrators the right to pollute the air that a majority of students and teachers respected enough to keep clean.

One year in a fit of budget cutting the superintendent of schools said to me, "You know, Madame, that a fifth year of French is exotic." I replied, "Sir, then twelve years of English study in an English-speaking society is idiotic. What have these English teachers been doing for twelve long years?" French V was not cut from the curriculum.

Rarely did I find an administrator who fully understood that the techniques of teaching a foreign language are different in some respects from other academic disciplines. Those who supported me did so on faith, which is the ultimate glue that will revive and renew our academic arena—faith in the future, faith in ourselves to improve, and faith in those who are willing to be held responsible and accountable.

Custodial staff is part of the title of this chapter. They are the unsung, undecorated people who line my memory. They kept my work area clean, moved cabinets, arrived earlier than usual to unlock school doors for a handful of teachers who kept unreasonable hours. I tried to show my thanks by never allowing my students to use the floor as a wastepaper basket and by regularly thanking them whenever I saw them. They were unfailingly courteous and helpful. They lined the hall to wish me a personal farewell the year I retired as we moved through the corridors in the graduating procession. They told me things wouldn't be the same. I see their faces still and feel as touched today by their sincerity as I was that evening.

The secretaries, the most underpaid and underappreciated of all support personnel, literally keep our schools from falling apart in a tidal wave of paper chaos. Their hours are longer, they have fewer breaks, and they bear more indignities from irritated superiors in our educational system than any others. I salute and thank them. They know the art of remaining calm in a whirlwind. May God bless them and accord them their pay. No other can.

Teachers should have a confidante who will listen to them and tell them the truth. Mine was the always the director of guidance. Guidance personnel, after all, hear most of the complaints. They should be trustworthy enough that they, too, can hear the truth about students as teachers see it. Keeping this confidante informed about all classroom procedures is a must. The director of guidance always justified my trust. All those I knew in this position were outstanding people of great integrity. I remember them with gratitude.

For all those engaged in the war on ignorance and the fine art of influencing our youth, I wish pleasant memories—when they have more time to reflect.

17

Retired Pay

At the end of every year, teachers confront agonizing decisions about the final grade for each student. Particularly agonizing is when the student's work is borderline between a "D" or an "F" since students receive credit on their permanent records even if they receive a "D," but no credit is given for an "F." It is easy to fall into the trap of intellectual conceit and to assume that the grades in a grade book measure all the learning that takes place in a year. At this time of year my vision always narrowed to view my own work, and despair often was the result. I hated the taste of failure that was mine if a student had persisted in doing nothing. I had to ask myself what will do the student the greatest good: a "D" the student knew was not merited, or an "F" that was a fair evaluation of the work or lack of work for the year. No "F's" in my grade book would make me feel even vaguely successful, but how I felt could not be part of the decision. I had to hope that the knowledge of earning and deserving the grade they received would be sweeter to students than a gift.

The awful grandeur of the idea of influencing for good the lives of my students always weighed heavily upon my mind when the end-of-the-year decisions had to be made. That mystical good would never be measurable and perhaps the results never seen, I reasoned in the early years of my teaching. I had to live on the faith I had in an idea of fairness and honesty.

Students very early returned to see me and report the events of their lives after high school. They were welcomed as my children and presented to the students of the class. I was always struck, however, with the realization that I could not always remember the final grade I had accorded to those students. The only thing I could remember well was the industry they had shown in studying. These guests would sometimes tell the class the grade they had received from me. I always protested that they were giving privileged information. Those who admitted to an "F" or a "D" actually seemed proud that I had not compromised my belief that something for nothing was unfair and demeaning to the receiver.

At Thanksgiving of my second year of teaching I received a telephone call from a former student then enrolled at the University of Mississippi. Kathy was a brilliant young lady, but her work did not glow in her class with me. She had *earned* a "D." She was calling for advice now and wanted to know if I thought she should major in French and Spanish and become a teacher. My quick response was, "Yes, Kathy, provided your goal is *mastery of your subject matter* and *dedication to teaching well.*" She began, but I did not hear from Kathy until the third quarter of her second year. The hour was late when she called. Kathy's thought evidently turned to me in the wee hours when sleep is troubled with unsolved problems. This time her situation was desperate. She had been dismissed from the University of Mississippi because she was caught sneaking into the dormitory via the window after curfew. I found it hard to believe that such a first offense would lead to dismissal, but I did not question her. I offered some supportive advice and a place to stay (she was in town) until she could make other arrangements. Times have changed, I understand, about living arrangements at many universities. Kathy did straighten out her life and was able to eventually enroll at Georgetown University (with no credit for previous work).

Another student comes to mind whose situation and behavior I remember vividly. Pat was in full rebellion at home. The War between the States was mild compared to what existed between Pat and her parents her senior year. Pat had joined the drug clique at school and her grades and choice of friends constantly troubled the home. Her unruly behavior caused trouble in the classroom as well. At Easter the crisis was upon us. Pat wanted to leave school early for the Easter break and was able to secure permission to do so in other classes. She met unbending opposition in her fourth-year French class. I had wanted to know what she was going to do with those extra days away from school. She was truthful. Then I posed a harder question: "Shall I dismiss all the other members of this class because you want to go to Carolina to waste your time on a beach with a bunch of teenagers who flock there to do drugs?"

Pat hardly hesitated before she shouted, "You mean you won't let me go?" My calm reply was, "I do not give you permission to go *early*. I cannot stop you from going."

Pat stalked from the room. She would not have waited for a note from me to the disciplinary principal. Her stay at the beach lengthened. She did not return to school except briefly. She did not graduate. Not long after, she returned to tell me that she was marrying a young man she had met on the beach. I wished her happiness and expressed my hope that she would never regret her decision.

A year later Pat knocked on my door during the class time of fourth-year French for seniors. She was without shoes, her clothes were dirty and ragged, her person unwashed. In her arms was her two-week-old daughter. I welcomed her warmly and invited her to speak to my class and to give the students any advice she might have. I held her daughter while she spoke with fervor and conviction: "Try not to make stupid mistakes. Listen to this old Dragon; she really does love you."

I had not expected this, but my students were impressed and thoughtful. Pat remained after class to tell me of her and her husband's struggle with earning a living. I asked her if she had used drugs during her pregnancy.

"Do you think I'm crazy? Of course not."

Two years later a different, cleaner Pat knocked on my door. Her daughter accompanied her. During this visit I learned that the husband had disappeared; peace had replaced warfare in the home to which she had returned and she had finished in night school the necessary courses for her high school diploma.

Pat and Kathy did not write letters, but their visits and telephone calls helped me feel less despairing each springtime as the eternal dilemma of teachers recurs: gift grade or the important lesson of teaching that we must discipline ourselves to receive earned rewards—otherwise there is no sweet savor in the remembrance of the doing.

Recognizing that we, as teachers, will never probe the depths of the soul and the ability to care in the young people we teach, we must, nevertheless, be content with orienting ourselves to teaching important lessons for life as well as the subject matter. Despair in the destiny of the human race will blind us to being firm in our moral responsibility to our charges. We must live on hope. We will never fully know or measure the ripples we may have caused in the lives of our students or whether we influenced them for good or whether we sank with only a small splash to the bottom of the pond of the mind.

The following letters, selected from many, give some evidence that I may have created a few ripples and probed some depths. I have many letters, but I had hundreds of students. How many remember me? Did I influence all of them for good? That will always be an enigma.

A few weeks ago I received a wedding invitation from two former students who are marrying each other. She is a practicing pediatrician and he is a hotel executive. He has his degree from Cornell University in Hotel Management. Incredibly, after many years, they still remembered me. Such invitations and letters warm me and sustain me in the belief that *loving my students* was the most important thing I did throughout my years of teaching. They surround my retired paycheck with the sweet incense of fond memories.

It is my hope that teachers who may read this book will be encouraged to renew their dedication to their students and to remain many years in the classroom.

* * *

November 1, 1961

Dear Mrs. Nelson,

My French course is very disturbing. I've discovered that the things that I was so cock-sure of after this summer I don't know! My mistakes are just plain dumb. I asked Dr. Susskind for help, and he's having me write little compositions which he is correcting. I've just lost interest in the course. It's partly because I haven't had enough time to put into it and it frustrates me to do a job only half way. I just can't seem to make time for anything. My Western Institutions mid-term was this morning; my English term paper is due on Monday, I have a tremendous French test next week and an oral report on Montaigne. I just turned in a Social Psychology paper, and the list runs on and on, but I don't mean to burden you. It's like being pulled in so many directions at once and you can only stretch so far.

The book in French that you gave me sits at home and I cry when I think of it. *La Peste* is only half finished, and I've read only a few of Rimbaud's poems from the book that I bought.

Virginia is too far to come home during the 3 full days of vacation that I have at Thanksgiving, but I hope to see you at Christmas time.

Soyez calme! Je ne vais pas me marier avant de finir le collège. Ayez de la patience pour moi. La Jeunesse est un temps plein de rêves.

Your days are so full, but please write to me when you can. I think of you often.

Love,
Bobbie

* * *

February 14, 1966

Dear Mrs. Nelson,

Jim's attitude toward school and his resulting failure in French has his father and me extremely distressed.

As we received *no* interim reports (due to Jim's failure to bring them home) we hoped this 9 week report card would reflect more effort and result in better grades. This is not the case; therefore, we believe it will be best for all concerned if Jim drops French II at this time and, if possible, enrolls again in French I.

I'm sure we could have benefitted from a conference with you before this half year became hopelessly lost, and I apologize for not eliciting your help. However, Jim has been less than honest about his progress in your class and we were led to believe he was doing better.

I'm calling Jim's counselor for advice on re-scheduling procedures. If you have any suggestions as to how to motivate Jim, we would certainly appreciate hearing them.

I am very sorry my son has wasted a semester of your time as well as his own. Thank you for your efforts.

E. K.

My note: Jim improved by doing two hours of French. He came to a French I and II and survived French II.

* * *

June 10, 1966

Dear Madame Nelson,

I am very sorry to hear you were ill this day. I came to school early in hopes that you would sign my yearbook and that we could say good-bye for the year.

At 8:05 A.M. we had homeroom and then a half hour later we reported to 4th period class. When I found that you were not there and that there was no substitute in the room I went outside to wait for the buses. Jackie O., Wendy, and I talked for maybe an hour or more. Subjects changed many times and we all agreed that we hoped you would feel better soon.

This has been quite a year for me and I have learned a lot. I have not succeeded as well in some of my classes as I would have liked to, but for some there is still another time. I do not know whether I would have preferred all my teachers to have been like you, yet I have been lucky in having at least one teacher a year who has been good for me. They have covered every field, elementary school (2 years), English, art, science, and now this year, French.

For me, French may never be a good subject, but its principles I can still learn and use. I have learned a necessary key to all work through respect. I have learned and must try to use the better rules of work that form a necessary and useful part of life. From these and other reasons, I can state that I have learned that self-determination and will-power are like a good general. He leads his men and forces them to do nothing he could not do himself. He puts all these "elements" to work in order to accomplish a goal or a job well done.

With many thanks for this year and hopes for the next, au revoir mon petit général.

Carol

* * *

August 9, 1966

Very dear Mary D.,

So much for the beginning. You know that you are that to me—very dear. Also, that this affinity and affection will remain even though more miles separate us one from the other. Strangely enough, when Bob received and accepted the call to Vanceboro, on July 31, my first thought was, "Oh, I won't be going to school with Mary D." and Bob's first remark was, "Honey, I know how much you are going to miss Mary D."

I have had a feeling all summer that something like this was going to happen. Of course, I hoped for it for Bob even while I wasn't looking forward to it for myself. Right after you left for France, we were invited down for the weekend. The following Sunday, the Church issued the call. We had been much taken with the people of the congregation, the little town, and, the proximity to the ocean which Bob so loves. During the following week, we spent many hours in prayer, meditation and discussion. We came to feel that we should go—even though formalities must be gone through, we had no doubt that the Church would call us. Thus, when it came, it was accepted. Last weekend, Patsy went down with us, and she was as pleased with the people and the town as were we. As she remarked, we had almost forgotten what fresh air smelled like and what garden-fresh food tasted like.

Don't faint, Mary D. Vanceboro is a "metropolis" of less than half the student body population of Fort Hunt High School. Except for Charlotte, Raleigh, Greensboro, Winston-Salem, and Asheville (and Wilmington), North Carolina is a state composed of small towns. Actually, the same can be said of Virginia too. Except for Atlanta, Louisville and Alexandria (and 3 1/2 years as a child in Tampa) I have lived in small towns of under 25,000. Most of them I have loved, too. I do not like the anonymity and the rush, rush, rush of truly urban life; of course, I must admit that I haven't been very anonymous around here, but I have been propelled along on the rush syndrome. Weighing the good and the bad, I'll take a town over a city any day. With transportation as it is, one can always go extra culture seeking. I didn't benefit much from all the advantages Washington has to offer because I was afraid to go over there!

So, the die is cast. On August 1, I went out to Fort Hunt to break the news to Mr. G. He was wonderfully understanding and told me that if we got back up this way there would always be a spot for me at Fort Hunt. Strange as it may seem, even in leaving I feel that we shall be back and that I shall be teaching again with you either at Fort Hunt or at West Springfield in two or three years. I wept copiously while we talked, and I kept talking about my association with you, Mary D., how very much it had meant to me personally, how much you had helped me professionally, what a fabulous person you are. He agreed with me wholeheartedly. I left, a sodden mass, and he walked with his arm around me out to my car. One very true thing he said was that I could feel so grief-stricken because I had put so much of myself into Fort Hunt, that I was leaving a part of myself here. He said that he has such a hard time trying to lead some new teachers into the realization that one gets out of teaching in proportion to what one puts into it—so many of them are interested in teaching to make car payments, etc. I couldn't tell anyone else goodbye. I had had it, emotionally.

In like respect, I believe it is fortunate for me that you are still in France. Were you here, naturally, I would come to see you to give you my news. And I would wail like a banshee, Mary D. The people I love, I love so wholeheartedly and I have to work always not to go to a like extreme with the people I do not "love." I just couldn't and wouldn't say "Goodbye" so I would have just spotted up your furniture with my tears. I shall try to behave better when I take this up to Howard. It's going to be terribly hard, even so, because I am fond of him. Shakespeare wasn't talking about me when he came out with "Parting is such sweet sorrow." All I can say is that I am forever grateful to have had the opportunity to know you and to become your friend. Moving away can't change that. It's continual history. Your kindness and generosity to me and to all of my family still leaves me at a loss for words to properly express my thankfulness and eternal indebtedness. My dear I told C. E. to try to keep you from unduly spinning your wheels, and to keep an eye on you for me. This she has promised to do for me. She admires and loves you too, Mary D., and she will be a good friend who is interested in ever becoming a better French teacher.

We shall leave either the 15th or 16th and I shall write you again before school starts. I shall be teaching remedial English in a special program sponsored by the government; though there is added grief because it isn't French, I have a satisfaction in realizing its great importance. I also feel lucky to have a position locally on such short notice. I'll study French like mad, and find a place to teach it another year.

Comme toujours,
M.

My note: Former colleague

* * *

le 12 septembre 1966

Chère Madame,

Hier soir j'ai essayé d'écrire à un ami en français. J'étais horrifiée de découvrir que j'avais oublié complètement le subjonctif! Le seul subjonctif qui restait dans ma tête était celui de l'espagnol!

Pouvez vous m'envoyer une liste des règles comme celle que vous nous donniez *autrefois* dans la classe de la cinquieme année? C'était une liste de quelques règles à propos de l'emploi du subjonctif. (Je l'ai perdue.)

Je pars pour Mt. Holyoke cette semaine, et mon adresse est.:

C. C.
Mount Holyoke College

* * *

October 17, 1966

(TELEGRAM)
Mrs. Mary D. Nelson,

NOUS ESPÉRONS QUE VOUS DEVIENDREZ MIEUX
Your Fourth Period Class

* * *

283

November 2, 1966

Dear Madame Nelson,

I am sure you must have many trying and frustrating days instilling French into your students, and especially working with a "goof-off" like Jay was. But you certainly did succeed somewhere along the way—his report just came today from Florida Southern College, and believe it or not, he had an "A" in French!

I don't know what he was doing during high school, but this is the best report I've seen in years—3 A's, 2 B's, and 1 C. I just hope he will keep it up and not backslide now.

So thank you for all you did for him; he always looked on you as a very good friend.

Sincerely,
Jane A.

* * *

October 1967
Radford College

Bonjour Mon professer,

I have a moment to write you, so I have decided to tell you a little bit about Radford College life. It's strange how just two years ago, you read us part of a letter sent to you by one of your former students. Now I am experiencing much of that life.

Because I heard college life was much different in comparison to high school, getting into the "groove," so to speak wasn't too hard. The heavy concentration of homework is more easily dealt with because of short school days. Monday, Wednesday, and Friday I have four classes (with a 3-hour break between the morning & afternoon sessions). On Tues. and Thurs. and Saturday I have only two classes, both before noon. As you can see, it can be "easy" as well as hard.

Testing doesn't come as often (my first series of tests was 5 weeks after classes began). In many instances, material covered on each test will not be *dealt with again on a final*. This is good, since so much extra reading is given other than the text. The freshmen here really have to work, as the first year contains few, if any, elective courses. My courses for the fall quarter are history, typing, business introduction, swimming, math and English.

Vacations, weekend trips and homecomings are really paramount here. Some kids have little chance of getting home on weekends unless they wish to skip part of Friday and Saturday classes. I can leave the evening of the 22nd of Nov. for Thanksgiving and again the 9th of Dec.

for Christmas. Christmas vacations, college style, are really something. We have most of a month free!

I hope the classes this year are going well for you. If you wish to write to me, this is my address:

P.O. Box 1856
Radford College Station
Radford, Virginia 24141

Sincerely (votre étudiante),
C. P.

* * *

May 24, 1968

Dear Madame Nelson,

Now that school is almost over and graduation is approaching, I have been reflecting over my high school days. I wanted to thank you for being my teacher. I just wanted you to know that you taught me a bit more than whatever French rubbed off on me during my days in your class. It is hard to define precisely what I learned, but I like to think it might have been a little responsibility and maturity.

I can well appreciate those hours I fretted, and regret the ones I frittered away in your class, which, in my case, I think was an education in itself. You were right, all along, and I did make it to college. I was accepted to the University of Virginia, but I chose Oregon State University and will be entering that school in the fall.

Last summer my family moved out here to California. I was fortunate enough to finish out my high school days at one of the better schools in the state. I've been doing well and, of course, I'm looking forward to graduation.

I'm certain that you've enjoyed another illustrious year as the "vieille dragon" of Fort Hunt. Seriously, I hope that it has been another great year for you. In any case, Madame Nelson, I felt as though I should tell you that I truly regard your French class as the most rewarding and beneficial of my four years of high school and I sincerely want to thank you for the experience!

Sincerely,
C. M.

My note: The year spent with me he complained that I expected too much work for him to earn a B. He received a C and claimed a C would keep him out of a university.

285

* * *

September 17, 1968
Florida State University

Chère Madame,

I know you are mentally kicking me for writing in English, but I haven't much time. I just wanted to let you know that I have just completed the Florida State University Advanced French Exam and *I could not have taken an easier test. I thought I was in French II again.* Now I am reassured that your class was worth every minute of burning flames from "la vieille dragonne." I am so thankful that I was fortunate enough to have you both for the very important French II and the strenuous mental exercise of French IV. Please let your classes know that you, "la vieille dragonne," are worth every minute. And don't let them become discouraged. Right now I am scheduled for French 301—Introduction to French Literature—a course usually followed by sophomores and juniors, and I plan to minor in French. Thank you again.

M. H., 1968 (a freshman)

P.S.   Vive la vieille dragonne, Le Cid, et Walter Schnaffs!!

P.S. Box 62, Magnolia Hall
Florida State University
Tallahassee, Florida 32306

* * *

February 28, 1969

PAR PROCLAMATION de la SOCIÉTÉ DES VACHES ESPAGNOLES:
Vendredi, le 28 février est officiellement déclaré FÊTE DE NELSON; car c'était à ce jour-là, dans le Jardin d'Eden (au centre de la France), en 1,111,066 Avant J.C., [B.C. in English] que LA VIEILLE DRAGONNE fut explosée de son volcan, pour établir la langue française.
Nous, les révolutionnaires de la S.V.E.—autrement dits LES SEPT IMMORTELS—ordonnons qu'à l'avenir cet *anniversaire de naissance Nelsonienne* soit célébré avec tous les rites et sacrifices convenables.

Joey	Susan S.
Madeleine A.	Chris A.
Judy R.	Rob W.
	Beth W.

My note: When one wishes to say that another speaks French badly one remarks: He speaks French like a Spanish cow. Vache is the word for

286

cow. This class was *not* composed of "Spanish Cows" but brilliant students. I had been ill several days and this was the get-well card from the class.

Translation: Friday, 28 February is officially declared Holiday of Nelson. It was on this day in the Garden of Eden in the center of France in the year 1,111,066 B.C. that The Old Dragon was exploded from her volcano to establish the French Language. We, the seven revolutionaries of the Society of Spanish Cows, or the Seven Immortals order that in the future this Nelson birthday shall be celebrated with all the rites and sacrifices suitable.

* * *

le 19 september 1969
vendredi

Dear Mme. Nelson,

I was going to attempt to write this letter "en français," but I had a change of heart—which was probably a wise decision with my scant vocabulary!

We live in a small country village called Mt. Holly Springs. To prove further how small a town this really is—we don't even have a number on our house! And with a small town, goes a small school which usually houses a meager course in foreign languages. The Boiling Springs Consolidated School (which includes grades 7–12 plus kindergarten) has a staff of *one* French teacher. I'm not taking ALM or the Mauger course, but some weirdo books called "Oui, je parle français!" I've quit knocking French teachers and the way they teach, but this lady I have now sure is a big difference from you! She must be fresh out of college because her pronunciation is almost first year. But she is easy and nice (extremely easy). Maybe that's it. Maybe I should be taking French III or something. But, whatever, if my father gets reassigned to the Washington D.C. area, I'm going to insist on having you! Some of my friends that have you now really like you—but "la vieille dragon" still lives. Well, I suppose I should say so long. Say "hello and good luck" to the class I was to be in. Express the good luck more than the hello!

Au revoir,
S. C.

* * *

287

About 1969

Dear Mme. Nelson,

We are all sitting around your room writing dialogues and generally bulling around and we just thought we'd write you a note to tell you what a fantastic teacher you are and how much we all think of you, because nobody ever tells you and we think somebody ought to tell you.

Bonne santé,

J.

G.

L. B.

My note: I was ill.

* * *

le 13 mai 1973

Ma Chère Madame,

Que je suis content d'avoir reçu votre bonne lettre, laquelle m'a bien soulagé et me donne beaucoup d'encouragement! Comme vous avez raison et bon sens! Nous passons en ce moment par une époque d'une grande sécheresse intellectuelle et spirituelle. J'ai l'impression que nous nous laissons mener par des coquins et des imbéciles.

Votre carte est si belle avec cette charmante peinture de Renoir! Et que j'admire et aime votre citation de Rivarol—"Tout ce qui n'est pas clair n'est pas français!"

En espérant bien vous revoir bientôt, je vous prie, chère Madame, de vouloir bien agréer l'expression de mes sentiments les plus chaleureux.

Calvin C.

My note: Colleague

* * *

September 4, 1973

My dear Madame Nelson,

How are you? Busy as usual? I hope that you had an enjoyable summer. My summer was quite enjoyable, having both its ups and downs. But it was all interesting. Exploring a new area fascinates me. I love the Chicago area, although the temperature may require some adaptation. I am looking forward to the commencement of school. My classes actually start the 25th, although I move in the dorms much earlier. I am planning to take the first quarter Russian, French advanced grammar and composition, or poetry analysis. I would prefer the first. I did not receive any credit for my French, but I got four semesters worth of placement. It seems unfair, but in Spanish I did get credit, although I'm basically at the same level as in French. I am taking Spanish also and a course called "Introduction to the Soviet Union." They should prove interesting. Then I am taking piano and Phys. ed. I am also continuing Karate. It is an A.A.U. program and I get so much credit per belt. I am going next week for my blue belt test. I am also going to be on their swim team. The Northwestern girls team is better than the boys'. I am also going to be on their diving team.

This summer was very productive. I worked as a lifeguard and earned $2,000. I read Camus' books (La Peste, La Chute et un autre dont j'ai oublié le titre). I also learned to speak Russian, actually only to read and write, as I have not yet heard it spoken. I hope to take second semester Russian although it is difficult to get the professor's consent as I have no Russian background to show him. All this is for my upcoming trip to the Soviet Union.

December 16 I am flying to Copenhagen and from there will proceed to Moscow. My best friend from Fort Hunt is there (she left in May) for a year and I plan to stay 3 weeks with her. I have to investigate the KGB.

I have planned my college schedule and unfortunately I am lacking several years. There is never enough time. Anyway, after 4 years I will graduate with my Masters; because of my high school record they will obliterate 6 necessary credits enabling me to receive both my Bachelors and Masters in 4 years—in Spanish. But, as I am already at the literature level of 2 languages and my year of Latin, I will be able to become fluent in French, Spanish, Russian, German, and possibly an oriental language.

The only courses I take outside of languages are psychology, which I love, sociology, history, astronomy, math, theology and philosophy. This is with 45 courses. And 30 some courses are in foreign languages. But I do not know if an MA in Spanish will get me into law school or a job with the CIA.

Well, say hi to Miss S. for me and all the level 5's. How lucky they are! Take care of yourself.

Love,
Pat J. (your ex-pupil)

* * *

November 30, 1973

Dear Mme. Nelson,

I am most apologetic for not being able to make it to your Holiday party last week. I was hoping I would be able to drop by to see you, but time just wouldn't let me. There are a lot of things that I want to talk to you about but a phone call wouldn't have sufficed, I'm afraid. Over Christmas, if your plans permit it, I would very much like to see you.

A point of interest . . . I'm taking a French literature course and I am considering double majoring in it. You know I'd keep it up though—no surprise. I'm even doing A– work.

Duke is a good school I suppose, but for some reason, I'm just not able to justify going through the stereotype "push-push" for grad school or a job after graduation that so many students are doing. There are too many things I want to do after school than jump into my business suit. I've considered perhaps picking up some education courses and trying to teach and/or coach on the high school level. I've even considered the School of Forestry and working for the National Park Service. Law is my ultimate objective—I know that for certain, but I'm in no rush. Well, I don't mean to confuse you also. These are things that are going through my head and I just wanted to discuss this with you sometime.

My running was going the best ever until in the middle of cross country season I had to pull *one* "all nighter." It destroyed my health and running. It really got me down, in the best shape of my life and I fell apart and got sick. Right now, I'll be trying to muster a "comeback" but our team is *so* good, it will be tough. I'm shooting for spring season (skip winter).

Exams are upon me and God will have to be on my side—I'm so far behind.

Well, thank you for your generous "ear" Madame and I hope to see you soon.

As I often remember you telling us of your former students and their advice, I might humbly suggest that you have some of your students consider staying out a year before entering school again. If they do something constructive, schools look favorably upon it.

C.
Duke University

* * *

1973

Ma Chère Madame Nelson,

J'espère que je pourrai trouver un professeur comme vous au Japon.

Vous m'avez appris beaucoup et je me souviendrai de la "vieille dragonne" à jamais. J'admirerai votre courage jusqu' à la fin de ma vie.

Je vous embrasse,
Michele

* * *

16 February 1974

Dearest Mme. Nelson,

Well, so much has happened since I really had a chance to sit down and talk with you, I hardly know where to begin to fill you in on my activities.

The most recent chapter was my semester spent in Washington area on a work study program from Cornell, at the Crystal City Marriott Hotel. In this program, I took a semester of studying on my own while working as assistant manager in each of three different departments of the hotel. While manager in one department of 65 employees, there was definitely a case of cross-cultural influence. We had 13 different nationalities and 8 different languages spoken. In most cases, the employee only spoke his native tongue, which was not English. So, I guess that's learning the hard way. The cold cruel facts of the dollars and cents of knowing multiple languages is becoming increasingly clear.

At any rate, the General Manager of the hotel gave me an excellent rating and wrote a letter to the President of the company recommending they follow my career and keep their eye on me for permanent post-grad employment. Not bad!

Oh yes, and about midway through the program, I became involved in a car accident and broke the steering wheel off with my face and arm. Not too much fun! My face was okay, but my arm (left, of course) was fractured multiply. They operated and screwed it back together with metal plates. So now the arm is as good as new except for a little stiffness and two rather gross scars the length of the arm. Thank heavens for my hairy arm.

And I guess you know (from my earlier postcard) that I just returned from a three-week trip to Scandinavia and the Netherlands. In the Netherlands, I visited Jennifer C., '71 also, and Secretary when I was 1st Vice President of the SCA. She is doing great and just as lovely as ever. She attends school at Nijenrode, an international business school, near Amsterdam. From there, I went to Stockholm to visit with friends made last summer while I was working at Grand Hotel, there. From Stockholm, I headed even farther north, above the arctic circle to Oulu, Finland, to see Liisa Kestitalo, a native Finnish laplander girlfriend whom I met last summer. This was my first stay in Finland (of any length) and I found it incredibly interesting. Unlike many other parts of

Europe, this rather remote section of Finland has remained fairly un-touched by tourists. In addition, due to the lack of political orientation (even less than Sweden) to either the west or east, the eastern influence comes through a bit more noticeably. Oh yes, virtually no English at all is spoken. That really caused some interesting moments when I had no translator. Meeting Liisa's parents was a real treat, too (no English do they speak). However, you'd be surprised at the amount of communi-cation through expressions, gestures and inflections, even when you don't understand the language. (This is when Liisa wasn't translating.) Oh yes, took in an authentic Finnish Sauna there. It is a Finnish institu-tion, as every house has one. You basically sit in your "birthday suit" for 1/2 hour in an oak-lined room, heating to 212° F by hot rocks. Then you run out through the snow and –25° air and jump in an ice covered lake for a swim. You repeat this process 3 or 4 times and then report inside (dressed) for beer and sausages, roasted on an open fire. That's great!

After Finland, I left to go 200 miles above the Arctic Circle to Nar-vik, Norway to see a school chum from Cornell. As you can imagine, with all these travels around the Arctic Circle, it snowed 10–15 inches per day and averaged about –15° to –35° F.

Well, after this I went to Milan, Italy to visit a big Leonardo Da Vin-ci exhibition there and to visit a certain hotel. That about wrapped up that trip, of course, I haven't told you much of the story, but at least you know what places I saw. And now, of course, I am back at school and heavily into course work. No telling where next summer's work will take me. I'd like to try Australia if I can dig up the money for airfare (as that's all I need with the business I'm in).

It's also that time of life to make the grad school decision. It's rough these days trying to evaluate correctly the value of such a degree, espe-cially with the economics of the country. However, they say the value of an MBA is on the upswing, while law is on the down.

At any rate, either way, I have a pretty good resume built for myself at grad time next year.

Well, the old lefty is getting rather stiff and cranky, so I'd better cool it. Keep plugging, and let your students know that it's incredible what use you might find one day for a language (or some other course you have little interest in), and believe me, it's next to impossible to start a language after you're already at college.

Well, so much for this. Drop me a line soon, OK?

Your friend,
B. C. ('71 FHHS)
Cornell University

* * *

April 4, 1974

Mr. Rodney T.
Principal of Fort Hunt High School

Dear Mr. T.:

Madame Nelson has proposed a new program in bi-level French in-struction for advanced students that will allow more individual instruc-tion and use of modern techniques. Our daughter, Ann Marie B., has expressed a strong desire to take such a course. She has been receiving French instruction since the third grade and is currently taking French III as a freshman at Ft. Hunt.

We urge that this course be made available next year if at all pos-sible, to encourage the further development of these students.

Sincerely yours,
Mr. and Mrs. Louis B.

My note: Such letters opened the way for me to try extremely experi-mental things.

* * *

1974
Christmas Card

Madame,

I hope you feel a lot better after seeing your children and then you should have a good time in the Middle East. I am sure I will see you next year.

Love,
R. E.

* * *

1974

Dear Madame Nelson,

I would like to thank you for making this year as meaningful as it has been for me. At the beginning of the year I came into your class expecting to learn only French and now at the end of the year, I leave your class with a much better understanding of the French language and something much more valuable—a better understanding of myself. You

293

helped me when I needed help and you were willing to do whatever you could to help me.

You gave me confidence when I needed it and you gave me the desire to keep going and to learn as much as possible and to accomplish. I am glad you are the type of teacher that you are—one who cares about her students, not just as students, but also as humans who need love and care. If there were more people like you, I think the world would be a much better place in which to live.

This year has been very worthwhile for me. Although my grades were not as good as they might have been, I can honestly say that I earned those grades in French and that I really learned. From this experience, I have learned that it is not the grade that really counts, it is how much you have learned and how well you have learned it.

The knowledge that you have given me will help me to become a better person and it will help me in the future knowing that I am capable.

Thank you for everything that you have done for me. I hope that you are able to find a position closer to home for your sake, but I hope that you will come back to Fort Hunt High School for my sake and the sake of all French students.

Merci mille fois,
L. M.

My note: I was thinking of transferring to another school. I didn't.

* * *

le 22 avril 1975

Dear Madame Nelson,

With classes winding down and exam time winding up, I thought I would pause and write the letter that I had been meaning to write for a long time.

I'm back taking French but this time for good and in a fascinating way. Besides taking a conversation course, I'm taking a Canadian Studies program with research in the area of the immigration of French Canadians to the U.S. around the time of the industrial revolution and that culture's survival in the U.S. If I am able to go to grad school, this is what I'll be studying. I want so badly to talk to you about it. I know you don't like the French Canadian accent, but it is a fascinating part of history that has been neglected too often. I might try to go to Europe for awhile if next year goes all right. At least there I can absorb the tongue and a bit of culture. I could go on for ages about this (I'm having *no* problem doing my research in French, I love it!)

Academically, this is my best semester, but in every other, it could be my worst. College can really be stifling to one's individuality sometimes. Maybe this is natural, but I am really disappointed in Duke. I once thought it to be progressive, tough and educationally oriented. It's none of that. The students are just as disappointing. I once looked upon my sister, who is 8 years older than I, with a silent respect during what our society calls the "turbulent" sixties and all her beliefs. Now, I wish I grew up with her. My generation, and my heavens, I do hate to generalize, is complacent, cut-throat and will be good American capitalists. Everyone is pre-med. How boring!

No one has stopped to become educated, they just want to be Mr. Doctor. Cheating has gone up 20% here, too. No one cares about Vietnam or Cambodia, nor their school, nor the strangers they pass on the quad. . . . Well, enough.

I want to talk to you, so I'll drop by the second week in May to see you at school.

It was so good to see you over Christmas and I look forward to seeing you again and hearing about how things are going!

Fondly,
C.
Duke University

My note: He became a lawyer and followed his congressman father.

* * *

Indianapolis, In.
May 21, 1975

Mr. Rodney T., Principal
Ft. Hunt High School
Ft. Hunt Road
Alexandria, Va. 22308

Dear Mr. T.,

I am taking the liberty of enclosing Application for Driver Training Discount—requiring certification that our son, Michael G. took a course in drivers' education. This was done while at Ft. Hunt High School, under the direction of Mr. T. J., three years ago.

We would greatly appreciate it if this form could be signed and returned to us. Michael's certificate attesting to his taking driving education has been misplaced through the years.

Forgive this reminiscing . . . but we all remember Ft. Hunt with much affection. From our youngest, who often mentions the planetarium and the field trips from Stratford Landing, to our two older boys who physically attended your school, to this parent, who attended the banquets and was impressed with your presentation of English classes. You provided an excellent background for inquiring minds, where learning could be a challenge and a joy. I hope the Ft. Hunt students of today are living up to their opportunities.

Michael, incidentally, will be attending Notre Dame's affiliate in Angers, France, for his sophomore year. The expert instruction and guidance given by Madame Nelson entrenched in Michael a firm comprehension of the French language, and a great love for it, thereby making it possible for him to receive this great honor.

With kindest regards,
Marguerite G.

* * *

September 2, 1975

I would like to take French II under Mme. Nelson 5th period and Spanish III under Miss L. 1st period. I presently have French 1st period (with no teacher at the moment) and Spanish 5th period. If it is possible, I would like to simply switch the two subjects in the time slots.

Annie W.

* * *

September 2, 1975

To whom it may concern:

As Annie W.'s mother, I request that she be allowed to join Mme. Nelson's fifth period French II class and Miss L.'s first period Spanish III class.

I feel that these simple changes in her schedule will be beneficial to my daughter's studies. These changes have been discussed and approved by both Mme. Nelson and Miss L., and we are all convinced of Annie's ability to handle this program change, and feel that it will be a better learning situation for her.

Sincerely,
Barbara W.

* * *

September 3, 1975
William & Mary University

Chère Madame,

I'm writing to you in English because my French is quite rusty. Hope you don't mind. I'll write again as the year progresses, peut-être en français.

Today was the first day of classes. I'm taking Geology, Calculus, Anthropology, Phys. Ed., and French (bien sûr). I was in the last group to register, but luckily was able to obtain most of the courses that I wanted . . . all except one—Le Français, naturellement. I wanted to take a composition course, which was mainly a review course for the most part. Well, the course was full by the time I got there, so I decided to take a higher level French. It deals with advanced readings. My professor's name is Don M. He studied at the University of Utah, so maybe you might know him. Anyway, we are reading four novels this semester: *La princesse de Clèves, Le barbier de Séville, Trois contes par Flaubert,* et *La peste.*

There are only 15 in the class. The professor began asking questions in French to see how much everyone knew. I panicked. I hadn't spoken French in nearly two years. Then all of a sudden I began to listen to some of the answers that the professor was receiving. Madame, I wish you were there. I couldn't believe it. There I was in a classroom with fourth-year French students (toutes femmes) who were speaking French as if they just completed *first-year French.* It was pitiful. Needless to say, the professor seemed quite satisfied. Anyway, you know me and how I rarely opened my mouth to partake in discussions, plus the fact of not taking French last year, which was a mistake, but I had to work. Well, when he came around to me I just blew him right out of the classroom. I was answering questions right and left. I couldn't believe it. My heart was almost bursting with anticipation. It made my day.

Tell your students the importance of conversation. Don't let them speak English behind your back. Starting Monday my professor has vowed he will not speak English in class; nor will the students. This will probably be my downfall because I never opened my mouth. If your students want to take French in college, they must speak, for the hardest French courses, at least at William & Mary, are the conversation courses. I think B. will be interested.

I'll write you again Madame. Je vous aime toujours,

John

* * *

University of North Carolina
Chapel Hill, N.C.
September 3, 1975

Bonjour Mme. Nelson!!!!!!!

Comment-allez vous? Moi, je suis enchantée avec l'université!!!! I have been here about two weeks now, and I can find my way around pretty well. The campus itself is beautiful, and everyone is friendly and eager to help a lost-looking freshman (*Me,* sometimes), although, other times, people think that I look like someone to ask for help, and I always try.

I am taking some very interesting courses, and I have high hopes for a great year. Most courses are large—200 students—but if you really need help, it is usually available. My schedule of classes is as follows:

Math 15—Pre-calculus
Psychology 10—introductory
Anthropology—Basic
Music—The Evolution of Jazz—Fantastic!!
Volleyball
Chemistry 11 and Lab—The professor is great!!!!!

The only course that worries me is the Anthropology. The prof is a young, quiet girl, who is overwhelmed by an auditorium of young kids. She is obviously very knowledgeable in her field, but she lacks the experience to get it across to her students. She doesn't follow the book or even explain it in her lectures, and tends to use the vocabulary of an anthropologist without defining any of her words (most cannot be even spelled correctly to be looked up later).

The rest of the classes should be really rewarding, and I hope to learn a lot. All my other profs are good speakers, and can easily hold the attention of 250 students for the class time.

As part of my financial aid package, I am working about 8 hours a week as a lab assistant. I work for a young Doctor in the Nutrition Department of the School of Public Health. I can make my own hours to a great extent, so it is not too hard to fit in with studies. Right now I am learning to use the various machines in the lab, but eventually I will be working directly with the white rats. That is, I will be feeding them and keeping a growth-rate chart for each rat. The job is not demanding, and it is a welcome change from sitting around my room. (Of course, I don't do too much of that . . .)

Maybe you have noticed by now that I am not taking any French. . . That is because I placed out of even 4th level!!! In more concrete terms, when I walked in this university I got 8 credit hours for French, and 4 for English!!!!!! 12 total credits! There are *very* few other students who placed out of both. In fact, my roommate from North Carolina had had four years of French in high school, but only placed into level 1 1/2–2. In English, you are only required to take two semesters, so that is all the credit anyone can get!!! I am really glad, because this leaves me time enough to take my math a little slower so that I can fully grasp all that I should. It also frees me and I am already taking two sophomore courses towards a physical therapy major.

Just to show you that I am not being *too* studious, I will tell you about my second "job." I can't really call it a job because it is a lot of fun. I am a disc jockey for the University radio station. WCAR is currently heard only in the dorms, but we hope to go FM by springtime. I have never worked a "board" before, so I am not super good yet, but I will be getting all the practice I want in the weeks to come.

I know you have heard this before, and you will probably hear it again, but tell all the kids who are dying in your class to *stick it out*. Believe me, the kids who are taking French in college are having a really rough time. Their backgrounds were scanty, and it is required that they take *SIX HOURS A WEEK*. This means going TWICE on one day!!!!!! It can really take away from time needed just to adjust to a new type of existence. In fact, so many of the North Carolina kids *have* to take the 6-hour course, that some were closed out until the next time it is offered. This generally means wasting time needed to get on with courses in your major. The requirement is not hard to place out of (you only have to place out of level two) so I am sure that any one of your students in level two or three could place out easily. Just tell Diggs and Ryan, that it is A LOT HARDER IN COLLEGE THAN IT EVER WAS IN LA VIEILLE DRAGONNE'S CLASSE.

Enough of that—how is the old CREW??? La Bande??? I hope that you get to see them all, even if they are no longer in French. Please say hello to them all for me!!! That class is certainly the one I will remember most fondly of any class at Fort Hunt. . . . I guess that you are probably not teaching Eric, or Steve, or Ryan, but tell anyone you see that I will be looking for them when I come home. . . .

Have you heard from Jennifer???? Or Fran?? I am sure that they both are doing just great.

It is funny, even now, I get to tutor some of the kids on my hall in French. They all come over to check something out, and I show them where the information is in all my books . . . yes, I brought my workbooks, my verb book, and my Petit Larousse. . . . If I ever left them home, I would probably have some kind of withdrawal symptoms.

It is really funny, it seems like only yesterday that I was sitting in your class, listening to you read a letter from some college student who had left Fort Hunt eons ago. . . .

How is Billy D.??? He was so smart, he just didn't want anyone to know it. . . .

Oh well, I hope you can excuse my typing and spelling errors. I want to go on and on, but my poor roommate wants to go to bed. I keep you and your classes in my prayers.

Avec amour,
Barb

My note: One of the elite students of the Athletic French Experiment.

* * *

le 8 septembre 1975

Chère Madame Nelson,

Bonjour! I've got a few minutes before my last class today, so I thought I'd drop you a line. So far, life at the University has been great—except for the day my parents brought me down (Aug. 31) and last Saturday (when my parents and all my brothers and sisters came for a short visit, and brought down some things). Those days I cried! I was in hysterics Saturday. I just couldn't stop crying for the life of me. I don't think you know this girl, but Mary B. came over and I spilled it all out. We were planning on going to the 5:15 P.M. Mass and we just made it! One of the other girls in my suite, Kathy D. (she's from Front Royal) also tried to calm me down and offered her consolation. She's a really sweet girl, and she's one of the other 2 girl engineers in my suite. I'm so glad there are some kind people around here.

The fact that UVA is a party school has really been proven to me. I don't understand how they manage, but they do! I don't have the energy nor the desire to go out and drink beer to get drunk. I only went to one party, and that was at a friend of a friend's house. It was nice. There was a big party for 4 dorms in front of our dorm, but it was like a zoo. There were so many people, and not enough space and the music was up sooo loud. It must affect some people in strange ways to be away from home. You should hear the volume of the stereos all day and night long. I find it hard to believe.

My roommate is a girl from McLean, Janet A. She's taking French, so I'll keep up by helping her! I'm in the Engineering School and they don't let us take much in the way of electives. They pre-register students. I have Calculus, Humanities, Chemistry, Chem. Lab, and a mini-course on lasers.

I'm going out for the field hockey team. Hopefully I'll make it. Try-outs start late this week. I'll be at tryouts 4–6, and the contract food place closes at 7. U. Hall where the practices are is a good 25 minutes from the food place by foot, so I'm going to really have to push.

How are your classes this year? How's Jenny doing as FHS [French Honor Society] President?

300

I've just returned from seeing the women's athletic locker room. It's really nice! There are 50–60 girls trying out for approximately 35–38 positions. I really want to make the team badly! I'm going to keep my fingers crossed.

My laser class isn't that bad. It's a little difficult for me to understand, but it's sort of interesting. I'm the only girl in a class of approximately 25. I feel sort of funny, if you know what I mean.

I haven't seen Linda A. very much, but she came by the other day. Yesterday she came by. If you remember Hal B., you might recognize the name John B. He's a year older than Hal, and is a transfer student from American University. He's sharing an efficiency with John K., and they have a kitchen. So, when my parents were here, we bought all I needed to make chocolate chip cookies. Mary B. and I made them yesterday. Yum! I gave John and Hal B. and John K. a lot of them and I took the rest home. They said they are going to take me to see the movie Nashville sometime. I can't wait!

Last night I sat home and wrote letters to my friend in TL and one to Celia. I've been writing to her a lot. I've spent so much money on books. It's terrible. I had to buy drawing equipment for Graphics. Well, time for homework. If you have time write and let me know how everything is. Especially let me know how you are, OK?

Avec beaucoup d'amour,
M. P.

* * *

October 6, 1975

Chère Madame,

As you can see, I'm applying for a Fulbright-Hays teaching assistantship in France. Since I did not really continue French in college beyond freshman year, I'm sending this form to you as a reference. My application is somewhat "en retard" due to circumstances beyond my control, i.e., they ran out of applications and I had to wait for the re-order to be filled.

If you could find time to fill out the remainder and send it off as soon as possible in the enclosed envelope, I would be much appreciative. You know that I have never forgotten the trip that I won, due largely to your excellent and undying instruction. Thank you again. I hope that if you have time, you might also drop me a line to catch up on lost time.

In haste with much love,
Guillaume
236 Edwards St.
New Haven, CT 06511

301

My note: He received six hours of college credit at Yale for his French in high school. He won first in the nation in the National French Contest at level III and spent the summer between junior and senior year in France at a private school where sons and daughters of royalty studied.

* * *

1975

Ma chère Madame,

Vous serez heureuse de savoir que je vais continuer mes études de français à Holyoke. On m'a mise dans des classes trop difficiles, je crains, mais je vais essayer. Je vais étudier "A Survey of French Literature" la première partie de l'année, et "French Literature of the 17th, 18th, and 19th Centuries" (je crois?) la deuxieme partie. Celles-ci sont des classes les plus difficiles pour les élèves de la première année, et j'ai un peu peur. (Je ne les ai pas choisies!) Mais, encore, je répète: je vais essayer!

Pardonnez-moi du français horrible de cette lettre! Je crains que j'aie tout oublié! Mais—j'espère que cette lettre vous montrerez, au moins, que je m'intéresse encore à "la belle langue."

Merci bien, encore une fois!

Je vous souhaite beaucoup d'élèves meilleurs que moi dans l'année prochaine!

Avec beaucoup d'affection,
C.

* * *

1975

Madame Nelson,

I'm sorry for kicking your door. I promise never to do it again!

Respectfully yours,
Pat

My note: Not my student but guilty just the same and reported by one of my students. I just heard the noise.

* * *

1975

Dear Mme. Nelson,

It was good to hear from you. You mentioned in your letter a trip you were planning to Grenoble for the summer. Is it only for high school students, or would it be at all possible for me to come? I wanted to go to the Sorbonne for next year, but my parents feel that one year is too long. I'm trying to write in English but French keeps popping in.

Anyway, from what you said the program sounds great. If there is any possibility, could you please send me the info? My parents would not let me go with any other chaperon, but they idolize you.

Last night our campus had a riot. This so-called "streaking" hit *NU* [French word for naked]. There were 500 guys running around nude and 1,700 onlookers. They invaded our dorm. It was *disgustingly* funny.

Well, Chicago is really beautiful now. I really miss Washington, though. I am definitely going to be a French major. Now, I have to write a 12-page critique of Baudelaire's poems.

Guess what? I just had a poem published in a book of poetry. I have also had several published in magazines.

Well, I will see you maybe—Take care.

Love,
Pat

* * *

January 1976

Chère Madame,

Joyeux Noel et bonne année! I'm sorry I haven't written in such a long time, but never fear, I am now remedying that situation.

I really could use your influence out here, Mme. Nelson. This French class business is going down the drain. There is no official French class. There are exactly nine French III students. The Board of Education, or whoever, says that is not enough to make up a real class. They did not hire a teacher to teach us. So what we do is go into a different room, while Mrs. Littleton teaches the French II's. My class is taught by Betsy, I don't know her last name. Betsy is a native of France and speaks the language fluently. She is also a senior and one of the nine students that make up the class. Now, Madame Nelson, don't get upset yet; there's more to come.

Mrs. Littleton makes up worksheets for us to work on. She also makes a week's assignment when there isn't a worksheet to do. Now, this is the humdinger: *We had one and only one test this quarter.* Whatever we make on the test is more or less our grade. *Madame Nelson, I wish you were there. They need you.*

The test was on the passé composé. I remember very clearly that never, never do you make the avoir verbs agree with the subject. (This is without direct object.) After we had gotten our tests and gone to our room, some of the kids wanted to know if it was all right to make the avoir verb agree with the subject. Let me tell you, I soon put a stop to that nonsense.

The people in my class are sitting down and memorizing the être verbs. They do not realize that they are the coming and going verbs. I tried to explain this but they don't seem to understand. You know, I just might come away with an "A" this quarter. I didn't do a single drop of work!

I must say, though, that I am learning a lot more vocabulary words here. All in all, I am pretty lucky because I have a firm background in the verb conjugation and that I'm going to have a firm vocabulary. Now, enough about French. I have other things to tell you about.

Classes here are so easy I'm embarrassed. Geometry is very easy, I'm going to get an "A" or "B," while I got a "C" there. Biology is a cinch. I have an "A" in that class. I got an "A" there. P.E. I will get a "B." You already know about French. World History is the one class I have to work in. We read our chapter and take notes Monday through Thursday and have our test on Friday. I think I'll get an "A" there. English is pretty easy also.

Now you know about the school situation. I can't take Drivers Ed. until the summer. During the summer, I am going to be taking a diving class, so that next year I can join the YMCA swim team and be a diver. I have heard that they desperately need divers and I figure I am just the person they need.

I had to write you care of Fort Hunt because I did not get your address. Well, that's all the news for now. I'll try to write you every quarter and keep you posted on the goings on. Merry Christmas and a Happy New Year, Madame Nelson.

Love,
J. K.
(your very faithful French student)

P.S. Please excuse my sloppy handwriting.

* * *

le 6 novembre 1976

Je crois que je mérite une B dans cette classe parce que j'essaie de faire le travail. Quelquefois je ne comprends pas, mais encore *j'essaie.*

J'aime le français, et je veux faire bien. J'espère que je peux continuer en français. J'ai fait des progrés.

D. P.

* * *

December 4, 1976

Mme. Nelson,

I hate to tell you this but I have an orthodontic appointment at Andrews today at 2:45 P.M. I can't make French class.

I'd like to explain my other two absences to you. I'm on the make-up crew for Mr. Gassek's production. Those 2 days a photographer from the *Alexandria Gazette* and from the *Mt. Vernon Globe* were here to take publicity pictures of the cast in full make-up and costumes. So, since they were coming at 4:00 and there were only 3 of us crew members and 7 characters to make up, we were pressed for time. I'm sorry I had to miss class and I realize I should have let you know beforehand, but it was on the spur of the moment and I was thoughtless.

I should really like to talk to you sometime, but I'm afraid you'll make me speak in French, and I just can't communicate. It's horrible! Here I am (just barely) in French 5 and I'm so stupid—I feel so—incompetent in my class. But it's mainly my fault. I'm lazy and I figure I'm so far behind now, why even try to catch up?

I need inspiration and lots of self-discipline to work hard on French. I've just lost interest. I don't understand it.

Well, really Mme. Nelson, I hated to seem insolent the other day, but I didn't know how to respond in French. After all this apology, I can't say that I won't miss class any more. I'm afraid there will be more last-minute things to be done with the play and since I'm involved . . .

But I do want to reform my ways and once again, love French. HELP!

C. H.

My note: Some extra help from me changed the picture. This student had too many extra-curricular activities. She was a good student and recovered.

* * *

1976

Ma chère Mme. Nelson!

Merry Christmas and a Happy New Year from Germany! Even

305

though we have only a few days left until Christmas, I'm still very busy at school.

I study biology in Regensburg and enjoy it a lot. We seem to be very lucky because we have a nice, cold winter with much snow. I went cross-country skiing a few times which is usually impossible around Ingolstadt. I will celebrate Christmas Eve with my parents here and then go to a ski resort in the mountains where most of my relatives will be spending Christmas this year.

I wish you all the best, have a very good time and take care.

Love,
Petra

My note: German exchange student but in my French III class.

* * *

January 31, 1977
Fulton, New York

Dear Mrs. Nelson,

Thank you for inviting me to your classroom. I enjoyed seeing a great teacher in action. Your humor and your command of the students were very impressive. Before I returned home I talked with Bruce of how grateful he should be for a teacher who takes an interest in him, and that he should respond by doing better work. He does appreciate you and likes you very much. I am hoping that somehow he will do much better.

Most sincerely,
His grandmother

P.S. I do thank you and appreciate your efforts with Bruce.

My note: This student spent his sophomore year with me in French II.

* * *

February 2, 1977

Dear Madame Nelson,

I was really sorry to see in Susan's report that she only made an "F" again. Oh my, what are we to do with her? I've been talking quietly to her all the time, and she always says she's alright. I just can't seem to get through to her at all and I and my husband too are really worried about her. She just doesn't seem to understand that she has to do better than that. She says she cares, and she wants to take her exams in May for the English General Certificate of Education in French. I will have some papers next week, that I would like for you to have a look at, and perhaps give her the kind of work that will be needed. I haven't shouted at her at all, both my husband and I ask her quietly if she understands and she always says yes, so maybe she is afraid to admit that she doesn't understand. I just can't tell. We have said that we don't think she'll be able to take her exam, but she desperately wants to and needs to. She desperately wants to do well in her work and makes herself think that she is doing good, although she isn't. That's why I think she will not admit to being a failure. I feel so sorry for her and all of us too are try-ing our hardest to make her understand.

Dear Madame Nelson, is there anything you can do and we will do all we can too. Thank you so much.

Yours very sincerely,
J. G.

My note: Her parents needed to change their attitude. They did, but Susan had to learn to work. They needed to believe in their daughter and be firm in their justifiable expectations.

* * *

June 1, 1977

Dear Mme. Nelson,

I can't let this year pass without telling you how much it has meant to us that you guided Cliff through four years of French at Fort Hunt.

This was surely the strongest program he had there. His, and our, respect for you is very deep and I would say that you are one of the three or four people who have made a difference in his life. He once told us that you are the only teacher who won't let a student rest on past performance, but instead you insist on progress. Such standards are rare and will almost disappear at Fort Hunt if you do, indeed, retire soon.

In the meantime, my daughter Jill arrives next fall. She *must* have Mme. Nelson!

Sincerely,
Mrs. B.

* * *

le 10 juin 1977

Chère Madame Nelson,

Merci mille fois! Je vous aimerai toujours!
Avec tout l'amour du monde, 5020 E, 2nd & 5th Periods

S. M.

* * *

December 19, 1977

Ma Chère Madame,

Comment allez-vous? Je vais bien mais je pense à Virginie beaucoup. Mon coeur est dans ce lieu-là.

Madame Nelson, I will have to switch to English because I am a bit rusty on my French. I started to take French IV this year but stopped because I did not feel I was learning French at all. The French upper levels here cannot compare to the ones at Fort Hunt.

Excuse me for starting with bad news but now I have some good news. I was accepted into the University of Virginia the last of November. I am very pleased because I wanted to go there. My French achievement scores have placed me out of the language requirement.

Michele and I are doing fine over here in Tokyo. Our school is on a different system of scheduling known as modular scheduling. We are not in class all during the day and are given a lot of free time. It is really no longer free time because the teachers give us enough homework to keep us busy.

Tokyo is all aglitter with Christmas. Although they are not clear on the spirit of Christmas, the Japanese are fully aware of the commercial aspect of Xmas. It is not unusual for us to hear Christmas music while we are shopping.

Our church is eagerly preparing for the Lord's birthday. It is a predominantly Chinese congregation with a small percent of Japanese and an even smaller percent of English-speaking people. Though we are small in number, we are strong in spirit and I am so glad for the chance to worship with the Asians. They are very enthusiastic in their faith.

I am going skiing with a group from our church and must confess that I am a little nervous because I have never been on the ski slopes in my entire life. It should be quite an experience in Japan. Madame Nelson, I bet you are a good skier coming from the West. It sure is a popular sport over here and I understand the slopes are very crowded during Christmas.

The Japanese make a big to-do over New Years. The family goes to the shrine to receive the priest's blessings. We live right across the street from the shrine so we shall be in the thick of things.

Madame Nelson, Michele is down with the flu right now and is unable to write her cards. She sends you a big hug and a "Bonjour." Grandmother also sends her regards.

Please forgive the late arrival of this card but I did not want the Christmas season to go by without telling you that we think of you and miss you. I hope your Christmas was joyful and may God bless you this New Year!

Love,
C. and M.

* * *

1977

Dear Madame Nelson,

How can I thank you for all you have given me. Although sometimes it may seem like your efforts are in vain, believe me, they are not. I see and I know the love you put into your work. That love, Madame, makes you the special teacher you are. It has inspired me and impressed me. When the years have long passed, your name shall not be forgotten because you are one teacher who loves her students—loves them so much that you want and expect the best for them.

Should something be accomplished with my life, credit goes to you for you have inspired me, directed me and guided me—no more could be asked of any teacher. It is clear that you are an A+ student of the greatest teacher of them all—Jesus Christ. I, too, have considered being a teacher because you have made me realize how truly fine and noble it is to plant knowledge in the minds of the young.

I know your harvest is abundant. With all sincerity I thank you for your wisdom, your concern and your love,

je vous embrasse,
Claire

* * *

June 15, 1978

Madame Mary D. Nelson
French Department
Fort Hunt High School
Alexandria, Virginia

Dear Madame Nelson:

Among the graduations our family has attended over the last ten

309

years, I think last Friday night's was the most memorable . . . not only for all the adults in the assembly, but also for all the children. To see and feel the dedication of a teacher who has truly loved her work and the children she has taught is to see a bit of the divine spark in us all.

Your audience was so moved by your sincerity, not a sound was to be heard except the wind. It was a beautiful experience for the Ritas, one and all. The class of '78 will never forget your farewell.

In instilling in young people the desire to aspire to greatness, you have helped them through these tremulous years and Margaret Rita has come out of your classroom much richer for the experience.

We are among the many grateful parents of students you have taught at Fort Hunt High School. We wish you much happiness in the future and hope you will never really "retire."

Sincerely,
Patricia B. R.

My note: I was asked to address the graduating class this year of my retirement.

* * *

le 7 juillet 1978

Chère Madame,

Mes salutations de Cedar Rapids, Iowa!

J'espère que cette lettre vous trouve en bonne santé. Et aussi que vous vous souviendrez que cela fait un mois que je n'écris aucun mot en français. Ma foi! Quelle honte!

De quoi vous occupez-vous maintenant? Avez-vous voyagé au Moyen Orient? Est-ce que vos "enfants" sont encore arrivés? Et votre jardin—comment pousse-t-il? Notre trajet s'est passé sans peine. Nous sommes parties le 15 juin et nous nous sommes arrêtées ce soir à Sandusky, Ohio. Le prochain jour nous sommes arrivées à Cedar Rapids où vivent ma soeur et son mari (C'est aujourd'hui leur anniversaire—2 ans). Nous avons passé la nuit chez eux puis nous continuions à Algona, notre destination. Tout est arrivé en bon état; rien ne s'est cassé. Nous nous y sommes arrangées, dans notre apartment. Quel tas de boîtes!!

Puisque je déménagerai à Cedar Rapids pour demeurer avec mon père, je ne cherche pas de travail. Donc je me lève tard, regarde la télé, et ai écrit près de quinze lettres à mes amis à Alexandria. Ils me manquent beaucoup. Mais le commencement veut dire exactement qu'on doit quitter des choses familières et se mettre au courant d'autres choses. Tout de même, on aura toujours ses souvenirs. Vous, Madame, serez un de mes plus grands.

En parlant des commencements, je vole à Cincinnati pour mon orientation jeudi et vendredi, le 10 et 11 juillet. Ce sera mon premier coup d'oeil du terrain de l'université. Je suis si enthousiasmée; après que je serai de retour, j'espère aller au travail. Je "peigne" les "want ads" chaque jour. Mon beau-frère connaît un homme qui est dans une agence d'emploi qui puisse m'aider. Et mon père a des amis.

Alors, j'espère qu'il n'y a pas trop de bêtises dans ces lignes! Ayez soin de vous-même. Rappelez-vous au bon souvenir à votre man.

Affectueusement,
Jennifer

P.S. Le paquet est un témoignage de ma gratitude.

* * *

August 8, 1978

Chère Madame,

I apologize for not writing in French, but I fear that it might have become slightly rusty over the summer.

I hope that you are enjoying yourself now. My vacation is nearing an end as I will be leaving for UVA the 26th of this month. I have good news—I scored a "4" on my Advanced Placement French test, which was considerably better than I had hoped for. As a result, I received six hours credit at UVA, as well as credit for two intermediate courses. In effect, I fulfilled the foreign language requirement completely. My achievement score had already exempted me from the language requirement, but the AP gave me the necessary credit hours. (Naturally I will continue my French!) I also received six hours credit in history, and was exempted from two beginning history courses as well as basic English.

Have you been to Europe this summer? One of my cousins, who is taking French, spent two weeks in England and France and enjoyed her trip immensely. I've seen many of my friends over the summer, including some from 2nd period Français this year. I stopped by the school yesterday and I miss not being with everyone, especially you, Madame. The only way I can picture you reading this letter is in class with one of your lower levels, encouraging them with letters from those who "survived."

I shall write again soon, hopefully en français! Je vous aime (I love you),

G. P.

* * *

1978
Christmas Card

Chère Madame,

I hope this Christmas finds you and Col. Nelson in good health and good spirits. This past year has been an eventful one for me, as you well know. I find that married life has brought us both greater challenges than we ever imagined. Of course, the rewards are equally increased, and I do believe I'm more content than I've ever been.

The distance from our immediate families is beginning to bother me. I rely on my family more than ever before, just to hear voices on the phone. I'm sure you can attest to the trials and tribulations of being far from your child and grandchildren. Michael and I both expect to eventually be in the D.C. area, but we'll have to see. We have a beautiful home, a dog and fantastic children. If we could pack them all up and take them with us. Soon enough we'll have our own, I'm sure. Have a wonderful Christmas. I'll be thinking of you.

Love,
Linda

* * *

1978

Madame,

Merci pour la lettre. I have some news for you. This fall I am going to start school part-time. Hopefully, I will be able to get a grant or loan. I think I'm going to start in pre-law.

Bobby is doing very well in school. He got a 4.0 last quarter. Right now he is preparing for mid-term exams (at the Air Force Academy).

I am not doing too badly either. Remember the pudgy girl trying to make it through school, who also bit her nails. I've stopped biting my nails, I now weigh 123 lbs. and can fit into a size 8–9 again. My next step is to stop smoking those filthy smelly cigarettes. I've cut down from a pack a day to a pack every three or four days. I've made a promise to myself that by April 3 I'm going to have stopped. That will be my 20th birthday. It's hard to believe I'm going to be 20. Fourteen, 15, and 16 seem like they were just around the corner.

I'm still writing a lot of poetry. This is one I wrote for Mom and Dad before I left. I think you'll like it.

"Once Upon A Time is how it all began, but no one ever told me how my life would end. Mother always told me to play things by ear, others believe it's just be happy while you can. These people have their opinions, but I have my own too, and one thing I believe, is what I must

312

do. Some say you're better off at home, others say get out while you can, and still others say be independent at home, it's grand. I'm just like any woman, and it's hard to say Good-bye, but I must leave to find my-self, what I want, and learn how to provide. I always told my mother, 'If I can't do for myself, how can I provide for others, a husband, more-over a child.' Mother just keeps hanging on saying that everything will work itself out, but I know the only way it will is if I help. I never want to hurt the people that I love, but I must do what I believe is right, even if it means saying Good-bye. People may try and stop me but it won't change my mind. I must find myself and what I am so I can survive. Life is like a puzzle to me and I just haven't found all the pieces. No one can do that for me, this I believe. So, if I hurt you, it's not inten-tional, for you see, I must do what I think is proper and make my way, find my goals, and work my way up my ladder. I'd like to say just once more, Once Upon A Time is how it all began, and if I can, I want it to be Happily Ever After in The End."

Take care and God be with you.

Love,
J. M.

Photo enclosed with inscription:

"Madame, you are the most fascinating, wonderful, friendly person anyone could have for a teacher. You spread your love to everyone and thought of us as your own. No one can ever repay you for your count-less hours of worry, love, and understanding."

* * *

March 13, about 1979

Dear Madame Nelson,

Bonjour! I hope that this letter finds you as healthy and happy as you sounded in the letter you sent me and what an interesting trip you had! I read your letter to the girls I live with and we all enjoyed it very much. Somehow I wasn't surprised to find that retirement hasn't slowed you down in the least.

You are probably wondering what the meaning of the enclosed sur-vey is. I would like to ask a favor of you. I'm doing a study of the pro-gram for gifted students for my School and Society class in the School of Education at UVA and this survey is a part of the project. Because you always have such interesting things to say, I wanted to mail you the survey I will be handing to Fort Hunt teachers this week and enclose an envelope so you can mail it back to me. I would greatly appreciate your

313

help with this. It is a subject that is of interest to me and I know to you also. (What a shame it would be if all upper-level languages were cut from the high schools!) Thank you very much.

I've been very busy this semester. I'm carrying 16 hours (including Karate) and working 20 hrs. a week at the Office of Admissions where I'm learning about the bureaucracy involved in getting accepted to universities. My French course this time is literature of the Middle Ages. I just finished La Chanson de Roland and am now reading Le Chevalier de la charrette. Très intéressant! Next, I'll probably take phonetics, simply because I rarely get the chance to speak in my literature classes.

I don't know if she told you or not, but S. R. is engaged. She'll be married in the summer of 1980 if all goes well and she finishes school (University).

Well, thank you again (in advance) for your help. I'll let you know how many other teachers share your views when I get the surveys back. Take care.

Love,
J.

* * *

1979
Christmas Card

Madame Nelson,

Joyeaux Noel!
I hope everyone is well at home. I am fine and so is Bobby. He is doing great at school. I was glad to receive your postcard and I even understood every word of it! I am going to start school next fall and you'll be happy to know that I'm going to start taking Français.

All my love, God be with you
J. M.

* * *

July 1, 1980

Dear Madame,

How are you? I am very much concerned about your health. I understood about Christmas by your letter. Our high school just started about two month ago.

I am in the second year. The other day our class went on an excursion to the sea. We were to draw a dragnet there and we had a good time.

An examination will be held on July 7th. We have a term examination for 4 days and have two subjects of examination on each day. Then we have the summer vacation.

It has been very hot in Tokyo. It is sweltering hot.

Today we had an American girl come to our school. I am very glad you wrote to me. I eagerly wanted to answer your letter, but school has kept me very busy. I am very sorry.

P.S. Thank you very much for sending me your picture.

[Japanese characters here]

My note: Megumi Fujima, Japanese student in Tokyo. I met her in Kyoto, Japan.

* * *

le 16 juillet 1980
from Mlle. B. B.

Chère Mme. Nelson,

Comment allez-vous? Je vais bien. Je suis arrivée à Charles de Gaulle à 0800 le 6 juillet, dimanche. J'ai pris le Métro de la Gare du Nord jusqu' à la Gare de Lyon. Puis, j'étais dans le train presque 8 heures, de Paris à Lyon et de Lyon à Annecy. C'était un peu long et j'étais fatiguée, mais le paysage était si joli. A Annecy, nous allons à la classe chaque matin, sauf samedi et dimanche, pour 3 heures (0830–1130). Il y a beaucoup de professeurs dans cette classe, et deux qui sont de Virginie. L'une vous connaît et elle s'appelle Stella N. et elle enseigne le français à Chantilly. Nous étudions la littérature, la poésie et les choses de la vie quotidienne comme les chansons et les journaux. Il faisait frais et pleuvait presque chaque jour. Pour la fête nationale, le 14 juillet, ils ont eu un feu d'artifice dans le champs tout près d'un beau lac—Aussi de 12 à 20 juillet, c'est le festival de la vieille ville d'Annecy et il y a toujours des bals, des ballets et de la musique qu'on peut voir. C'est une ville très pittoresque. Ce samedi je vais à Chamonix pour voir Mont Blanc. Ce sera seulement pour la journée.

Jack D. est dans une autre classe et il va bien aussi.

Hier soir j'ai vu un film français, *"La cage aux folles."* C'était vraiment différent d'un film américain et un peu bizarre.

Je serai ici jusqu'au 31 juillet quand je prendrai le train pour Paris. Mon avion sort de Paris le 1 août. J'espère que vous aurez un bon été.

Vous m'avez beaucoup aidée dans mes études françaises à Ft. Hunt et je vous remercie pour tout!

Love,
B. B.
Annecy-le-Vieux, France

My note: Both my former students then at Naval Academy—B. B. and Jack D. both chosen by the academy to study in France because of their proficiency in French.

* * *

December 14, 1980

Chère Madame,

For years I have been meaning to tell you how much you mean to me, and yet I somehow never got around to it. Only my mother has had a greater influence on my life than you. Although our religions differ, you possess the great qualities that form the basis of both our beliefs. Your high sense of morality—your sense of honesty, the willingness to work and to give unselfishly of yourself to others, along with endless patience, was and *is* a beautiful model for myself and others.

When former students tried to persuade you not to retire they did not mean to be selfish. It is just that you gave so much meaning to our lives that the thought of others not being able to share this unique experience as we did seemed such a great loss. Unfortunately, such a beautiful human being is rare in today's world. Many speak, but rarely are their actions louder than their words.

I feel awkward writing this letter, as even the best poet could not express properly my feelings for you.

Please give me a call (000–0000) or drop me a line. I know you are busy, but it would mean a lot.

May God bless you.

Shalom,
Mlle. Roi

* * *

University of Virginia
1980

Dear Madame Nelson,

I have just completed my student teaching (high school English) and I wanted to take this opportunity to once again thank you for everything that you taught me. The more I learned about teaching, and the more teaching I did, the more I appreciated what an incredible job you did with all of us. I learned more about French with you than in any of my college classes (which is probably why I am only getting a secondary certification in it; I feel uncomfortable teaching French, although I probably could have done it when I walked out of your class). More important than that, though, I learned how to teach by being your student. Funny that tiny little me never had a serious discipline problem while so many of my peers did—but I know the atmosphere of mutual respect and cooperation that (usually) existed in my classroom was possible because I spent so much time in yours. Thank you so much for that—I'm sure my students would also want to thank you for making me such an understanding (and demanding) teacher.

If I ever do become a "good teacher," I'm sure I will have gotten that way thanks mostly to you. I hope you and your family have a very joyous Christmas.

Very sincerely,
J. S.

* * *

1980
Christmas Card

Chère Madame,

I have been student-teaching this semester (as has Judy S.), and loving it. I have established a good relationship with so many of my students. I may not have imparted any worldly knowledge but I was able to give love and a little confidence to my kids. That's why I am happy—because I really love them. I'm so eager to start a real teaching career!

I hope the year has been a good one for you and your family. Have a Merry Christmas and a Happy 1981. God bless you.

Love,
Mel

* * *

August 1985

Dear Madame Nelson,

I have taught myself long enough now to know how unlikely it is

317

that you would remember me, for it has been perhaps eight years since Mlle. S. sat in your French 6 class, but I decided to write to you anyway for two reasons. The first is simply to say "thank you."

I'm not talking about the knowledge of the French language I gained from four years with you; although I understood how considerable it was when I took my place as a freshman in college with advanced college students and felt no pressure at all as I followed literature courses rather than the grammar and comprehension courses other freshmen seemed to need.

Instead I want to thank you for what else you taught me. From you I learned many things that helped me—indeed, that help me still. Discipline, of course—the one thing I see my students lacking every day and the thing they resent the most when I try to teach it to them. The value of hard work, and the pleasure that comes from simply doing a job well. I am as demanding a teacher of English as I remember you being of French, Madame, and my students have given me a name I knew you would enjoy hearing: the Barracuda. Respect for myself and for my peers, and now for my students, but a respect that stems from rigor, at least in the classroom and not from the fun and games I see so many other teachers substituting for hard work (with praise from "education experts"). These and many other things I learned from you.

Without a doubt I model myself on you when I teach, and I am told I am a fine teacher. Thank you for that and for the four years of devotion and love that I only now can understand you gave to all of us.

That is my first reason for writing to you, but I have often begun this letter without finishing it in the past. My reason for doing so now is that I also have a favor to ask of you. I have been teaching English for four years and during that time, I have also obtained my Master's degree in English; for you see, Madame, literature was my first love despite my enjoyment of French. I am probably going to begin work on a Ph.D. in English within the next few years, if all goes well, but in the meantime, the county I work for has asked me to finally put to use all those French courses I took—and I did minor in French.

I'll be teaching two classes of French I next year along with my two sections of English, and I would like to ask you for some advice to prepare myself. I slipped over to the University for a conversation class (to refresh myself) and I am working through Schaum's French grammar to remind myself of the rules I have forgotten. But my real fear is this: How does one *begin* teaching a foreign language? I remember the weekly verb quizzes, the dictations, the recitations, but those came in French III, my first year with you. Where should I begin with a class that has never heard a word of French? How can I start from zero? My textbook is terrible, Madame; it is so clearly designed for lazy, unmotivated students and equally lazy teachers that even the directions to the teacher are insulting. (For example, on page 62, the book reminds the

318

teacher to tell students that "There is usually liaison in the expression quand est-ce que . . .?" and that the *d* is pronounced as a *t*.) I must use it, but what else can I do? Or should I throw it out the window, especially since there is almost no grammar in it (the latest trend, as you know, is to ignore grammar) and hope I don't get caught? Madame, I'm turning to you knowing that the least word of advice would be most helpful, and I thank you for letting me benefit from your knowledge once again.

Let me also fill you in on what has passed in my life since we last spoke. I did go to UVA as I mentioned, and although you were quite right about "le snobisme," I fell in love with the countryside and stayed to work in a country school. I love it here—my husband and I live in an old farm house in a very peaceful spot and I can't imagine moving back to Washington. Besides, as I said, the University has kindly given me the chance to return for more study, which I hope to do soon. By the way, you would like my husband. I took your advice and married a man as smart as I am (but don't tell him I said that!).

I hope this letter finds you in marvelous health and happily teaching in the church school you mentioned. Please take care and if you find the time to write, I would be very grateful to you, Madame.

Yours,
J. S.

* * *

September 1, 1985

Dear Madame Nelson,

Thank you for the note that was waiting for me when I returned from vacation. The book had arrived just before I left, so I was able to look over it while I was away, and I pulled much of my first lesson from it (vocabulaire). The trouble I've been having since school started a week ago is that the French department, unlike the English department I'm used to, insists that all teachers stay together and teach exactly the same thing. For example, I must report each week on *what page* of that textbook I sent you I'm on. I am not pleased about this and I simply refuse to use the "activity masters" and tests that come with the book. Instead, I'm sneaking in vocabulary quizzes every Monday (verb quizzes once we get to verbs, and why the book waits so long to introduce them, I can't imagine) and oral presentations of some kind every Friday (dialogues now, discours later). So far, no one has complained, but I am troubled that the first quiz showed my students as either very good or very bad; all the grades were either A/B or F. I hope this is typical of French I the first week, and that the students just don't believe—yet—that they need to study "trente minute chaque soir." And I also hope the department head won't care that I'm "stressing grammar" which is not allowed this year. We'll see.

Madame, I would very much like to come visit you—thank you for the offer! I'm afraid it would be difficult this month, but I am hoping to be in your area for a family gathering in October. Would this be possible? I will call on you as soon as my plans are firm to check the time. I know by then I will have already struggled through a month, but if you will let me throw my problems at your feet, I would be most grateful!

I am very sorry to hear about Col. Nelson's ill health and I hope this letter finds him better. Did you know that the last time you had our class over for the Christmas party, he took us all downstairs to show off your files? Ask him if he remembers.

Meanwhile, I will continue to use my memories of your class to direct my teaching. And, Madame, I now have *two* pairs of red shoes, which I wear in your honor.

Pardonnez-moi—je sais que je dois écrire en français, mais j'ai encore peur de votre grand stylo rouge, après presque dix ans. Je vous dis un grand merci!

J.

* * *

1985

Ma Chère Dame, [My Lady—Michel knew the difference between Madame and the two words.]

Tonight I was going through my yearbook and I found this. Ma Dame, you gave me so much in the short span of two years. When I think back to my years in high school, I now see all of the teaching you gave me. And it is amazing how much more you taught than French. You taught me love, honor and responsibility!

One of the greatest joys I had recently, happened at work when a wonderful woman came in and could not speak English. I felt so proud that I was capable of helping someone who was visiting from France.

Madame, after graduating, I chose not to go to college. I upset many friends and relatives because I gave up a drama scholarship, but I felt I could never make it to Broadway.

Today I have my own ceramic business. I find the greatest pleasure in teaching something to someone which they were positive they could not do. Currently our business is growing very quickly and I can think of nothing I would rather do.

But back to the reason I'm writing. I would like to return *this* to you as a refund for all you have done for me. I would love to hear from you.

Hope all is well.

Tout mon amour,
M.P.

My note: He returned a check I had given him as a gift at Christmas. He was one of my student assistants as well as my student.

* * *

March 19, 1986

Dear Madame Nelson,

When I received your letter informing me of the death of Col. Nelson, I cried and could not bear to finish reading until the following day. We all grieve for you and feel a sense of loss. I cannot tell you how much I appreciate the effort of writing your letter—it was surely a difficult ordeal.

I have been thinking of you so much lately and of the Colonel—for that is how all of your students think of him—the "Colonel." It is a warm and happy memory. When one is in 10th grade and faces "La Vieille Dragon" every day, one wonders "What kind of man could this Col. Nelson be to be married to such an intimidating person as Mme.?" Formidable indeed! And once past the adolescent first impressions, I learned that you both were two of the most loving, caring people I'd ever known. Enter an intimidation of another kind—that I could never live up to your (collective) standards. And it was not that you *judged;* you just *were.* I suppose that some of that adolescent immaturity is still there.

I am so grateful for your dinner invitation of some years back. My Michael became more than a name to you, and Col. Nelson became more than the man married to Madame to us. That evening is another fond memory we will always cherish.

Death makes us assess our own lives. It also forces us to say what is normally hidden before we lose the opportunity. I have long felt, and now must openly say, that you have had the most profound effect of any person on my life, outside of my family. Your influence has extended to every corner of my life, and for that effort, concern, and caring, I thank you. And be assured that for those of us who *finally* tell you what your life has meant to us, there are a hundred more you affected in a similar manner.

I often wonder what I will "do" when my children are older and I return to the work force—the oft-heard "What will I be when I grow up?" For several years I have intended to sit down with you. I suspect that you could help me shed some light on my future direction. I have always been fascinated by your teaching methods—how did they evolve? Could I learn them? Should I teach? Every time I mentally explore my possibilities, I return to teaching, and I'm not sure if it is a flirtation or serious. When I think of all the nameless, want-to-be-popular, boring teachers I had, I scream to myself, "I can do better than that!" With the snap of the finger, I could name only two of my high school teachers—you and Mr. Levy. With a little thought, more come to mind, but it's not much of a showing for four years of high school.

Our home life is very fulfilling. Kathleen will soon be 4, Deborah is almost 20 months, and they are both bright, fascinating children. I have children here all day long and they provide me with delight and occasional aggravation. I care for four families' children—all part-time so as to avoid raising someone else's child. Mike is traveling a great deal this spring, but it has made him even more sensitive and attuned to the children and me. He has a bond with Deborah that is the most precious thing to see and feel. He was gone for a great deal of Kathleen's infancy, and being my first child, Kathleen and I naturally are close. Deborah, on the other hand, loves me, depends on me, and spends her whole day with me, but when Daddy comes home, the whole world stops. It's a wonderful sight!

My parents and brothers and sister are all well. My sister and her family will return home from four years in Rome this summer. She is expecting a second child in August, prior to returning. We are excited about their homecoming, needless to say.

May I pay you a visit within the next month or so? My schedule is not as flexible as I would hope because of my child care, but I am free Thursday mornings or the weekend, or evenings, for that matter. I do hope we can arrange something.

Please take care of yourself. I know you have a world full of friends and loved ones who care about you.

Love,
L. S.

* * *

Arlington, Va.
5 January 1987

To Whom It May Concern:

I studied French under Mme. Mary D. Nelson for two years out of ten. I was a high school valedictorian, went on to complete a French major and enter Phi Beta Kappa at the University of Virginia, and am considering becoming a teacher. I have found the text by Mme. Nelson to be a true and thorough representation of her technique. It is an exceptional method of teaching.

Mme. Nelson is one of those rare memorable teachers; the most important teacher I had in 16 years. From the moment one walked through her door, education took on a whole new meaning. For some students like me, she affected our lives and gave us direction past formal education. For others, she was "La Vieille Dragon." Everyone left her classroom with a strong knowledge of the French language and culture, and more important, nobody would ever forget her.

The national drive for better teachers makes this book timely. Mme. Nelson has taken her vast teaching experience and explained her methodology in detail. I have experienced it and and I know it works.

I am sure that both experienced and novice teachers will gain from this book. It is not a theoretical discussion written in an ivory tower. Mme. Nelson understands teaching in the broadest sense, and has now done a wonderful service by recording this knowledge.

I look forward to its publication.

Sincerely,
Linda Anne Allen Schoelwer

* * *

February 13, 1987

Chère Madame Nelson,

This work is truly inspired! It embodies so much valuable advice and important guidelines. Every teacher—not only French teachers—could profit from "Order in the Classroom," "Techniques," "Beginnings," "The Essence of Method," "Problems," and "Grading and Communication." These are well-thought-out procedures that have been very clearly expressed and should serve as a model for all teachers.

The part that is specifically devoted to French teaching is also a model that all French teachers should aspire to imitate.

Your book is already an unquestionable success—I rejoice in the prospect of its publication. Thank you for sharing the pre-publication copy—I am very impressed!

My best wishes for you and the book accompany this note.

Sincerely,
Jane Goll
Headmistress, Westminster School
Annandale, Virginia

* * *

Madame Nelson,

I can't thank you enough for giving your time, knowledge, and enthusiasm to my fourth period class. It is such a shame that this could not be shared with the entire student body. You are a truly wonderful lady.

Many, many thanks.

P. M.

My note: Colleague in English Literature

* * *

March 22, 1980

Dear Madame Nelson,

I want to express my deep appreciation for the time and interest you took answering my questionnaire. Your answers are not only extremely enlightening, but will form the basis for my thesis.

I agree completely with you, although I know I don't really have enough experience to judge for myself. Your letter will be invaluable to me as I face the problems of teaching, which you so especially handled and I shall certainly keep it among my reference books. Now, if I could only learn the rest of your secrets, what a good teacher I would be!

I shall try, at any rate, and put into practice the other "law" I learned from you—a good teacher must love her students.

Thank you again for your help.

Love,
J.

* * *

1975

Chère Madame,

L'année passée, un jour au moment où vous étiez en train de me gronder—je ne me rappelle plus exactement pourquoi—vous m'avez dit, "Il s'agit de manque de respect." Je n'ai pas compris, et donc je ne vous ai pas crue. Je vous crois bien maintenant. Grâce à Dieu et Mlle. Wilbur, et bien sûr, grâce à vous, (et avec l'aide de quelques-uns de mes amis) je viens ce soir d'arriver enfin à comprendre cette idée de 'respect.'

Peut-être que vous ne sauriez pas croire que j'y suis. A ce point, c'est tout naturel que vous ne me croyez plus; vous n'avez aucune raison de me croire. L'épreuve se fera avec du temps. Mais si maintenant vous me croyez ou non, il m'a fallu tout de même vous le dire, et vous remercier (et vous féliciter). Merci pour être l'enseigneuse que vous êtes.

Joey

My note: This student had an I.Q. of 158. She rarely made written errors. She cut class to get *extra* attention from me. During the two hours that she cut she went to the football stadium and paraded around in order to be seen. Her two zeros for cutting class gave her an average of 89.

Translation of above: Last year when you were scolding me (I do not remember exactly why), you said to me: "It is a question of lack of respect." I did not understand and therefor I did not believe you. I believe you now. Thanks to God and Mlle. Wilbur, and certainly, thanks to you (and with the help of some friends) I finally succeeded this evening in understanding this idea of respect.

Perhaps you would not be able to believe that I am there [that I understand]. At this point, it is completely natural that you no longer believe me; you have no reason to believe me. Proof will come with time. But if now you do believe me or not, it has been necessary just the same, to tell you and to thank you and to congratulate you. Thank you for being the teacher that you are.

* * *

May 19, 1978

Ms. Mary D. Nelson
Fort Hunt High School
8428 Fort Hunt Road
Alexandria, Virginia 22308

Dear Madame Nelson:

I have just heard from Maria Wilmeth that you are retiring. These occasions are always ones of mixed emotions for me when I know the success of the individuals involved.

I have crossed paths with you on a number of occasions, and I have heard about you from others as far back as the days of Jean Payne. I know that you have helped many students to enjoy much success in learning French. I am sure that the attention which you have given to your students has motivated many who might not have been so interested under less exciting teachers. I also know that you have been very active in foreign language affairs and have exercised much leadership among your colleagues.

I am therefore sorry to see you leaving Maria's and the state's troops; at the same time, retirement and time for ourselves is what all of us should enjoy as much of as possible. You have my best wishes for your years of leisure and my gratitude for all that you have done for the course of foreign languages.

You may wish to keep in touch with old friends and the profession, and I invite you to attend the state conference each year if you would like to do so.

This year it is at the Omni in Norfolk on October 13 and 14.

Cordially,
(Ms.) Helen P. Warriner
Supervisor of Foreign Languages
for Virginia

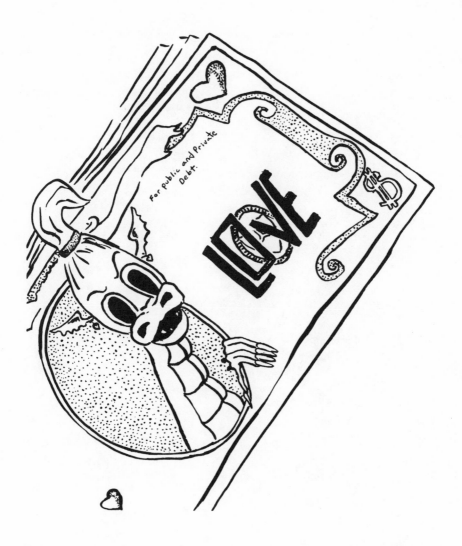